ORDINARY VICTORIES

MANU LARCENET
ORDINARY VICTORIES

Joann SFAR • Lewis TRONDHEIM • Manu LARCENET
Dungeon
Parade
Vol. 1: A Dungeon Too Many

Dungeon
Parade
Vol. 2: Day of the Toads

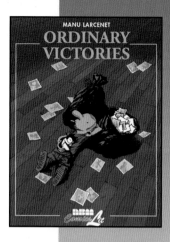

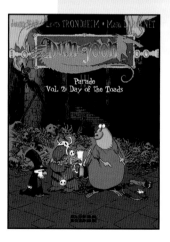

MANU LARCENET

ORDINARY VICTORIES

What is Precious

colors by Patrice Larcenet

With the rather obvious intent of not getting royally sued which would leave him shirtless, the author would like to thank Studio Ghibli for the use of the plush "Totoro," and Emmanuel Guibert and Joann Sfar for dialogue taken from Sardine in Outer Space.

ISBN-10: 1-56163-533-2
ISBN-13: 978-1-56163-533-7
© Dargaud 2007, 2008 by Larcenet
www.dargaud.com
© 2008 NBM for the English translation
Translation by Joe Johnson
Lettering by Ortho
Printed in China
3 2 1

Ordinary Victories

3. What is precious

I've been beat up
I've been thrown out
but I'm not down.
The Clash

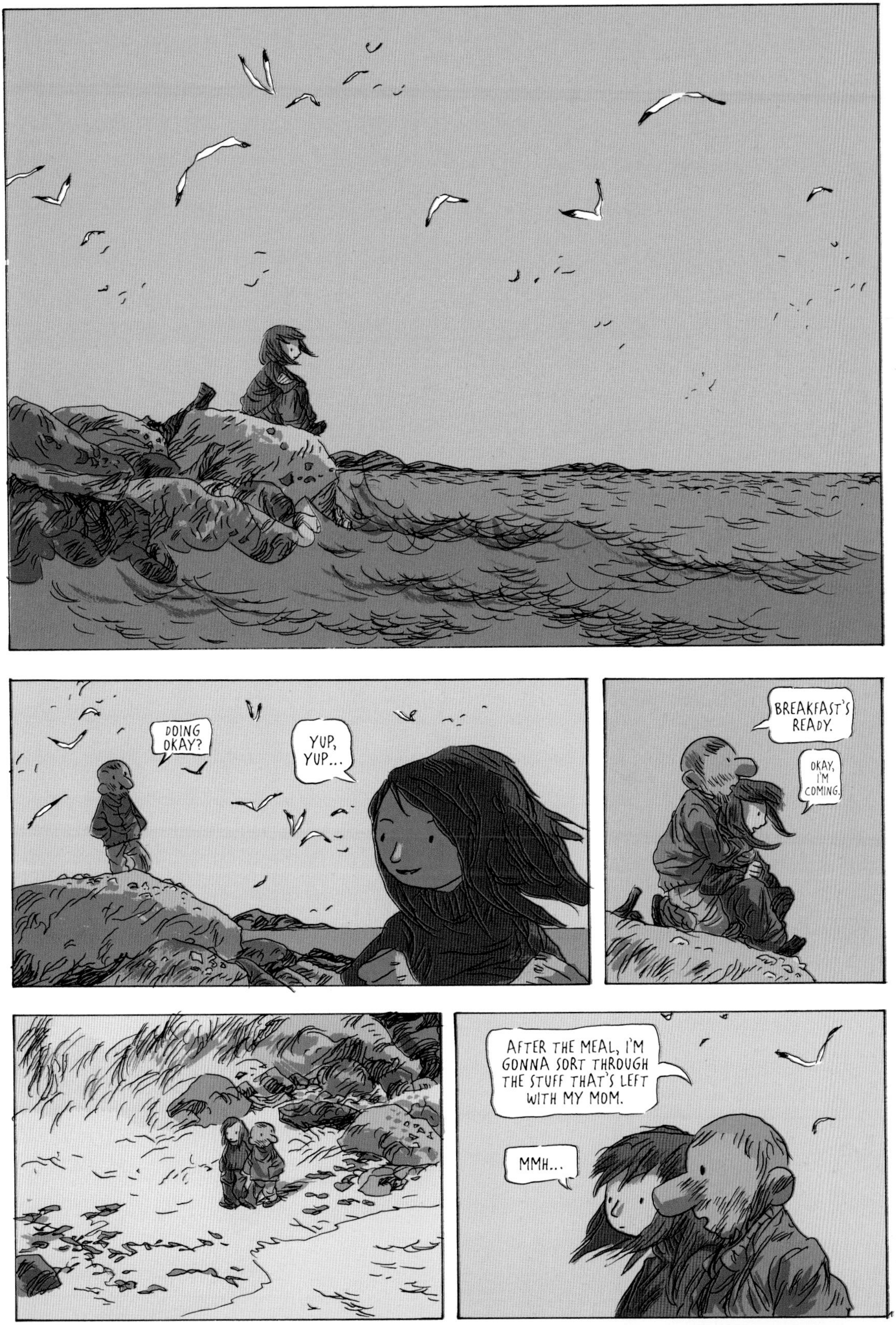
DOING OKAY?
YUP, YUP...
BREAKFAST'S READY.
OKAY, I'M COMING.
AFTER THE MEAL, I'M GONNA SORT THROUGH THE STUFF THAT'S LEFT WITH MY MOM.
MMH...

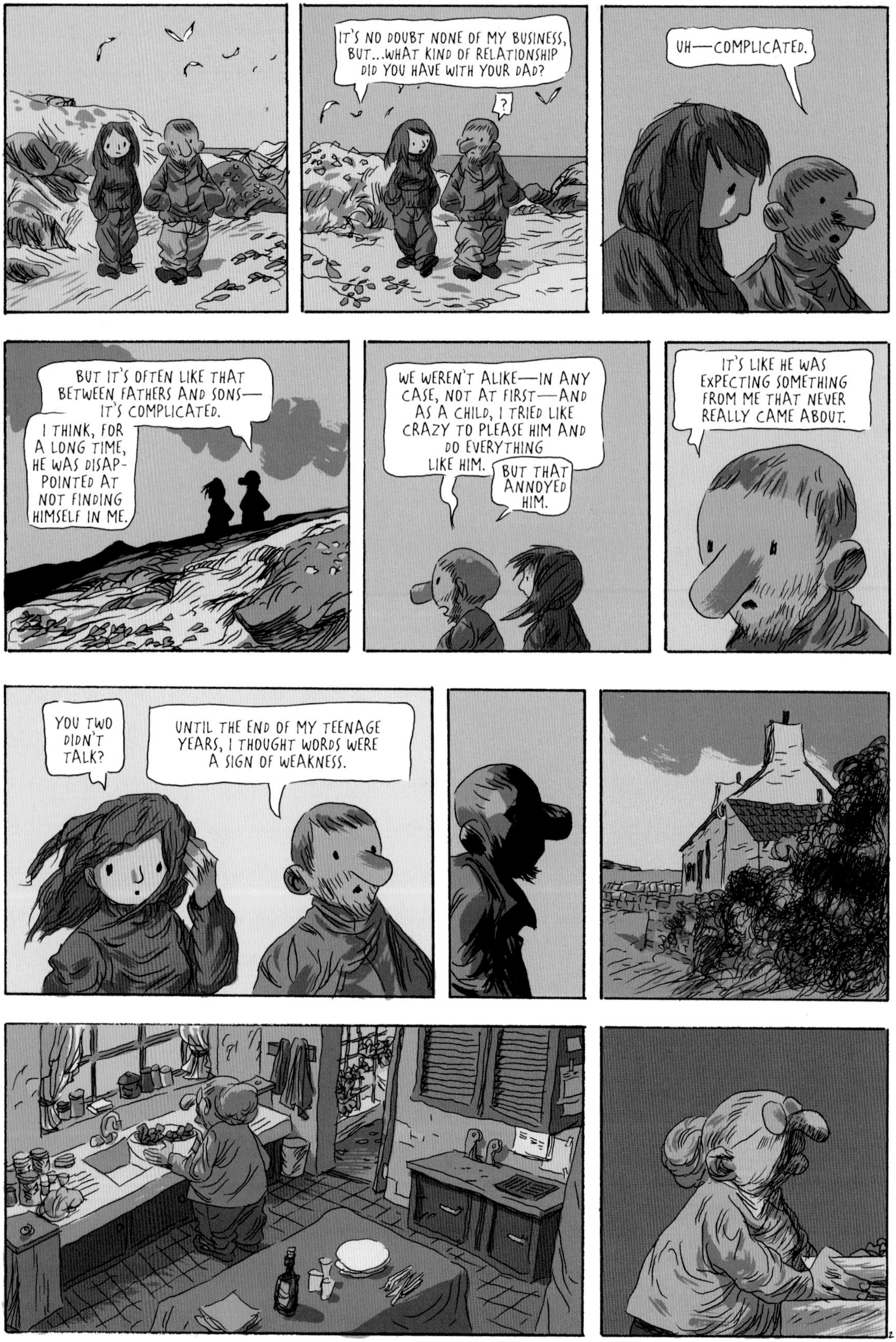
IT'S NO DOUBT NONE OF MY BUSINESS, BUT...WHAT KIND OF RELATIONSHIP DID YOU HAVE WITH YOUR DAD?
?
UH—COMPLICATED.
BUT IT'S OFTEN LIKE THAT BETWEEN FATHERS AND SONS—IT'S COMPLICATED.
I THINK, FOR A LONG TIME, HE WAS DISAPPOINTED AT NOT FINDING HIMSELF IN ME.
WE WEREN'T ALIKE—IN ANY CASE, NOT AT FIRST—AND AS A CHILD, I TRIED LIKE CRAZY TO PLEASE HIM AND DO EVERYTHING LIKE HIM.
BUT THAT ANNOYED HIM.
IT'S LIKE HE WAS EXPECTING SOMETHING FROM ME THAT NEVER REALLY CAME ABOUT.
YOU TWO DIDN'T TALK?
UNTIL THE END OF MY TEENAGE YEARS, I THOUGHT WORDS WERE A SIGN OF WEAKNESS.

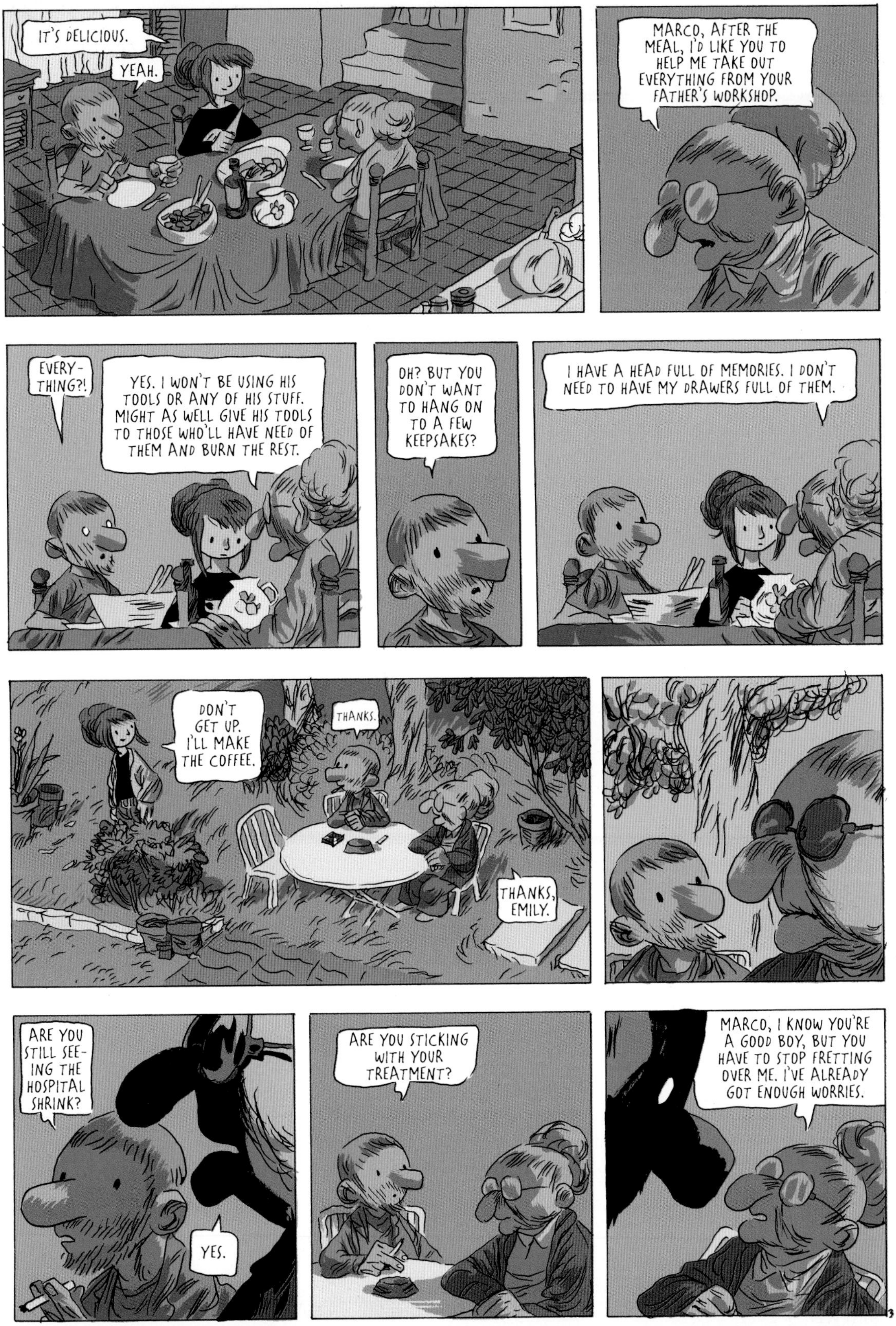
IT'S DELICIOUS.
YEAH.
MARCO, AFTER THE MEAL, I'D LIKE YOU TO HELP ME TAKE OUT EVERYTHING FROM YOUR FATHER'S WORKSHOP.
EVERY-THING?!
YES. I WON'T BE USING HIS TOOLS OR ANY OF HIS STUFF. MIGHT AS WELL GIVE HIS TOOLS TO THOSE WHO'LL HAVE NEED OF THEM AND BURN THE REST.
OH? BUT YOU DON'T WANT TO HANG ON TO A FEW KEEPSAKES?
I HAVE A HEAD FULL OF MEMORIES. I DON'T NEED TO HAVE MY DRAWERS FULL OF THEM.
DON'T GET UP. I'LL MAKE THE COFFEE.
THANKS.
THANKS, EMILY.
ARE YOU STILL SEE-ING THE HOSPITAL SHRINK?
YES.
ARE YOU STICKING WITH YOUR TREATMENT?
MARCO, I KNOW YOU'RE A GOOD BOY, BUT YOU HAVE TO STOP FRETTING OVER ME. I'VE ALREADY GOT ENOUGH WORRIES.

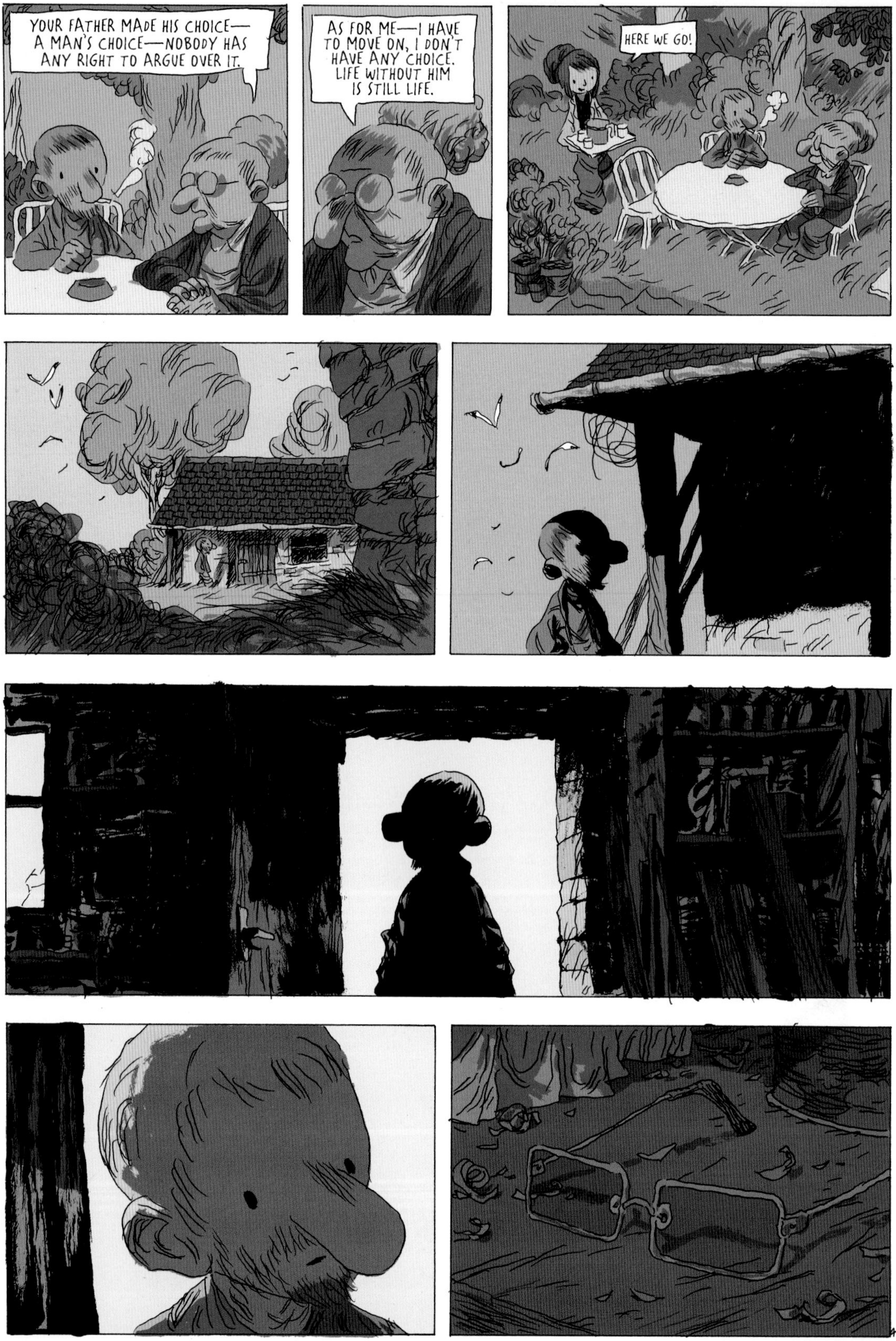
YOUR FATHER MADE HIS CHOICE—A MAN'S CHOICE—NOBODY HAS ANY RIGHT TO ARGUE OVER IT.
AS FOR ME—I HAVE TO MOVE ON, I DON'T HAVE ANY CHOICE. LIFE WITHOUT HIM IS STILL LIFE.
HERE WE GO!

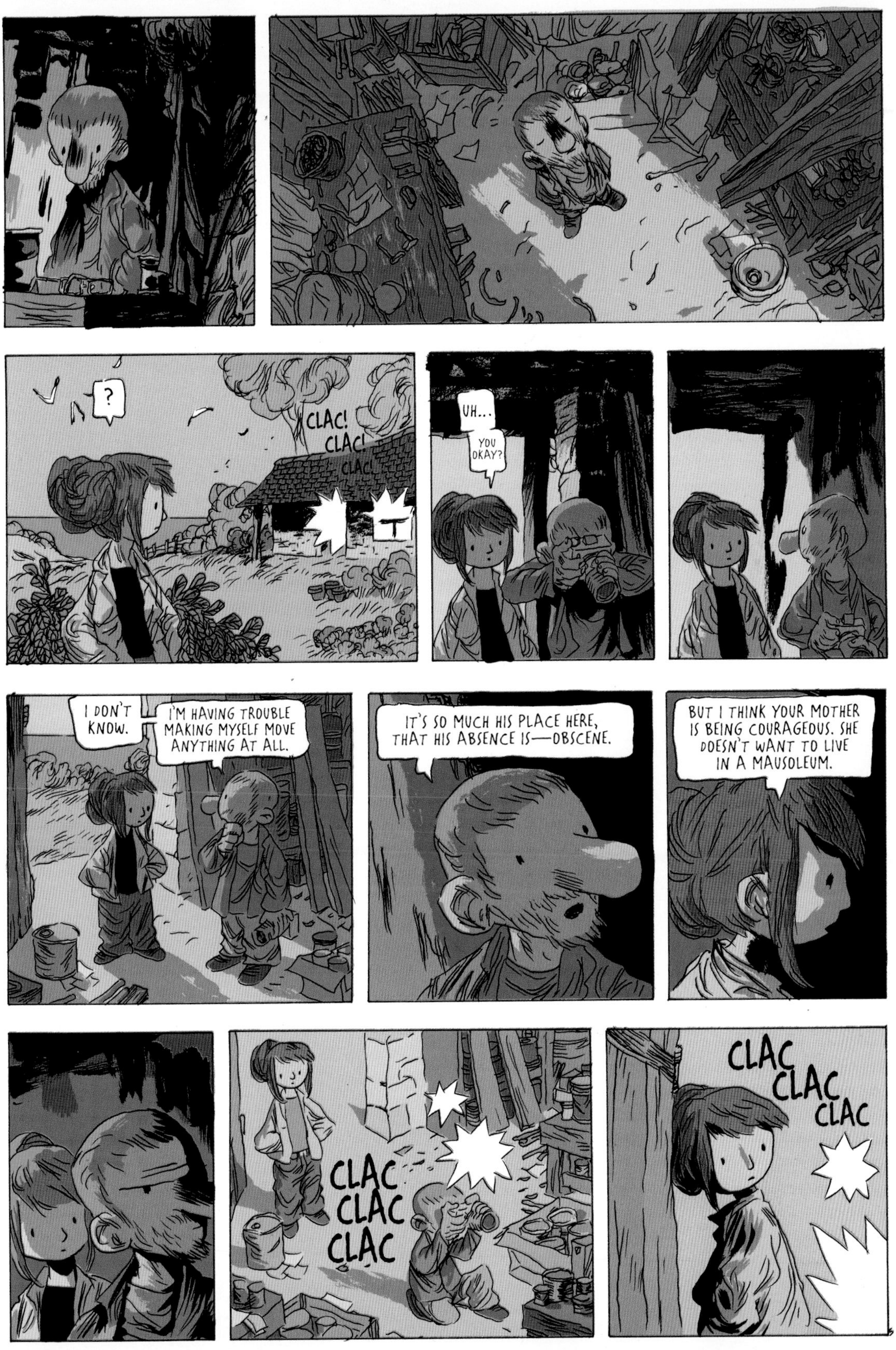

?
CLAC! CLAC! CLAC!
UH...
YOU OKAY?
I DON'T KNOW.
I'M HAVING TROUBLE MAKING MYSELF MOVE ANYTHING AT ALL.
IT'S SO MUCH HIS PLACE HERE, THAT HIS ABSENCE IS—OBSCENE.
BUT I THINK YOUR MOTHER IS BEING COURAGEOUS. SHE DOESN'T WANT TO LIVE IN A MAUSOLEUM.
CLAC CLAC CLAC
CLAC CLAC CLAC

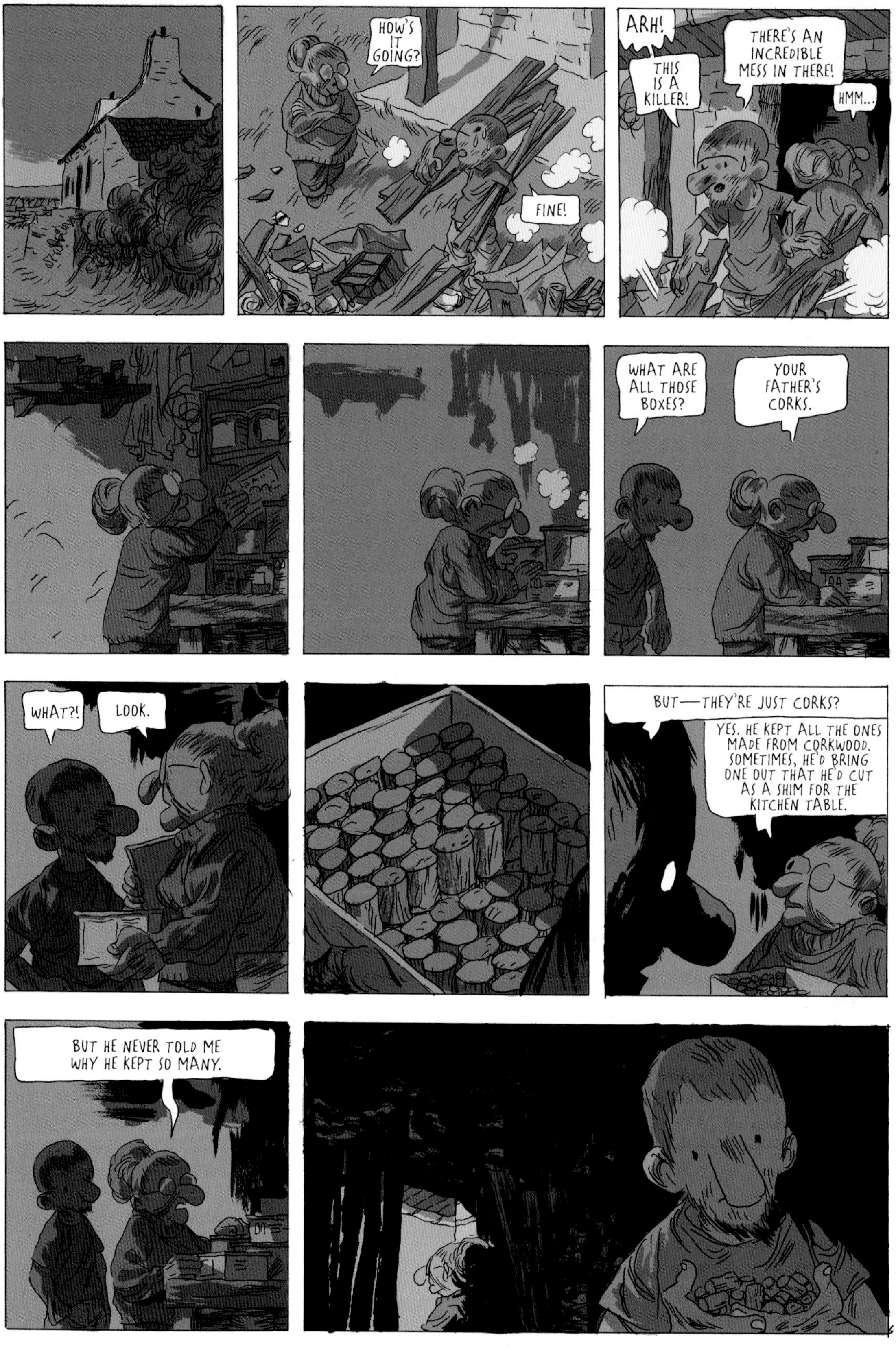
HOW'S IT GOING?
FINE!
ARH!
THIS IS A KILLER!
THERE'S AN INCREDIBLE MESS IN THERE!
HMM...
WHAT ARE ALL THOSE BOXES?
YOUR FATHER'S CORKS.
WHAT?!
LOOK.
BUT—THEY'RE JUST CORKS?
YES. HE KEPT ALL THE ONES MADE FROM CORKWOOD. SOMETIMES, HE'D BRING ONE OUT THAT HE'D CUT AS A SHIM FOR THE KITCHEN TABLE.
BUT HE NEVER TOLD ME WHY HE KEPT SO MANY.

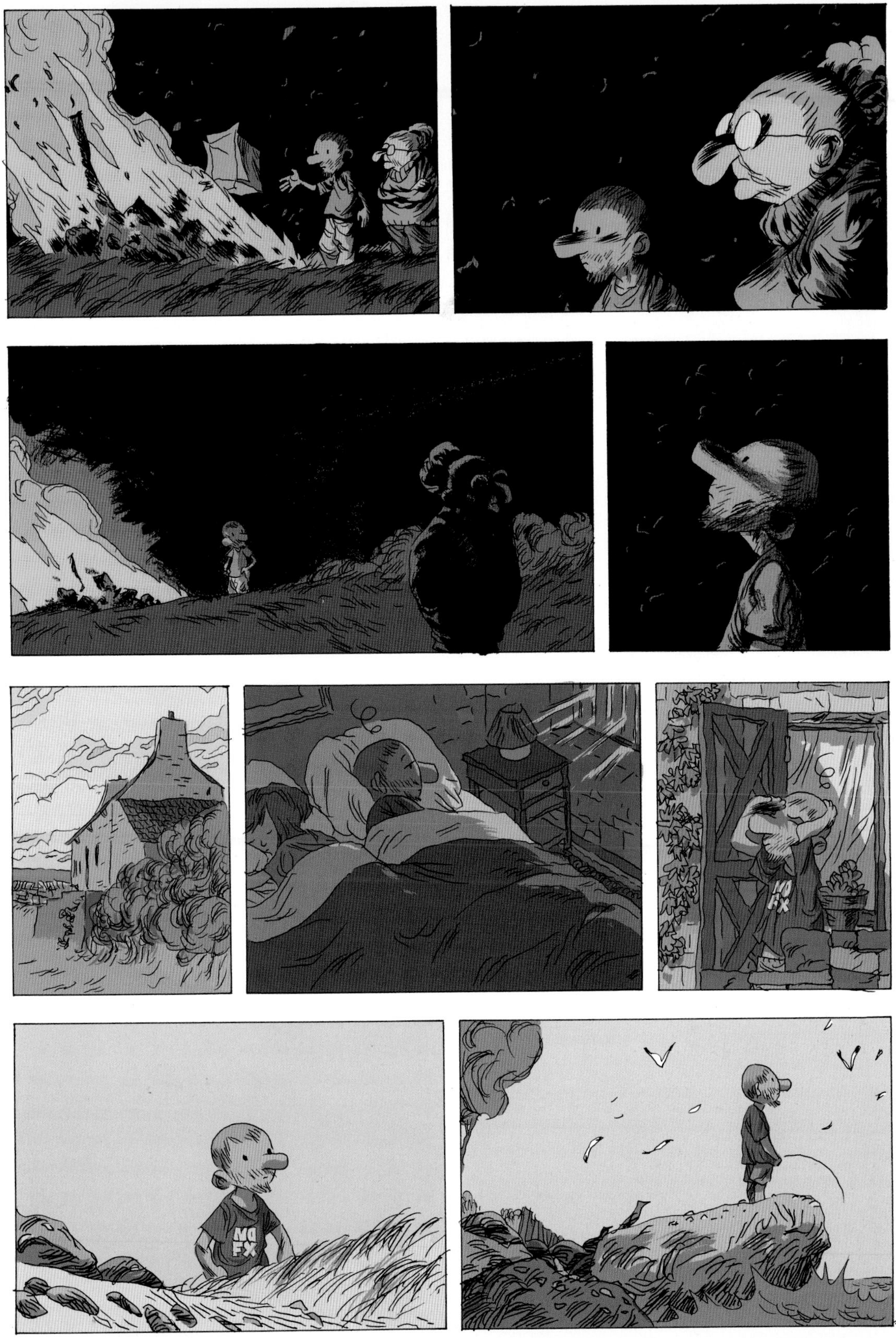

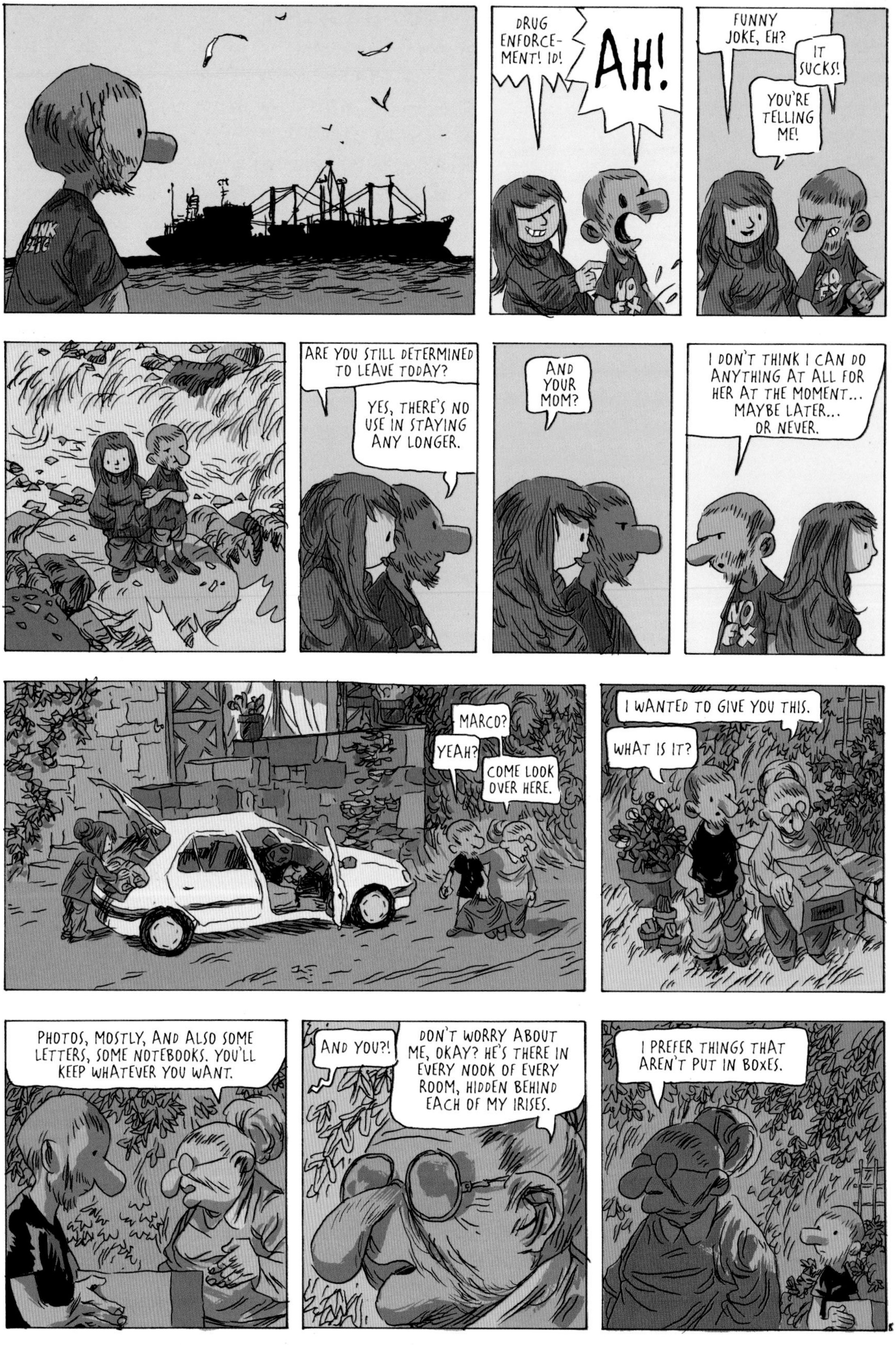

DRUG ENFORCEMENT! ID!
AH!
FUNNY JOKE, EH?
IT SUCKS!
YOU'RE TELLING ME!
ARE YOU STILL DETERMINED TO LEAVE TODAY?
YES, THERE'S NO USE IN STAYING ANY LONGER.
AND YOUR MOM?
I DON'T THINK I CAN DO ANYTHING AT ALL FOR HER AT THE MOMENT... MAYBE LATER... OR NEVER.
MARCO?
YEAH?
COME LOOK OVER HERE.
I WANTED TO GIVE YOU THIS.
WHAT IS IT?
PHOTOS, MOSTLY, AND ALSO SOME LETTERS, SOME NOTEBOOKS. YOU'LL KEEP WHATEVER YOU WANT.
AND YOU?!
DON'T WORRY ABOUT ME, OKAY? HE'S THERE IN EVERY NOOK OF EVERY ROOM, HIDDEN BEHIND EACH OF MY IRISES.
I PREFER THINGS THAT AREN'T PUT IN BOXES.

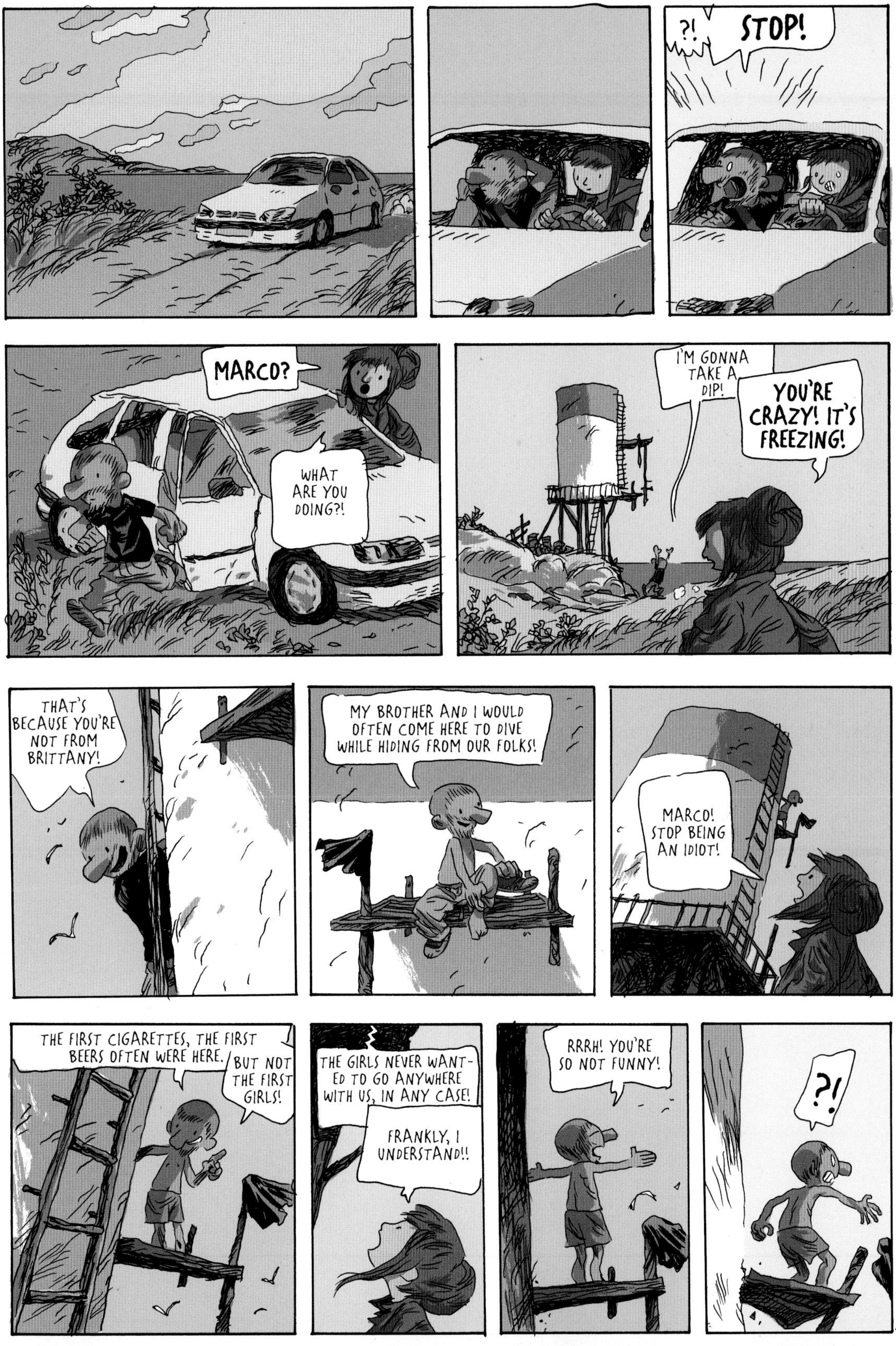
?!
STOP!
MARCO?
WHAT ARE YOU DOING?!
I'M GONNA TAKE A DIP!
YOU'RE CRAZY! IT'S FREEZING!
THAT'S BECAUSE YOU'RE NOT FROM BRITTANY!
MY BROTHER AND I WOULD OFTEN COME HERE TO DIVE WHILE HIDING FROM OUR FOLKS!
MARCO! STOP BEING AN IDIOT!
THE FIRST CIGARETTES, THE FIRST BEERS OFTEN WERE HERE.
BUT NOT THE FIRST GIRLS!
THE GIRLS NEVER WANT-ED TO GO ANYWHERE WITH US, IN ANY CASE!
FRANKLY, I UNDERSTAND!!
RRRH! YOU'RE SO NOT FUNNY!
?!

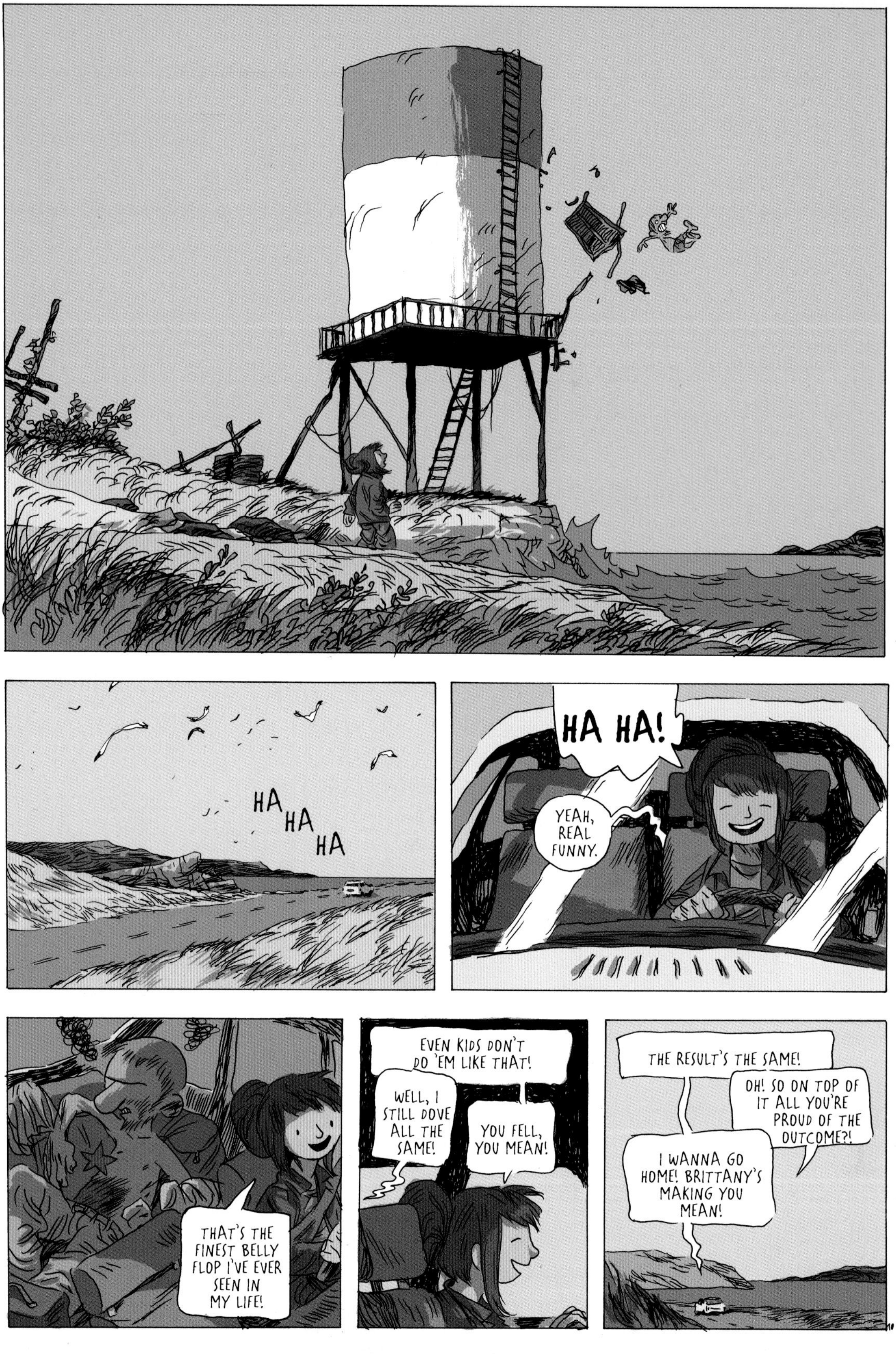
HA
HA
HA
HA HA!
YEAH, REAL FUNNY.
THAT'S THE FINEST BELLY FLOP I'VE EVER SEEN IN MY LIFE!
EVEN KIDS DON'T DO 'EM LIKE THAT!
WELL, I STILL DOVE ALL THE SAME!
YOU FELL, YOU MEAN!
THE RESULT'S THE SAME!
OH! SO ON TOP OF IT ALL YOU'RE PROUD OF THE OUTCOME?!
I WANNA GO HOME! BRITTANY'S MAKING YOU MEAN!

MY FATHER IS DEAD.

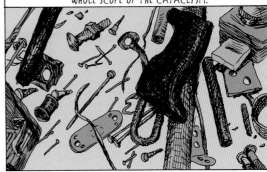

I DON'T THINK I FULLY GRASP YET THE
WHOLE SCOPE OF THE CATACLYSM.

ONCE I'M NO LONGER DEADENED BY THE BRUTALITY
OF HIS PASSING, PERHAPS THEN I'LL GET A GLIMPSE
OF ALL THE INTIMATE RANGE OF GRIEF.

EVER SINCE I WAS A KID, TO WARD OFF FEAR, I'D IMAGINED
THIS MOMENT IN ALL OF ITS DETAILS. I FANTASIZED
ABOUT IT SO MUCH THAT, ONCE IT ARRIVED...

...I WAS RELIEVED.

STRANGELY, IT'S AS THOUGH I'D TOLD MYSELF:
"OKAY, SO IT'S HAPPENED. THAT'S ONCE LESS HORROR TO
LIVE THROUGH, THAT'S ONE THING CHECKED OFF."

BUT IN THOSE INNUMERABLE, MORBID FANTASIES,
THOSE STAGINGS, IN ALL THAT RITUAL PREPARATION,
THERE'S SOMETHING OF WHICH I WAS UNAWARE...

...NOTHING PREPARES YOU FOR THE HORROR'S PERMANENCY.

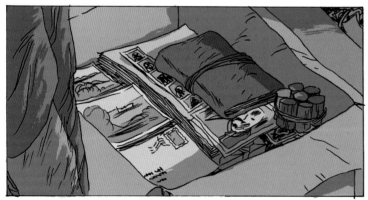

WEE
WEE
WEE

HELLO? ANNE-MARIE, HOW'S IT GOING?

YES...

WELL — THAT DEPENDS.

WHY?

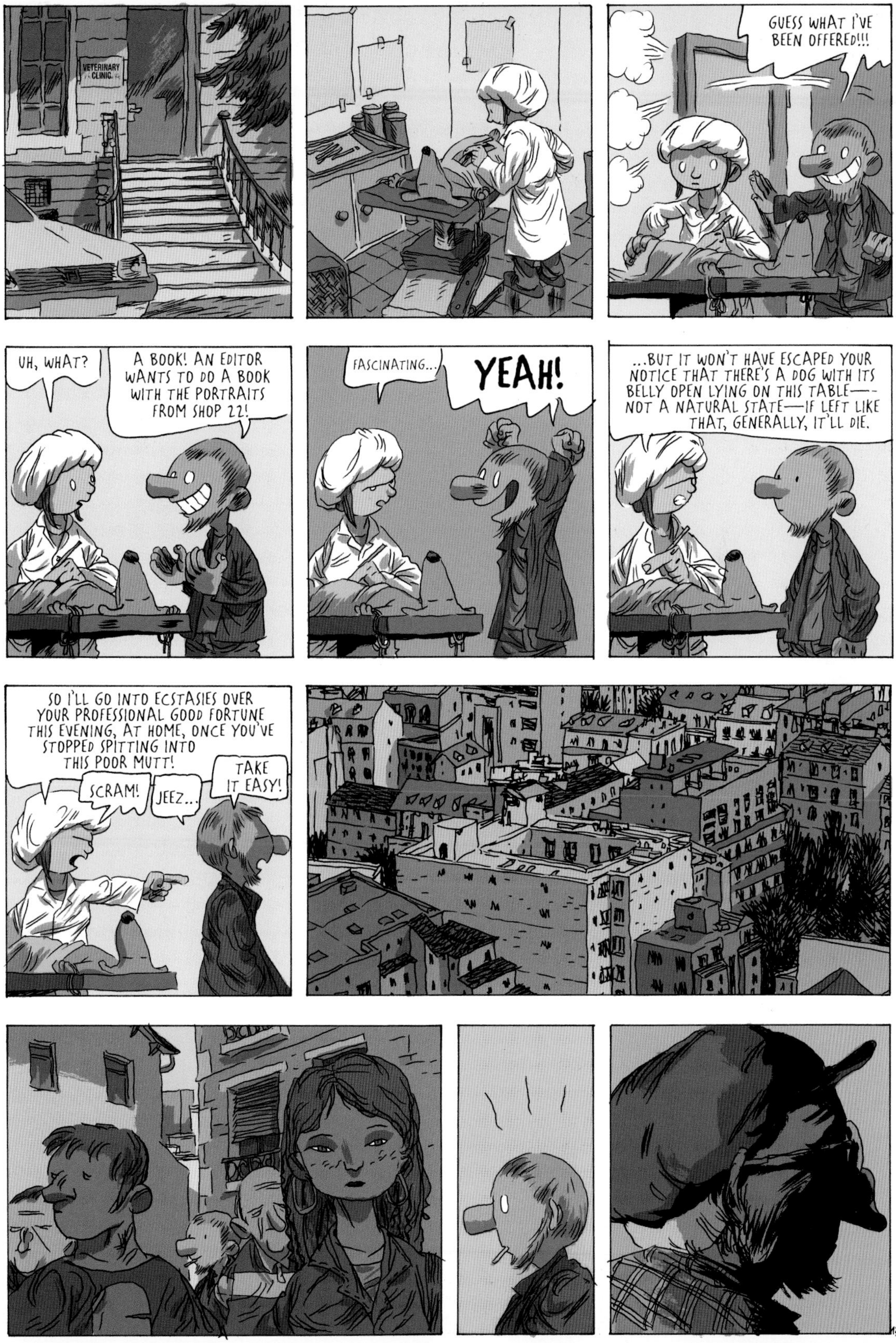
VETERINARY CLINIC
GUESS WHAT I'VE BEEN OFFERED!!!
UH, WHAT?
A BOOK! AN EDITOR WANTS TO DO A BOOK WITH THE PORTRAITS FROM SHOP 22!
FASCINATING...
YEAH!
...BUT IT WON'T HAVE ESCAPED YOUR NOTICE THAT THERE'S A DOG WITH ITS BELLY OPEN LYING ON THIS TABLE—-NOT A NATURAL STATE—IF LEFT LIKE THAT, GENERALLY, IT'LL DIE.
SO I'LL GO INTO ECSTASIES OVER YOUR PROFESSIONAL GOOD FORTUNE THIS EVENING, AT HOME, ONCE YOU'VE STOPPED SPITTING INTO THIS POOR MUTT!
SCRAM!
JEEZ...
TAKE IT EASY!

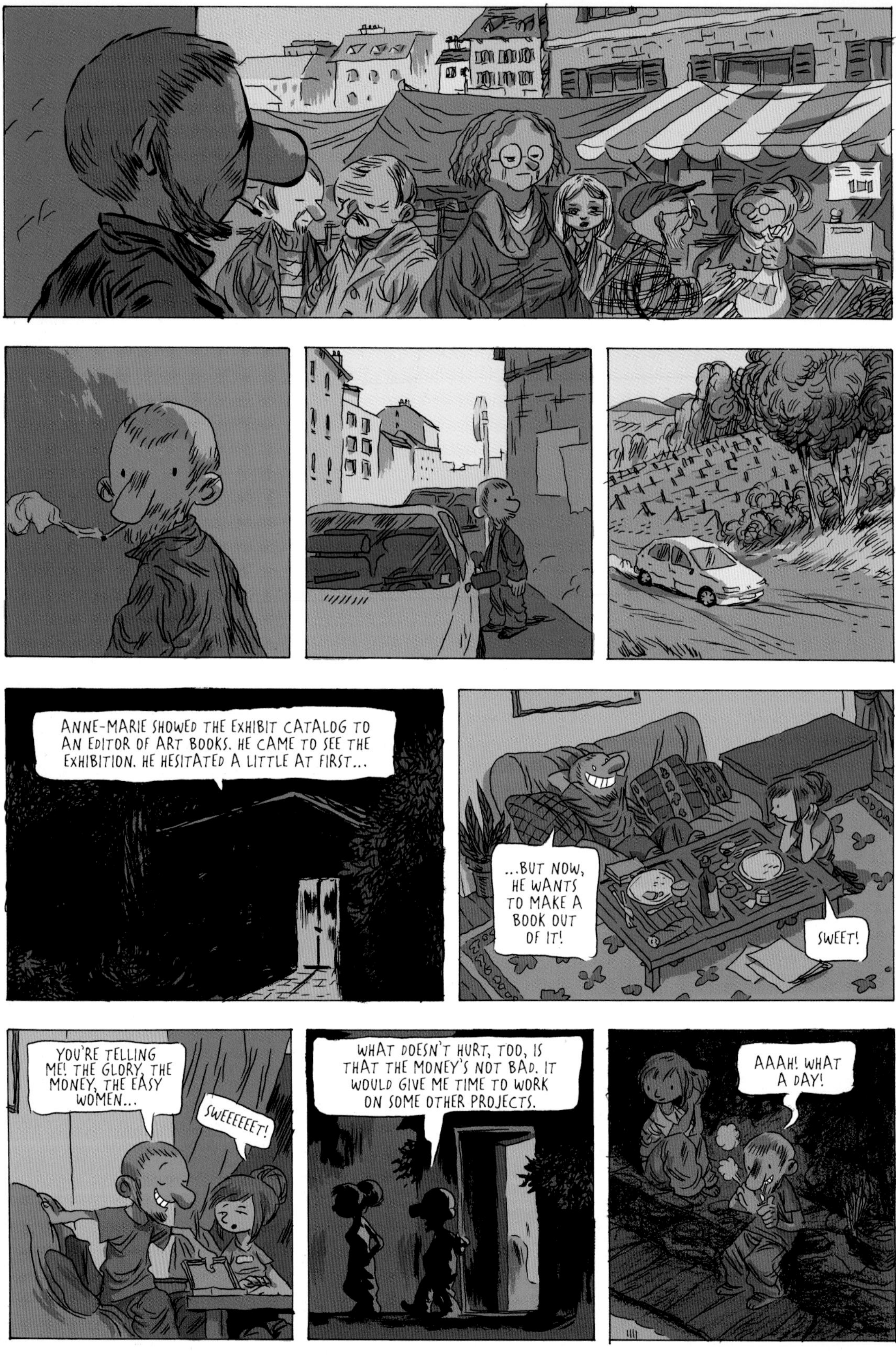
ANNE-MARIE SHOWED THE EXHIBIT CATALOG TO AN EDITOR OF ART BOOKS. HE CAME TO SEE THE EXHIBITION. HE HESITATED A LITTLE AT FIRST...
...BUT NOW, HE WANTS TO MAKE A BOOK OUT OF IT!
SWEET!
YOU'RE TELLING ME! THE GLORY, THE MONEY, THE EASY WOMEN...
SWEEEEEET!
WHAT DOESN'T HURT, TOO, IS THAT THE MONEY'S NOT BAD. IT WOULD GIVE ME TIME TO WORK ON SOME OTHER PROJECTS.
AAAH! WHAT A DAY!

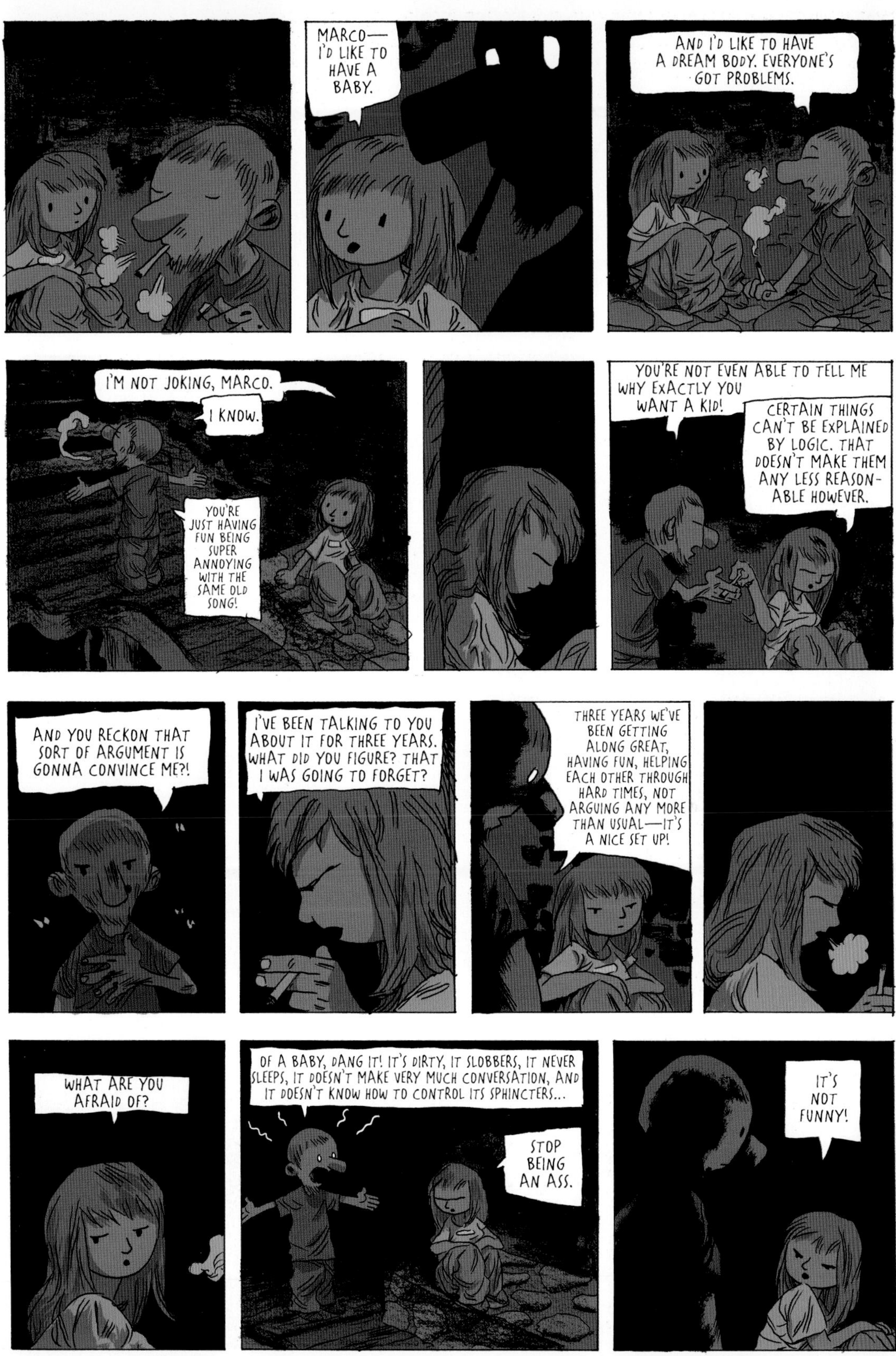
MARCO— I'D LIKE TO HAVE A BABY.
AND I'D LIKE TO HAVE A DREAM BODY. EVERYONE'S GOT PROBLEMS.
I'M NOT JOKING, MARCO.
I KNOW.
YOU'RE JUST HAVING FUN BEING SUPER ANNOYING WITH THE SAME OLD SONG!
YOU'RE NOT EVEN ABLE TO TELL ME WHY EXACTLY YOU WANT A KID!
CERTAIN THINGS CAN'T BE EXPLAINED BY LOGIC. THAT DOESN'T MAKE THEM ANY LESS REASONABLE HOWEVER.
AND YOU RECKON THAT SORT OF ARGUMENT IS GONNA CONVINCE ME?!
I'VE BEEN TALKING TO YOU ABOUT IT FOR THREE YEARS. WHAT DID YOU FIGURE? THAT I WAS GOING TO FORGET?
THREE YEARS WE'VE BEEN GETTING ALONG GREAT, HAVING FUN, HELPING EACH OTHER THROUGH HARD TIMES, NOT ARGUING ANY MORE THAN USUAL—IT'S A NICE SET UP!
WHAT ARE YOU AFRAID OF?
OF A BABY, DANG IT! IT'S DIRTY, IT SLOBBERS, IT NEVER SLEEPS, IT DOESN'T MAKE VERY MUCH CONVERSATION, AND IT DOESN'T KNOW HOW TO CONTROL ITS SPHINCTERS...
STOP BEING AN ASS.
IT'S NOT FUNNY!
15

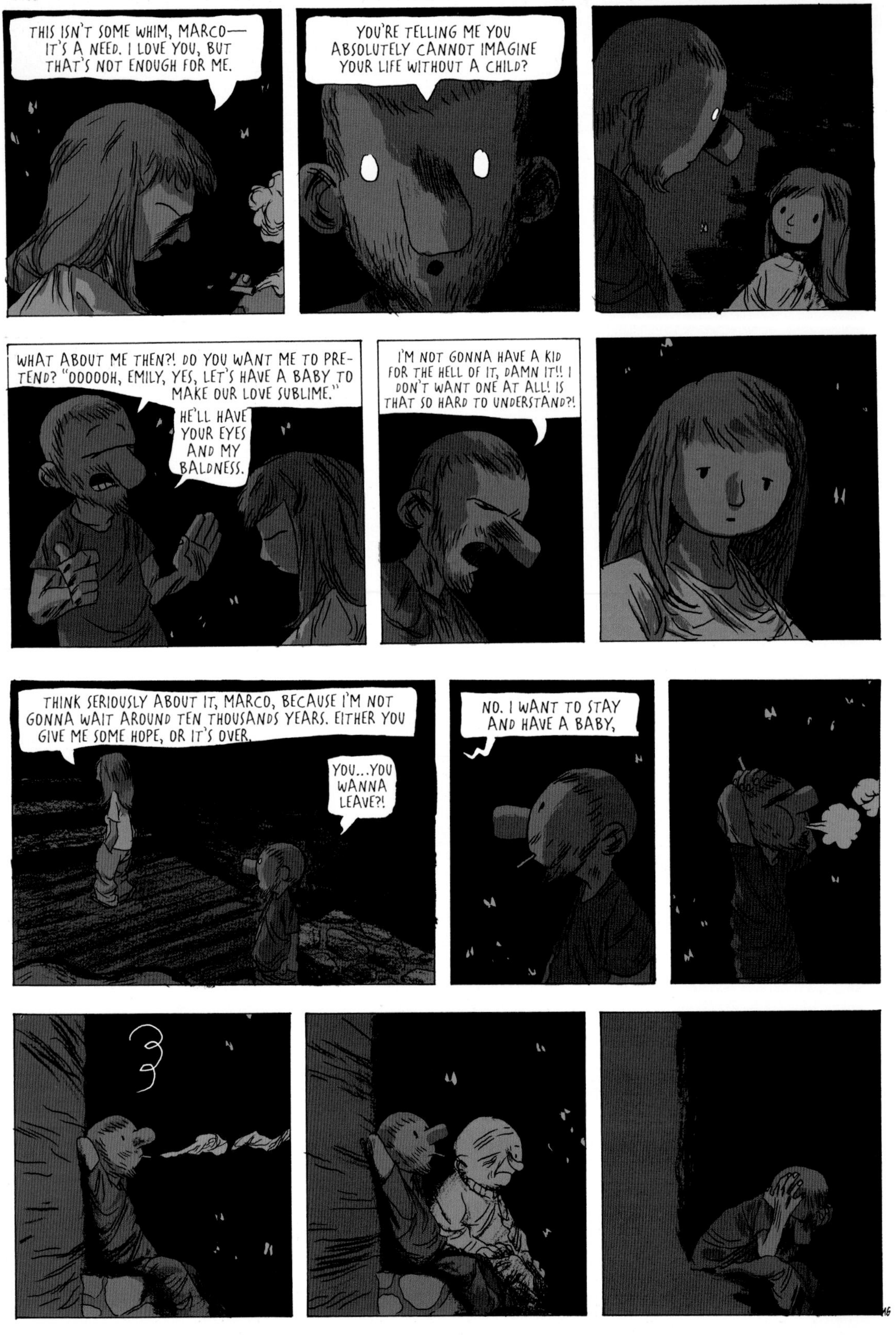
THIS ISN'T SOME WHIM, MARCO— IT'S A NEED. I LOVE YOU, BUT THAT'S NOT ENOUGH FOR ME.
YOU'RE TELLING ME YOU ABSOLUTELY CANNOT IMAGINE YOUR LIFE WITHOUT A CHILD?
WHAT ABOUT ME THEN?! DO YOU WANT ME TO PRETEND? "OOOOOH, EMILY, YES, LET'S HAVE A BABY TO MAKE OUR LOVE SUBLIME."
HE'LL HAVE YOUR EYES AND MY BALDNESS.
I'M NOT GONNA HAVE A KID FOR THE HELL OF IT, DAMN IT!! I DON'T WANT ONE AT ALL! IS THAT SO HARD TO UNDERSTAND?!
THINK SERIOUSLY ABOUT IT, MARCO, BECAUSE I'M NOT GONNA WAIT AROUND TEN THOUSANDS YEARS. EITHER YOU GIVE ME SOME HOPE, OR IT'S OVER.
YOU...YOU WANNA LEAVE?!
NO. I WANT TO STAY AND HAVE A BABY,

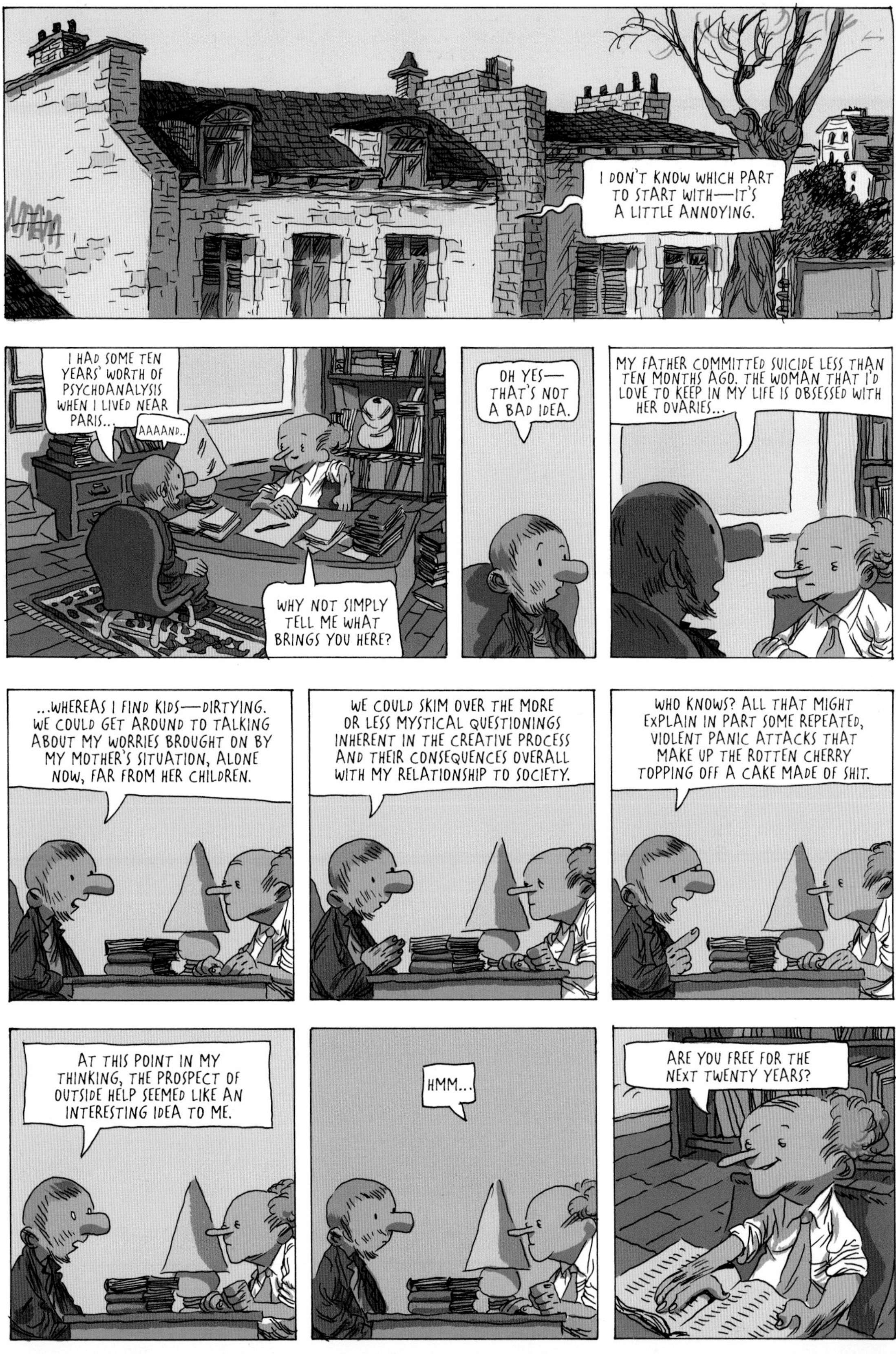
I DON'T KNOW WHICH PART TO START WITH—IT'S A LITTLE ANNOYING.
I HAD SOME TEN YEARS' WORTH OF PSYCHOANALYSIS WHEN I LIVED NEAR PARIS...
AAAAND..
WHY NOT SIMPLY TELL ME WHAT BRINGS YOU HERE?
OH YES—THAT'S NOT A BAD IDEA.
MY FATHER COMMITTED SUICIDE LESS THAN TEN MONTHS AGO. THE WOMAN THAT I'D LOVE TO KEEP IN MY LIFE IS OBSESSED WITH HER OVARIES...
...WHEREAS I FIND KIDS—DIRTYING. WE COULD GET AROUND TO TALKING ABOUT MY WORRIES BROUGHT ON BY MY MOTHER'S SITUATION, ALONE NOW, FAR FROM HER CHILDREN.
WE COULD SKIM OVER THE MORE OR LESS MYSTICAL QUESTIONINGS INHERENT IN THE CREATIVE PROCESS AND THEIR CONSEQUENCES OVERALL WITH MY RELATIONSHIP TO SOCIETY.
WHO KNOWS? ALL THAT MIGHT EXPLAIN IN PART SOME REPEATED, VIOLENT PANIC ATTACKS THAT MAKE UP THE ROTTEN CHERRY TOPPING OFF A CAKE MADE OF SHIT.
AT THIS POINT IN MY THINKING, THE PROSPECT OF OUTSIDE HELP SEEMED LIKE AN INTERESTING IDEA TO ME.
HMM...
ARE YOU FREE FOR THE NEXT TWENTY YEARS?

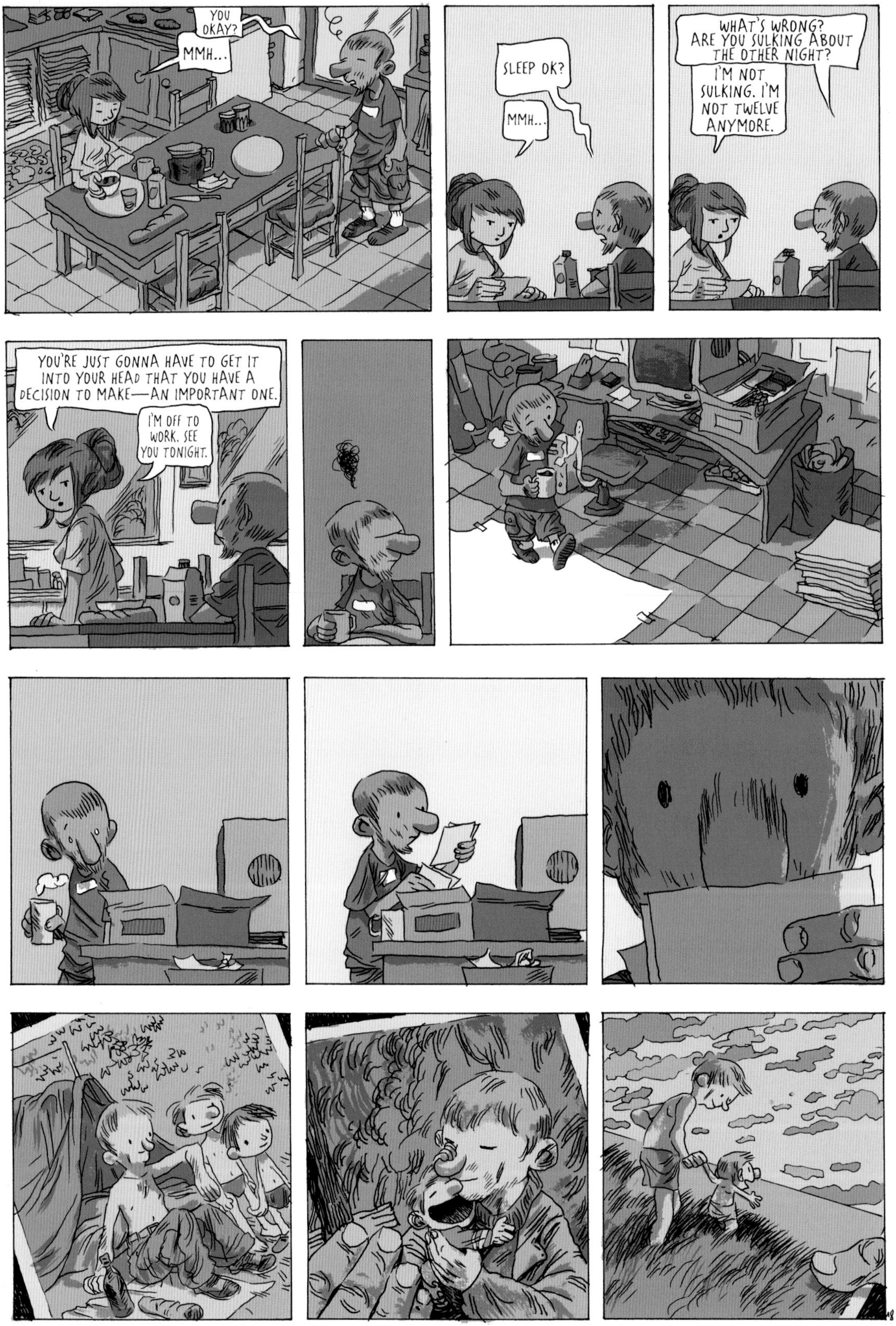
YOU OKAY?
MMH...
SLEEP OK?
MMH...
WHAT'S WRONG? ARE YOU SULKING ABOUT THE OTHER NIGHT?
I'M NOT SULKING. I'M NOT TWELVE ANYMORE.
YOU'RE JUST GONNA HAVE TO GET IT INTO YOUR HEAD THAT YOU HAVE A DECISION TO MAKE—AN IMPORTANT ONE.
I'M OFF TO WORK. SEE YOU TONIGHT.

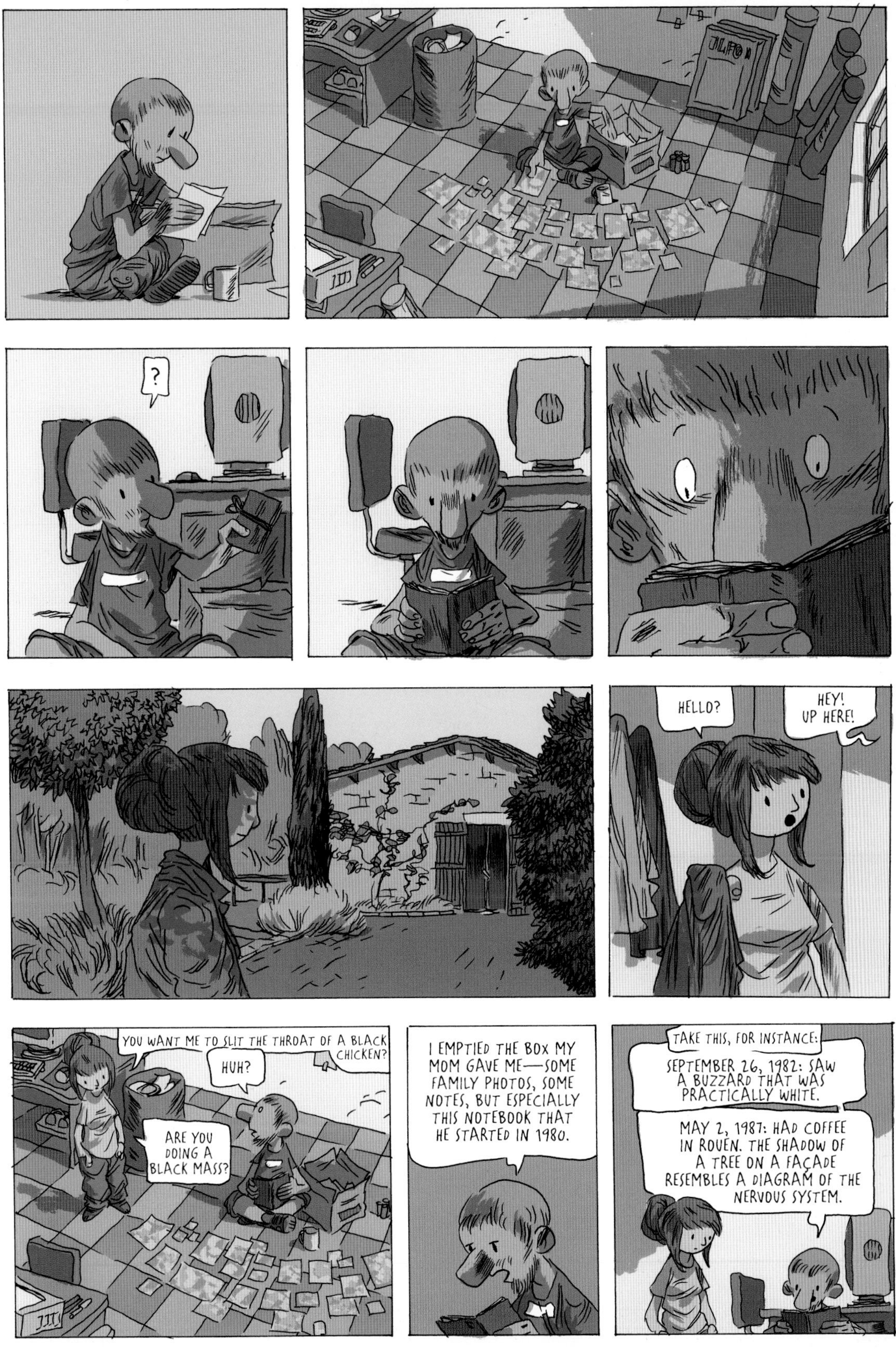
?
HELLO?
HEY! UP HERE!
YOU WANT ME TO SLIT THE THROAT OF A BLACK CHICKEN?
HUH?
ARE YOU DOING A BLACK MASS?
I EMPTIED THE BOX MY MOM GAVE ME—SOME FAMILY PHOTOS, SOME NOTES, BUT ESPECIALLY THIS NOTEBOOK THAT HE STARTED IN 1980.
TAKE THIS, FOR INSTANCE:
SEPTEMBER 26, 1982: SAW A BUZZARD THAT WAS PRACTICALLY WHITE.
MAY 2, 1987: HAD COFFEE IN ROUEN. THE SHADOW OF A TREE ON A FAÇADE RESEMBLES A DIAGRAM OF THE NERVOUS SYSTEM.

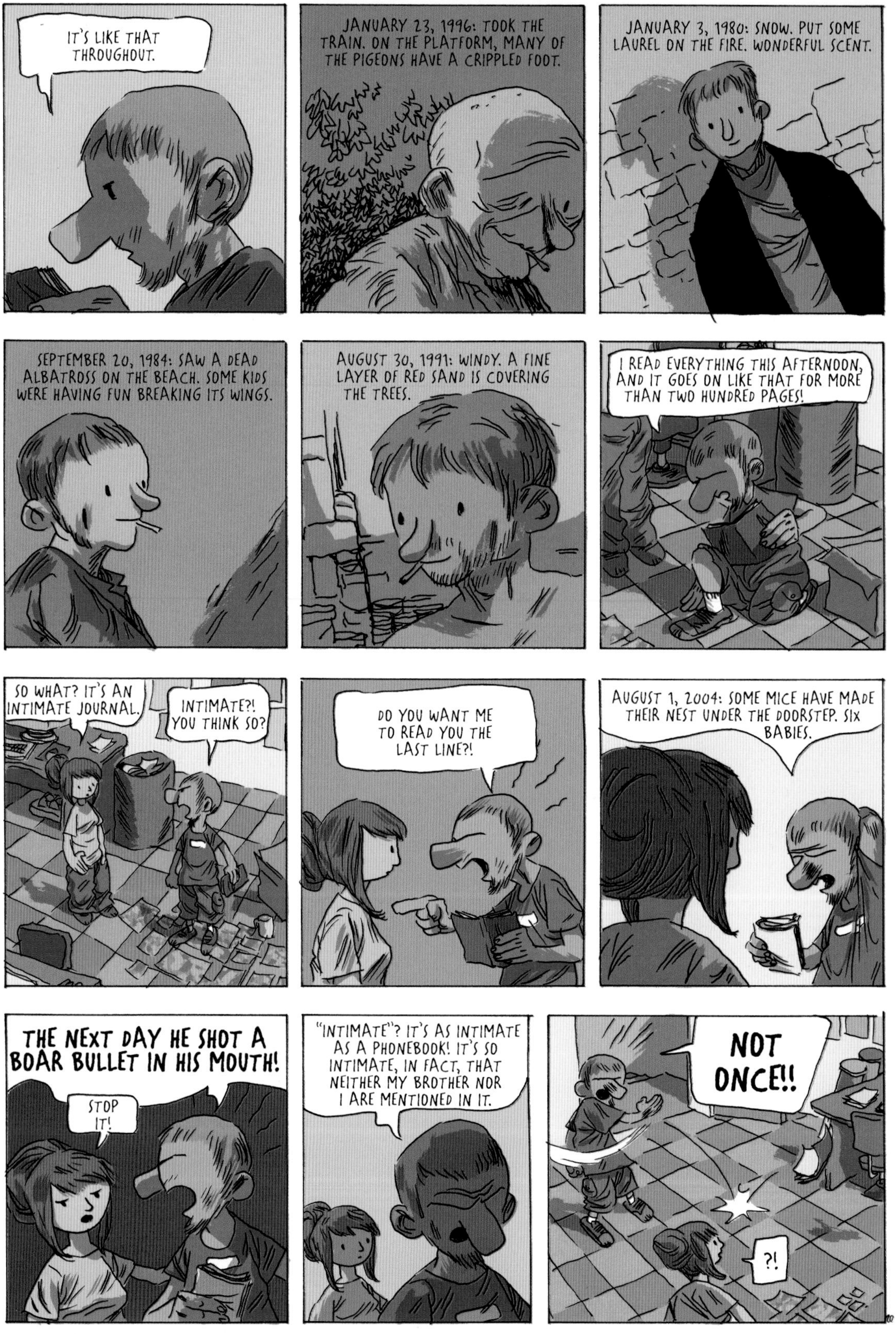
IT'S LIKE THAT THROUGHOUT.
JANUARY 23, 1996: TOOK THE TRAIN. ON THE PLATFORM, MANY OF THE PIGEONS HAVE A CRIPPLED FOOT.
JANUARY 3, 1980: SNOW. PUT SOME LAUREL ON THE FIRE. WONDERFUL SCENT.
SEPTEMBER 20, 1984: SAW A DEAD ALBATROSS ON THE BEACH. SOME KIDS WERE HAVING FUN BREAKING ITS WINGS.
AUGUST 30, 1991: WINDY. A FINE LAYER OF RED SAND IS COVERING THE TREES.
I READ EVERYTHING THIS AFTERNOON, AND IT GOES ON LIKE THAT FOR MORE THAN TWO HUNDRED PAGES!
SO WHAT? IT'S AN INTIMATE JOURNAL.
INTIMATE?! YOU THINK SO?
DO YOU WANT ME TO READ YOU THE LAST LINE?!
AUGUST 1, 2004: SOME MICE HAVE MADE THEIR NEST UNDER THE DOORSTEP. SIX BABIES.
THE NEXT DAY HE SHOT A BOAR BULLET IN HIS MOUTH!
STOP IT!
"INTIMATE"? IT'S AS INTIMATE AS A PHONEBOOK! IT'S SO INTIMATE, IN FACT, THAT NEITHER MY BROTHER NOR I ARE MENTIONED IN IT.
NOT ONCE!!
?!

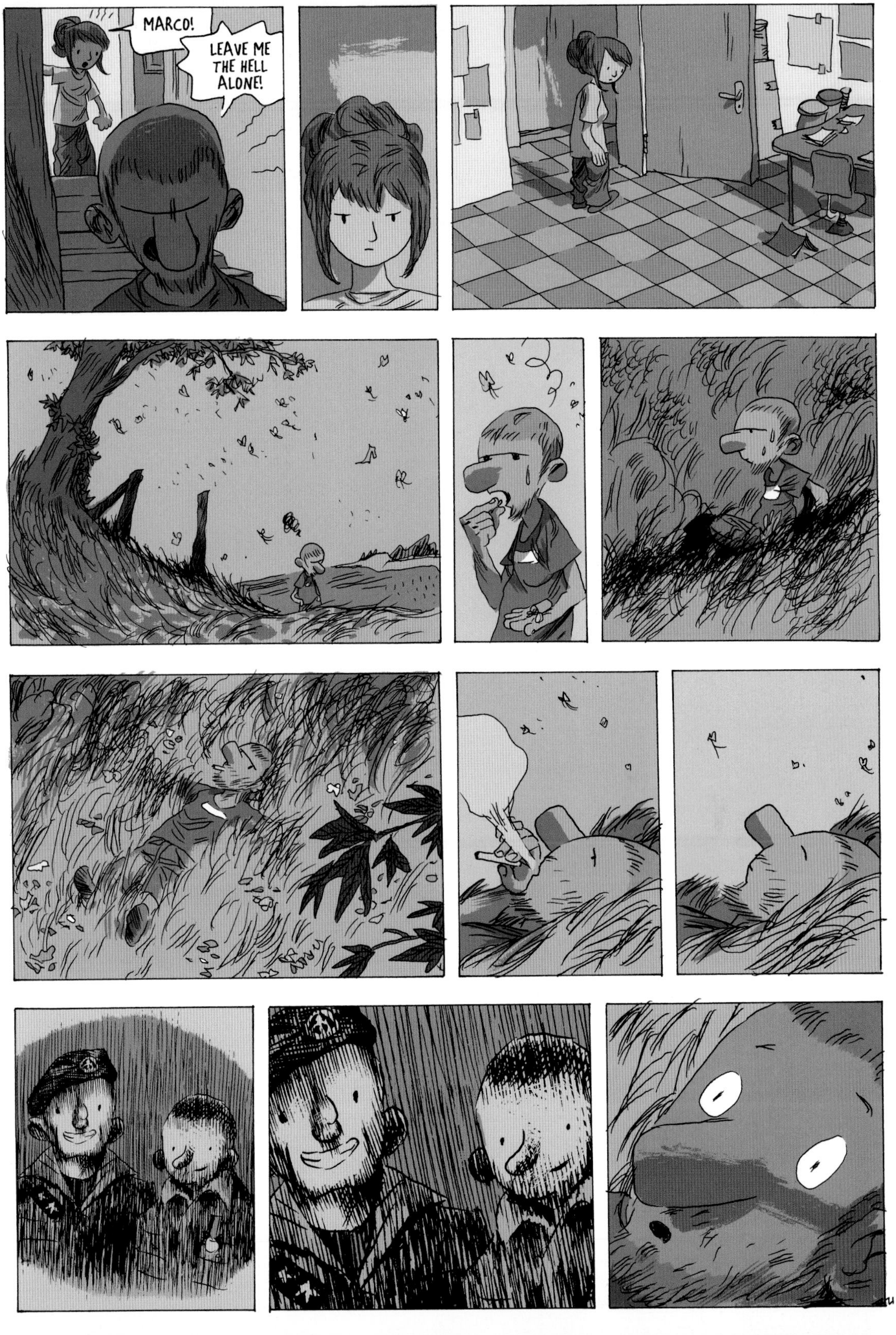
MARCO!
LEAVE ME THE HELL ALONE!

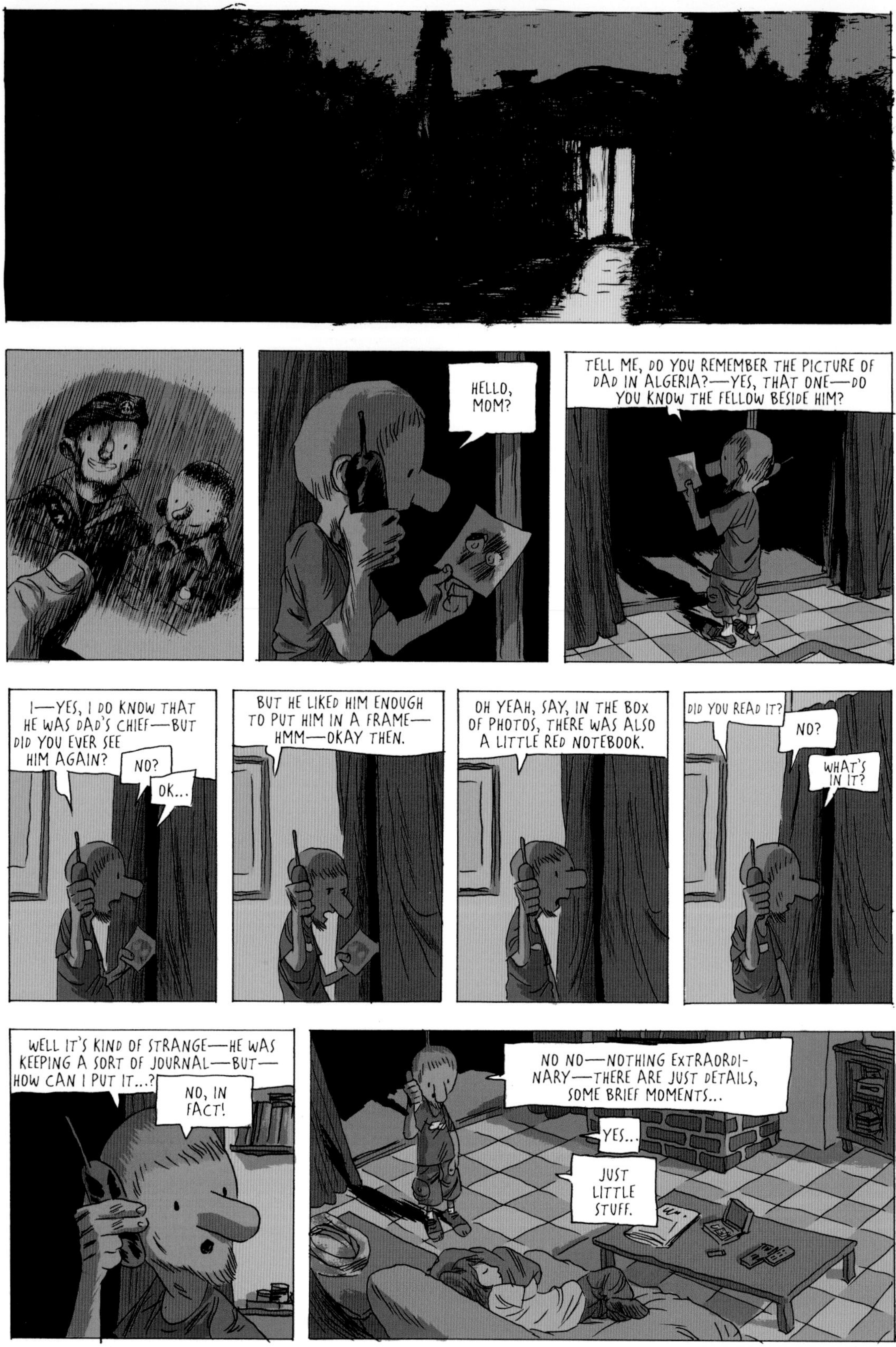
HELLO, MOM?
TELL ME, DO YOU REMEMBER THE PICTURE OF DAD IN ALGERIA?—YES, THAT ONE—DO YOU KNOW THE FELLOW BESIDE HIM?
I—YES, I DO KNOW THAT HE WAS DAD'S CHIEF—BUT DID YOU EVER SEE HIM AGAIN?
NO?
OK...
BUT HE LIKED HIM ENOUGH TO PUT HIM IN A FRAME—HMM—OKAY THEN.
OH YEAH, SAY, IN THE BOX OF PHOTOS, THERE WAS ALSO A LITTLE RED NOTEBOOK.
DID YOU READ IT?
NO?
WHAT'S IN IT?
WELL IT'S KIND OF STRANGE—HE WAS KEEPING A SORT OF JOURNAL—BUT—HOW CAN I PUT IT...?
NO, IN FACT!
NO NO—NOTHING EXTRAORDINARY—THERE ARE JUST DETAILS, SOME BRIEF MOMENTS...
YES...
JUST LITTLE STUFF.

EVEN WHEN SICK, EVEN DIMINISHED, EVEN NAKED, FOR A LONG TIME, I COULD ONLY SEE THE INFALLIBLE, INDESTRUCTIBLE FATHER-FIGURE IN MY DAD.

A FEW MONTHS BEFORE HIS DEATH, A STRANGE PROCESS HAD GOTTEN UNDER WAY: RENUNCIATION.

I WAS GIVING UP THE IDEAL FATHER, THE ONE WHO WOULD TAKE MY LITTLE BOY'S HAND AND WOULD SAY THE RIGHT WORDS AT THE RIGHT TIME.

I THEN STARTED TO SEE THE MAN IN THE FULLNESS OF HIS LIFE AS A MAN AND TO SHOW HIM TENDERNESS MORE OPENLY.

WHAT WAS UNTHINKABLE AS A CHILD BECAME A REALITY OF ADULTHOOD: "FATHERS ARE MORTAL."

ENVISIONING BEING A FATHER ISN'T ONLY RESIGNING ONESELF TO THE IDEA OF ONE'S OWN DEATH...

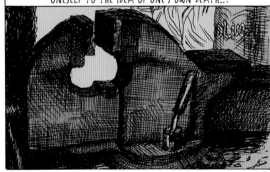

...IT'S ALSO RENOUNCING ONE'S LIFE AS AN IMPERFECT MAN IN ORDER TO BECOME A FANTASY FIGURE WHO HAS NO RIGHT TO MAKE MISTAKES.

WHO WAS THE MAN IMPRISONED WITHIN MY FATHER?

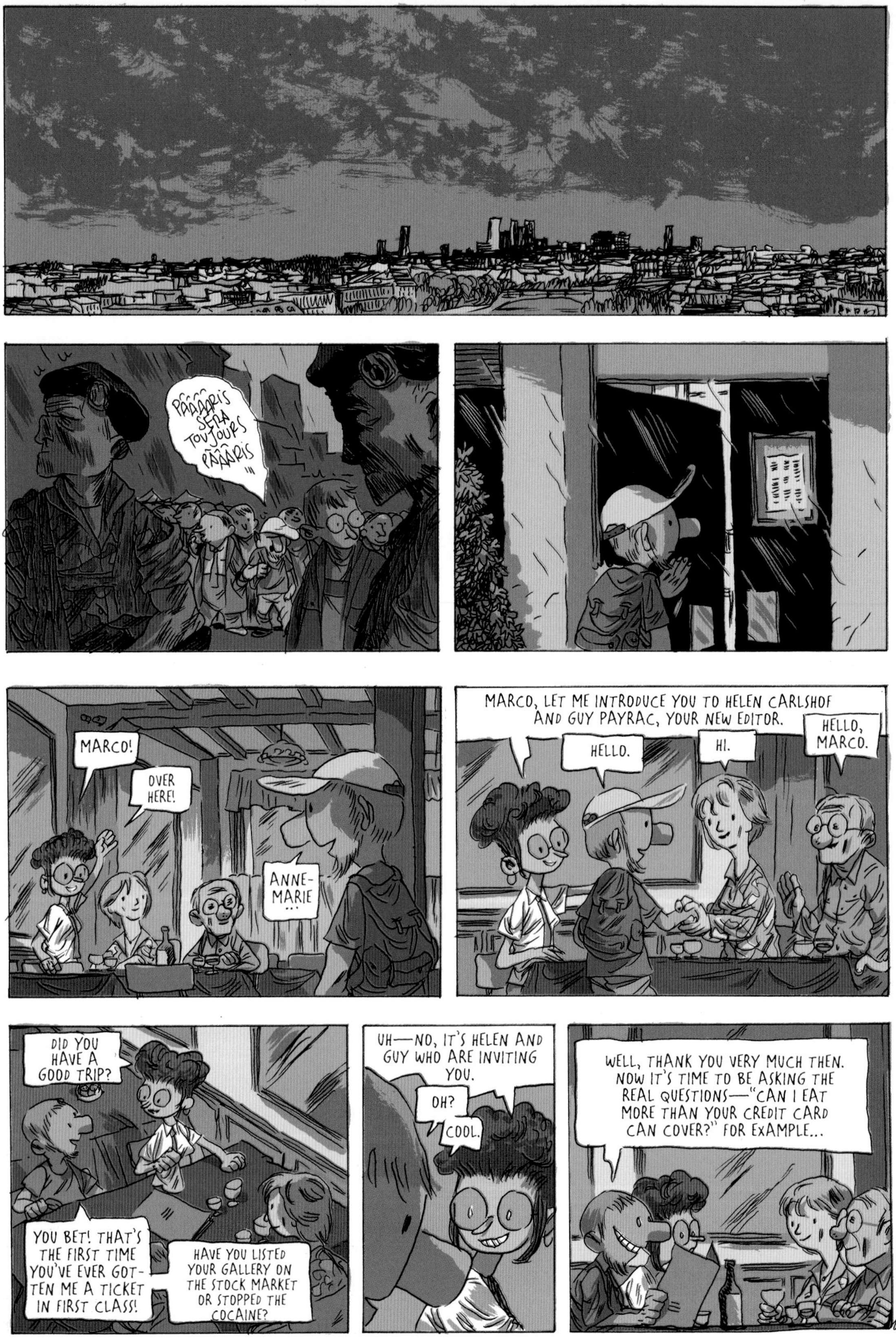
PÂÂÂRIS SERA TOUJOURS PÂÂÂRIS
MARCO!
OVER HERE!
ANNE-MARIE...
MARCO, LET ME INTRODUCE YOU TO HELEN CARLSHOF AND GUY PAYRAC, YOUR NEW EDITOR.
HELLO.
HI.
HELLO, MARCO.
DID YOU HAVE A GOOD TRIP?
YOU BET! THAT'S THE FIRST TIME YOU'VE EVER GOT-TEN ME A TICKET IN FIRST CLASS!
HAVE YOU LISTED YOUR GALLERY ON THE STOCK MARKET OR STOPPED THE COCAINE?
UH—NO, IT'S HELEN AND GUY WHO ARE INVITING YOU.
OH?
COOL.
WELL, THANK YOU VERY MUCH THEN. NOW IT'S TIME TO BE ASKING THE REAL QUESTIONS—"CAN I EAT MORE THAN YOUR CREDIT CARD CAN COVER?" FOR EXAMPLE...

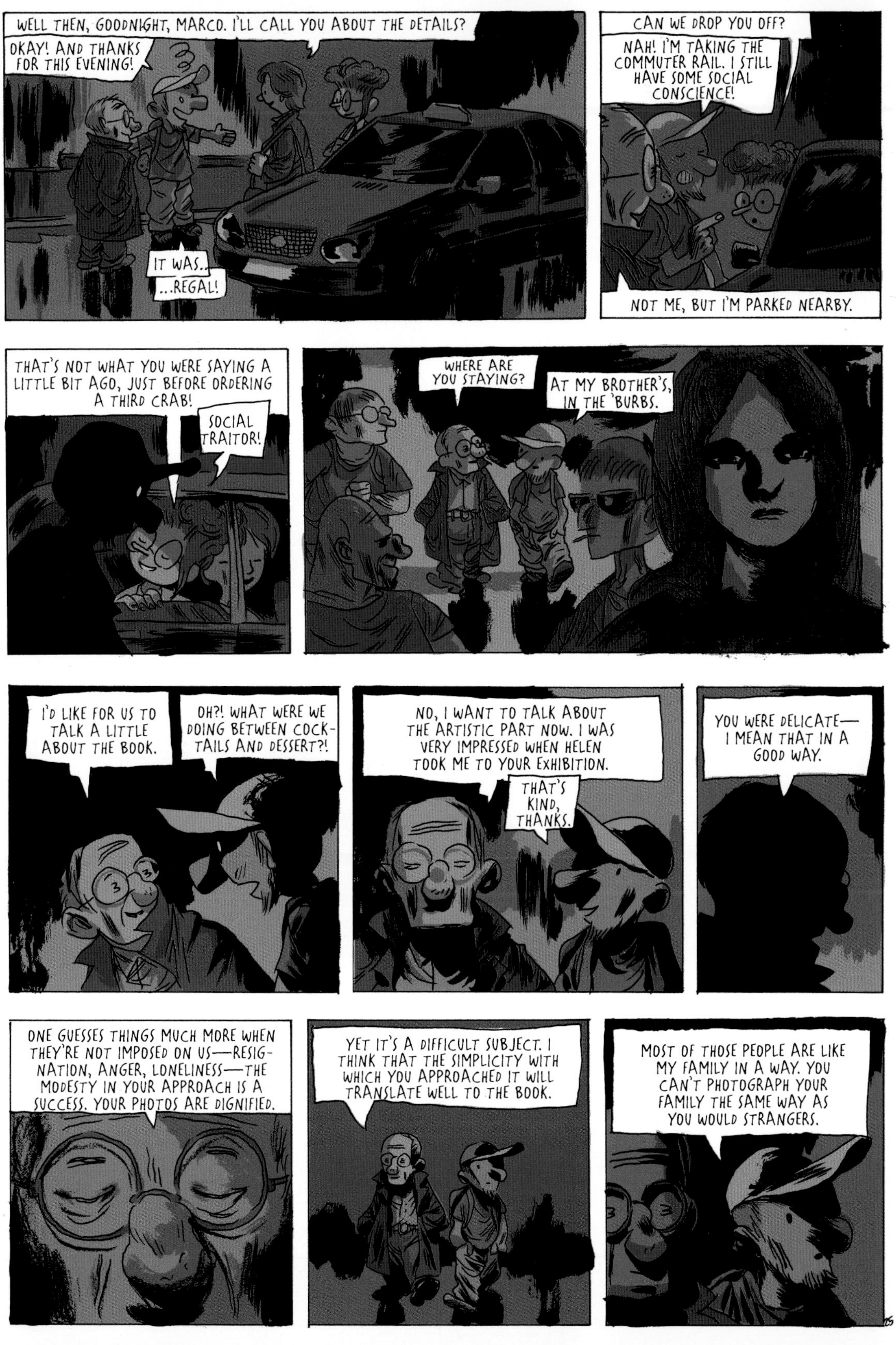
WELL THEN, GOODNIGHT, MARCO. I'LL CALL YOU ABOUT THE DETAILS?
OKAY! AND THANKS FOR THIS EVENING!
IT WAS...
...REGAL!
CAN WE DROP YOU OFF?
NAH! I'M TAKING THE COMMUTER RAIL. I STILL HAVE SOME SOCIAL CONSCIENCE!
NOT ME, BUT I'M PARKED NEARBY.
THAT'S NOT WHAT YOU WERE SAYING A LITTLE BIT AGO, JUST BEFORE ORDERING A THIRD CRAB!
SOCIAL TRAITOR!
WHERE ARE YOU STAYING?
AT MY BROTHER'S, IN THE 'BURBS.
I'D LIKE FOR US TO TALK A LITTLE ABOUT THE BOOK.
OH?! WHAT WERE WE DOING BETWEEN COCK-TAILS AND DESSERT?!
NO, I WANT TO TALK ABOUT THE ARTISTIC PART NOW. I WAS VERY IMPRESSED WHEN HELEN TOOK ME TO YOUR EXHIBITION.
THAT'S KIND, THANKS.
YOU WERE DELICATE— I MEAN THAT IN A GOOD WAY.
ONE GUESSES THINGS MUCH MORE WHEN THEY'RE NOT IMPOSED ON US—RESIG-NATION, ANGER, LONELINESS—THE MODESTY IN YOUR APPROACH IS A SUCCESS. YOUR PHOTOS ARE DIGNIFIED.
YET IT'S A DIFFICULT SUBJECT. I THINK THAT THE SIMPLICITY WITH WHICH YOU APPROACHED IT WILL TRANSLATE WELL TO THE BOOK.
MOST OF THOSE PEOPLE ARE LIKE MY FAMILY IN A WAY. YOU CAN'T PHOTOGRAPH YOUR FAMILY THE SAME WAY AS YOU WOULD STRANGERS.

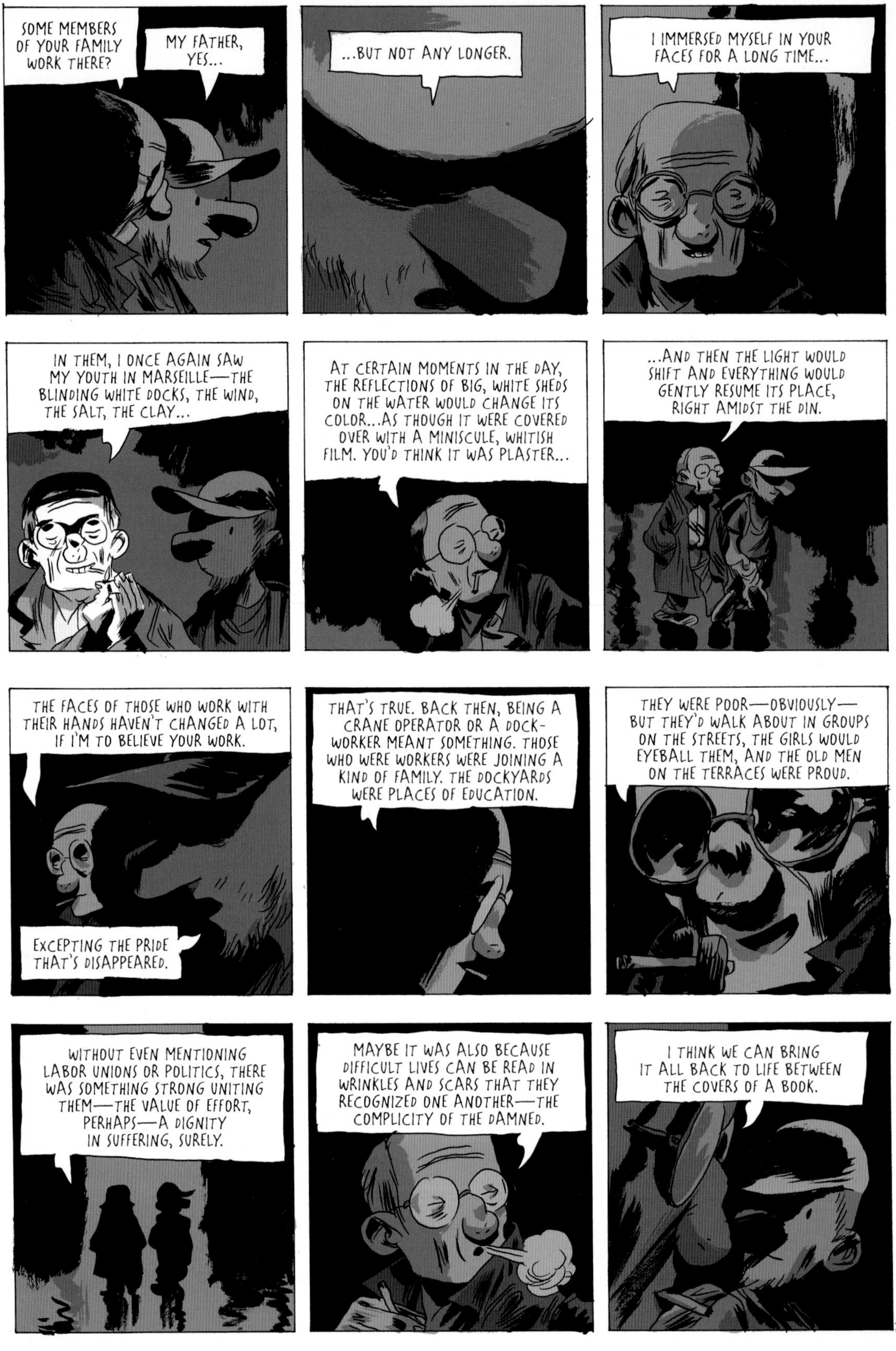
SOME MEMBERS OF YOUR FAMILY WORK THERE?
MY FATHER, YES...
...BUT NOT ANY LONGER.
I IMMERSED MYSELF IN YOUR FACES FOR A LONG TIME...
IN THEM, I ONCE AGAIN SAW MY YOUTH IN MARSEILLE—THE BLINDING WHITE DOCKS, THE WIND, THE SALT, THE CLAY...
AT CERTAIN MOMENTS IN THE DAY, THE REFLECTIONS OF BIG, WHITE SHEDS ON THE WATER WOULD CHANGE ITS COLOR...AS THOUGH IT WERE COVERED OVER WITH A MINISCULE, WHITISH FILM. YOU'D THINK IT WAS PLASTER...
...AND THEN THE LIGHT WOULD SHIFT AND EVERYTHING WOULD GENTLY RESUME ITS PLACE, RIGHT AMIDST THE DIN.
THE FACES OF THOSE WHO WORK WITH THEIR HANDS HAVEN'T CHANGED A LOT, IF I'M TO BELIEVE YOUR WORK.
EXCEPTING THE PRIDE THAT'S DISAPPEARED.
THAT'S TRUE. BACK THEN, BEING A CRANE OPERATOR OR A DOCK-WORKER MEANT SOMETHING. THOSE WHO WERE WORKERS WERE JOINING A KIND OF FAMILY. THE DOCKYARDS WERE PLACES OF EDUCATION.
THEY WERE POOR—OBVIOUSLY—BUT THEY'D WALK ABOUT IN GROUPS ON THE STREETS, THE GIRLS WOULD EYEBALL THEM, AND THE OLD MEN ON THE TERRACES WERE PROUD.
WITHOUT EVEN MENTIONING LABOR UNIONS OR POLITICS, THERE WAS SOMETHING STRONG UNITING THEM—THE VALUE OF EFFORT, PERHAPS—A DIGNITY IN SUFFERING, SURELY.
MAYBE IT WAS ALSO BECAUSE DIFFICULT LIVES CAN BE READ IN WRINKLES AND SCARS THAT THEY RECOGNIZED ONE ANOTHER—THE COMPLICITY OF THE DAMNED.
I THINK WE CAN BRING IT ALL BACK TO LIFE BETWEEN THE COVERS OF A BOOK.

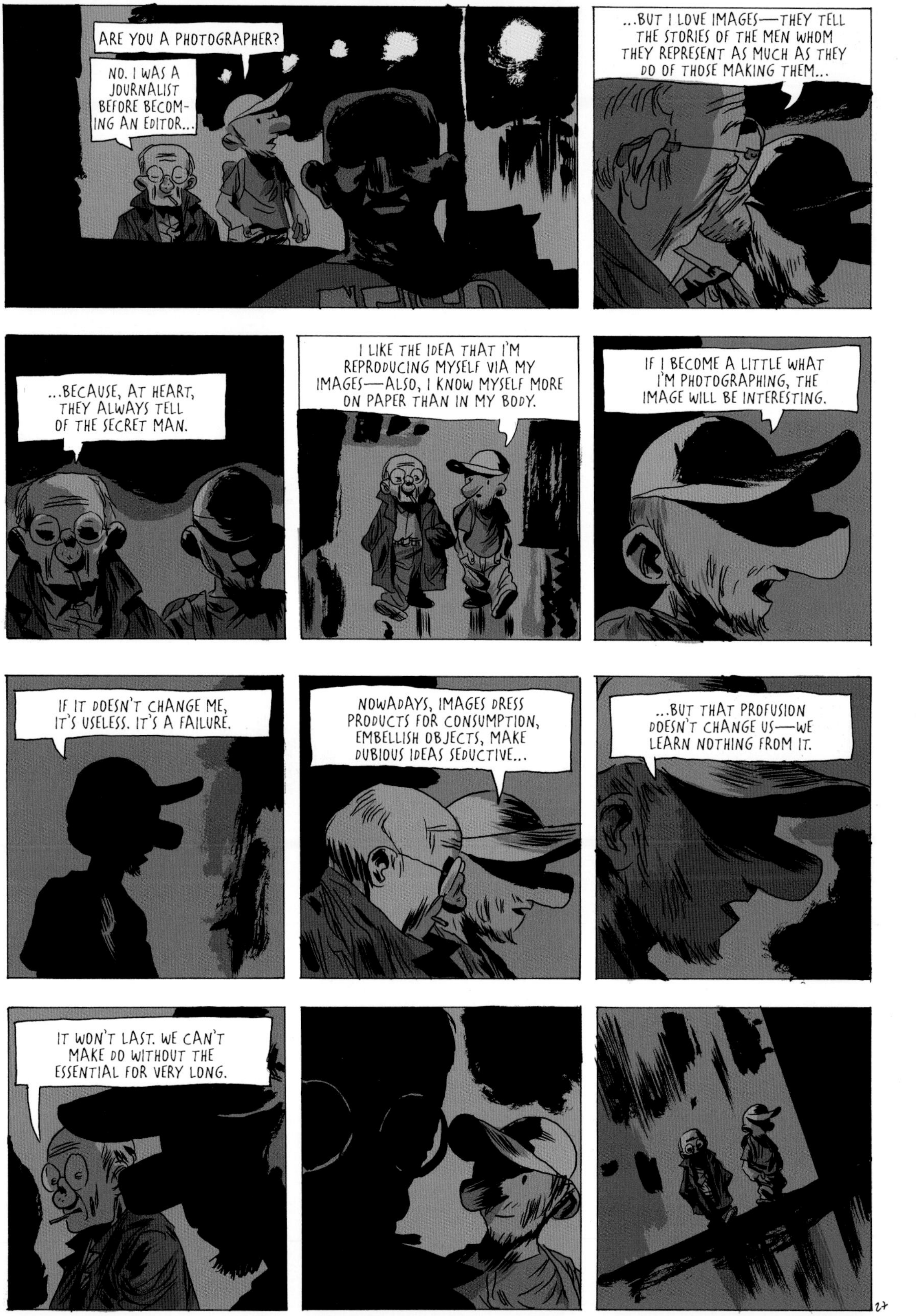
ARE YOU A PHOTOGRAPHER?
NO. I WAS A JOURNALIST BEFORE BECOMING AN EDITOR...
...BUT I LOVE IMAGES—THEY TELL THE STORIES OF THE MEN WHOM THEY REPRESENT AS MUCH AS THEY DO OF THOSE MAKING THEM...
...BECAUSE, AT HEART, THEY ALWAYS TELL OF THE SECRET MAN.
I LIKE THE IDEA THAT I'M REPRODUCING MYSELF VIA MY IMAGES—ALSO, I KNOW MYSELF MORE ON PAPER THAN IN MY BODY.
IF I BECOME A LITTLE WHAT I'M PHOTOGRAPHING, THE IMAGE WILL BE INTERESTING.
IF IT DOESN'T CHANGE ME, IT'S USELESS. IT'S A FAILURE.
NOWADAYS, IMAGES DRESS PRODUCTS FOR CONSUMPTION, EMBELLISH OBJECTS, MAKE DUBIOUS IDEAS SEDUCTIVE...
...BUT THAT PROFUSION DOESN'T CHANGE US—WE LEARN NOTHING FROM IT.
IT WON'T LAST. WE CAN'T MAKE DO WITHOUT THE ESSENTIAL FOR VERY LONG.

YOU KNOW, IT'S BEEN A VERY DIFFICULT TIME FOR US...MAYBE HE JUST NEEDS TO BE ALONE A LITTLE.

I GUESS SO...BUT HE'S CHANGED...HE'S GONE MORE AND MORE. HE SOMETIMES DOESN'T EVEN COME HOME AT NIGHT.

HAVE YOU TALKED WITH HIM?

HE REFUSES TO.

HE AVOIDS ALL CONVERSATION. YOU KNOW YOUR BROTHER. IF HE DOESN'T WANT TO TALK...

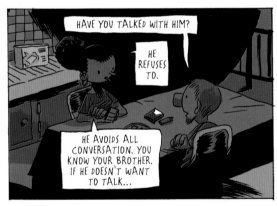

IT'LL BE ALL RIGHT.

YEAH..

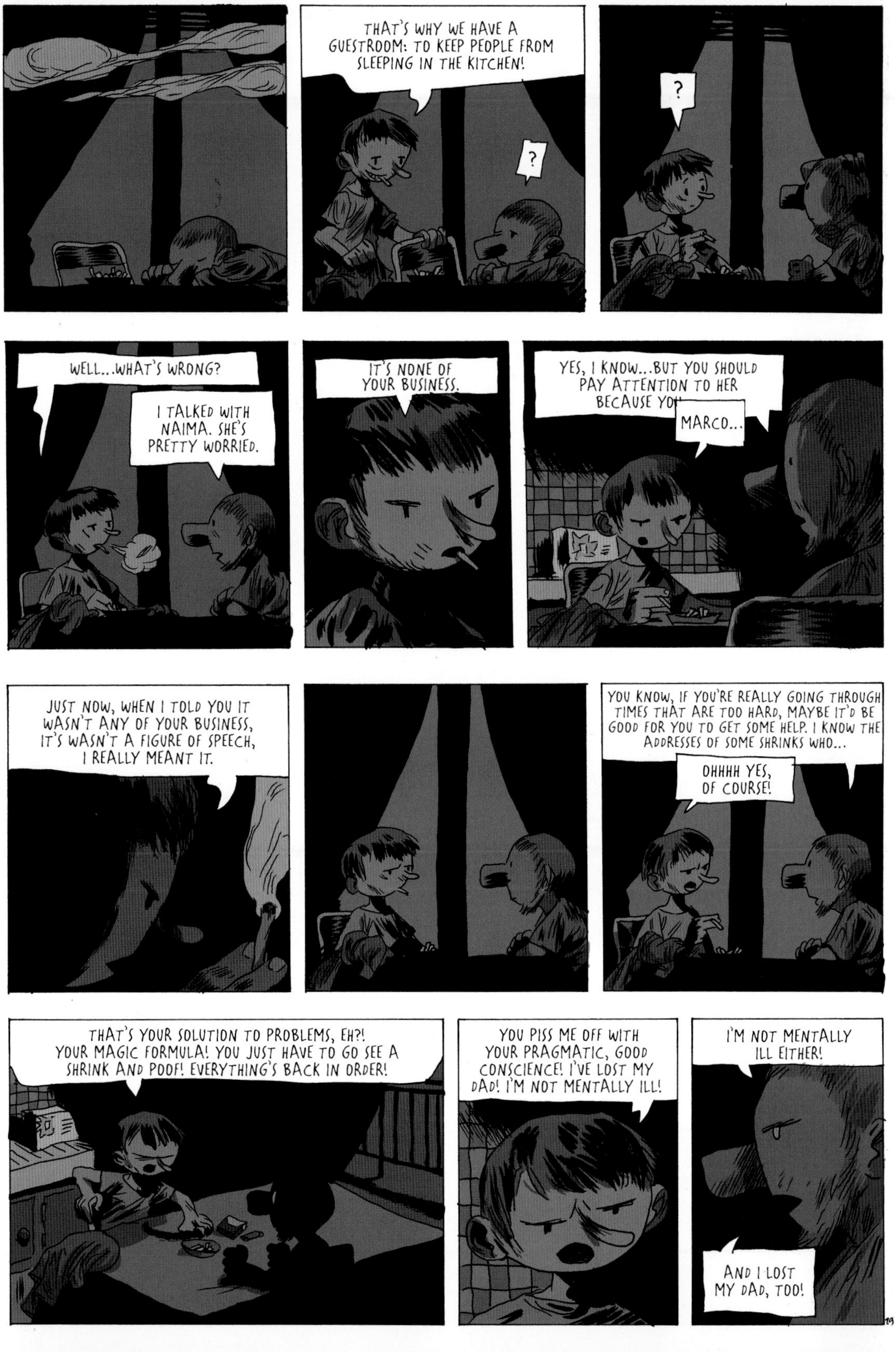

THAT'S WHY WE HAVE A GUESTROOM: TO KEEP PEOPLE FROM SLEEPING IN THE KITCHEN!
?
?
WELL...WHAT'S WRONG?
I TALKED WITH NAIMA. SHE'S PRETTY WORRIED.
IT'S NONE OF YOUR BUSINESS.
YES, I KNOW...BUT YOU SHOULD PAY ATTENTION TO HER BECAUSE YO
MARCO...
JUST NOW, WHEN I TOLD YOU IT WASN'T ANY OF YOUR BUSINESS, IT'S WASN'T A FIGURE OF SPEECH, I REALLY MEANT IT.
YOU KNOW, IF YOU'RE REALLY GOING THROUGH TIMES THAT ARE TOO HARD, MAYBE IT'D BE GOOD FOR YOU TO GET SOME HELP. I KNOW THE ADDRESSES OF SOME SHRINKS WHO...
OHHHH YES, OF COURSE!
THAT'S YOUR SOLUTION TO PROBLEMS, EH?! YOUR MAGIC FORMULA! YOU JUST HAVE TO GO SEE A SHRINK AND POOF! EVERYTHING'S BACK IN ORDER!
YOU PISS ME OFF WITH YOUR PRAGMATIC, GOOD CONSCIENCE! I'VE LOST MY DAD! I'M NOT MENTALLY ILL!
I'M NOT MENTALLY ILL EITHER!
AND I LOST MY DAD, TOO!

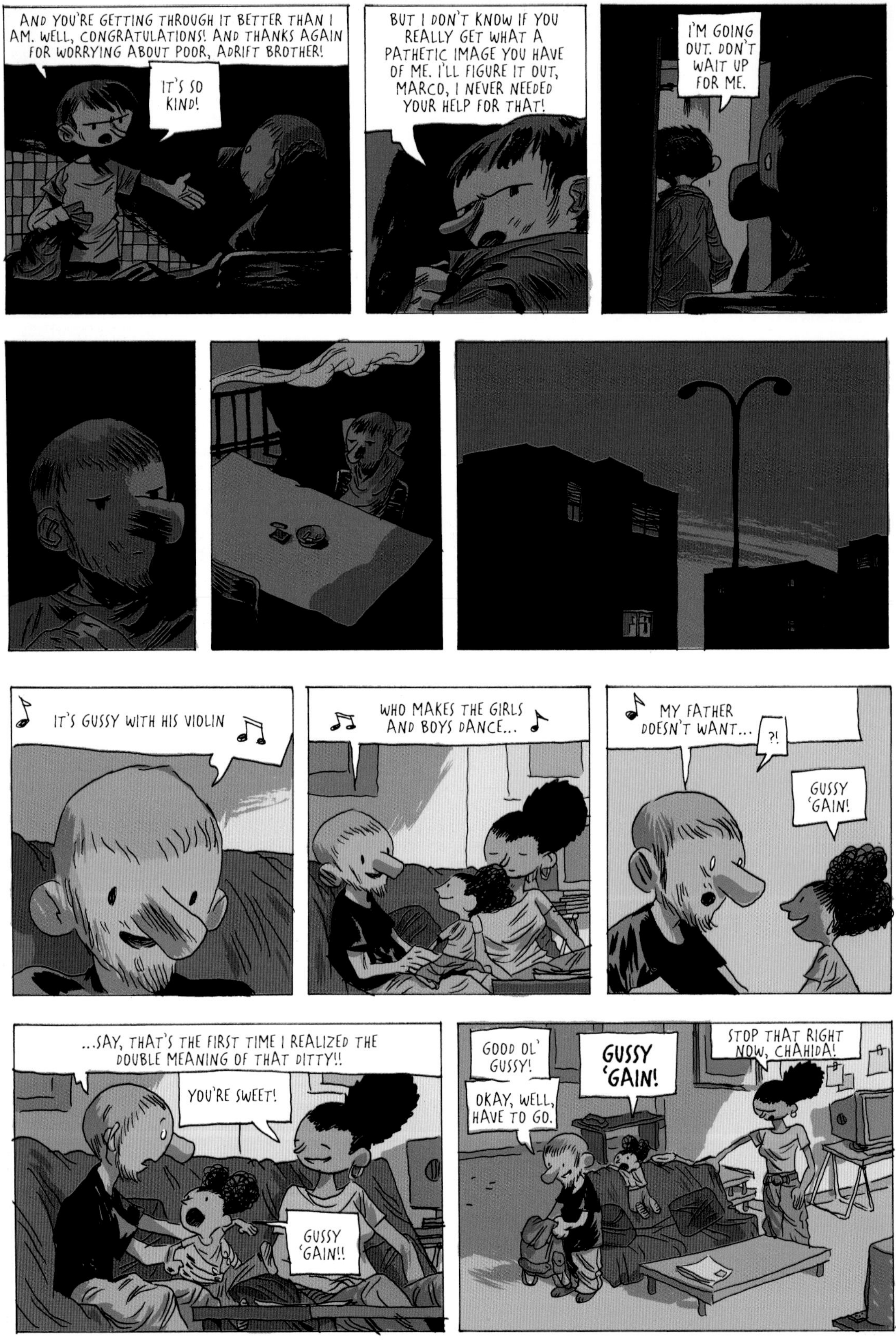
AND YOU'RE GETTING THROUGH IT BETTER THAN I AM. WELL, CONGRATULATIONS! AND THANKS AGAIN FOR WORRYING ABOUT POOR, ADRIFT BROTHER!
IT'S SO KIND!
BUT I DON'T KNOW IF YOU REALLY GET WHAT A PATHETIC IMAGE YOU HAVE OF ME. I'LL FIGURE IT OUT, MARCO, I NEVER NEEDED YOUR HELP FOR THAT!
I'M GOING OUT. DON'T WAIT UP FOR ME.
IT'S GUSSY WITH HIS VIOLIN
WHO MAKES THE GIRLS AND BOYS DANCE...
MY FATHER DOESN'T WANT...
?!
GUSSY 'GAIN!
...SAY, THAT'S THE FIRST TIME I REALIZED THE DOUBLE MEANING OF THAT DITTY!!
YOU'RE SWEET!
GUSSY 'GAIN!!
GOOD OL' GUSSY!
OKAY, WELL, HAVE TO GO.
GUSSY 'GAIN!
STOP THAT RIGHT NOW, CHAHIDA!

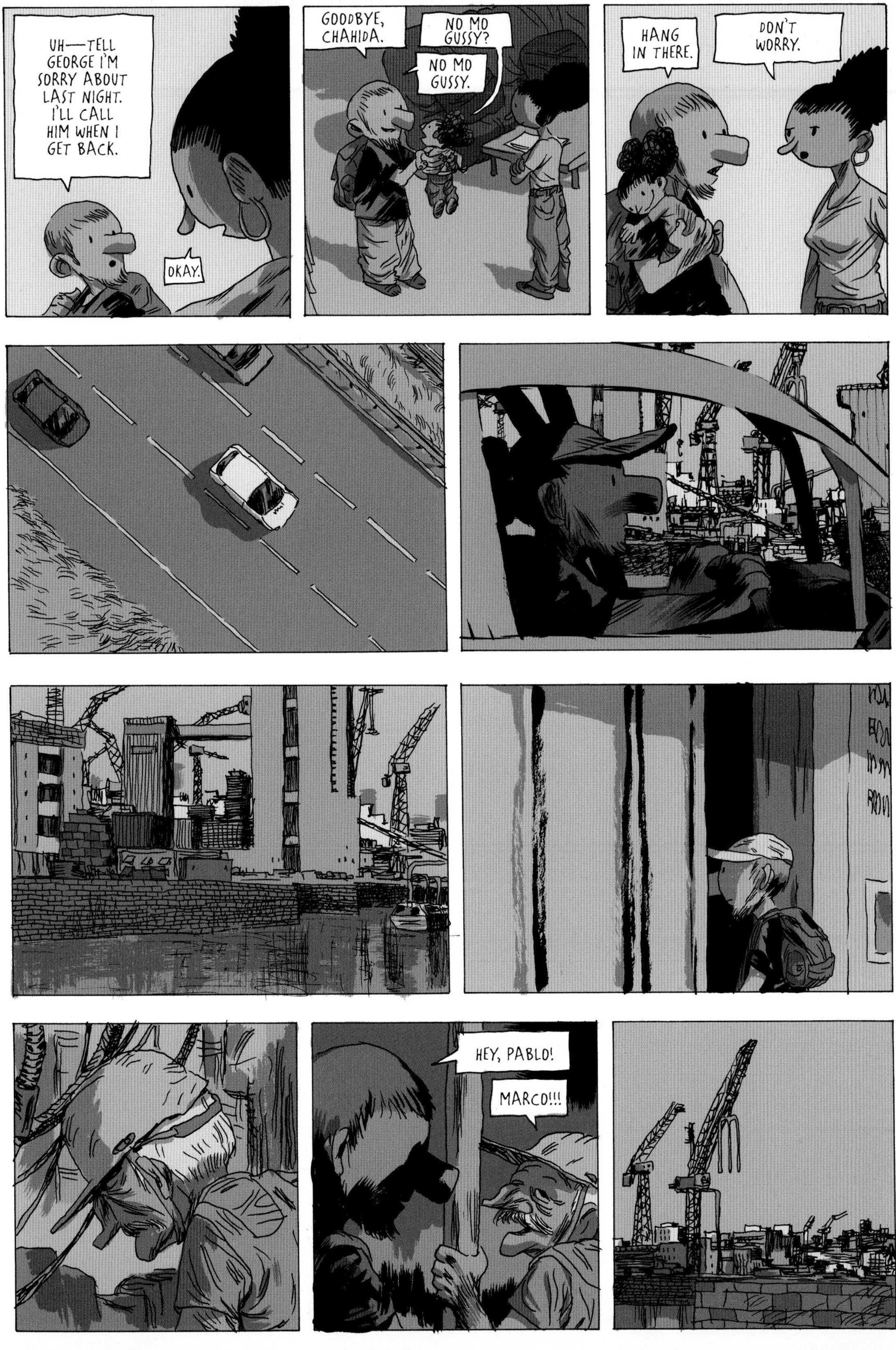
UH—TELL GEORGE I'M SORRY ABOUT LAST NIGHT. I'LL CALL HIM WHEN I GET BACK.
OKAY.
GOODBYE, CHAHIDA.
NO MO GUSSY?
NO MO GUSSY.
HANG IN THERE.
DON'T WORRY.
HEY, PABLO!
MARCO!!!

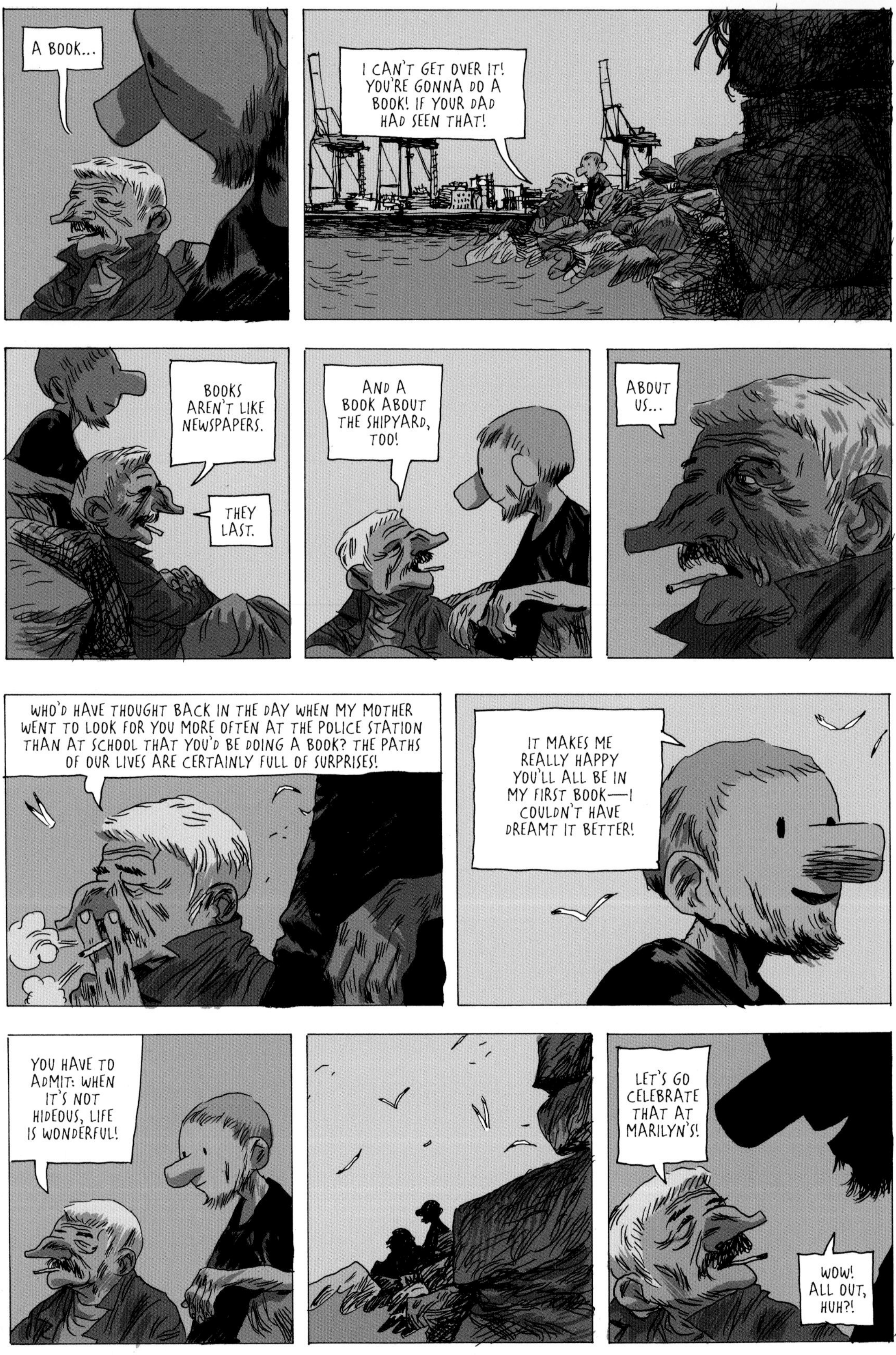

A BOOK...
I CAN'T GET OVER IT! YOU'RE GONNA DO A BOOK! IF YOUR DAD HAD SEEN THAT!
BOOKS AREN'T LIKE NEWSPAPERS.
THEY LAST.
AND A BOOK ABOUT THE SHIPYARD, TOO!
ABOUT US...
WHO'D HAVE THOUGHT BACK IN THE DAY WHEN MY MOTHER WENT TO LOOK FOR YOU MORE OFTEN AT THE POLICE STATION THAN AT SCHOOL THAT YOU'D BE DOING A BOOK? THE PATHS OF OUR LIVES ARE CERTAINLY FULL OF SURPRISES!
IT MAKES ME REALLY HAPPY YOU'LL ALL BE IN MY FIRST BOOK—I COULDN'T HAVE DREAMT IT BETTER!
YOU HAVE TO ADMIT: WHEN IT'S NOT HIDEOUS, LIFE IS WONDERFUL!
LET'S GO CELEBRATE THAT AT MARILYN'S!
WOW! ALL OUT, HUH?!

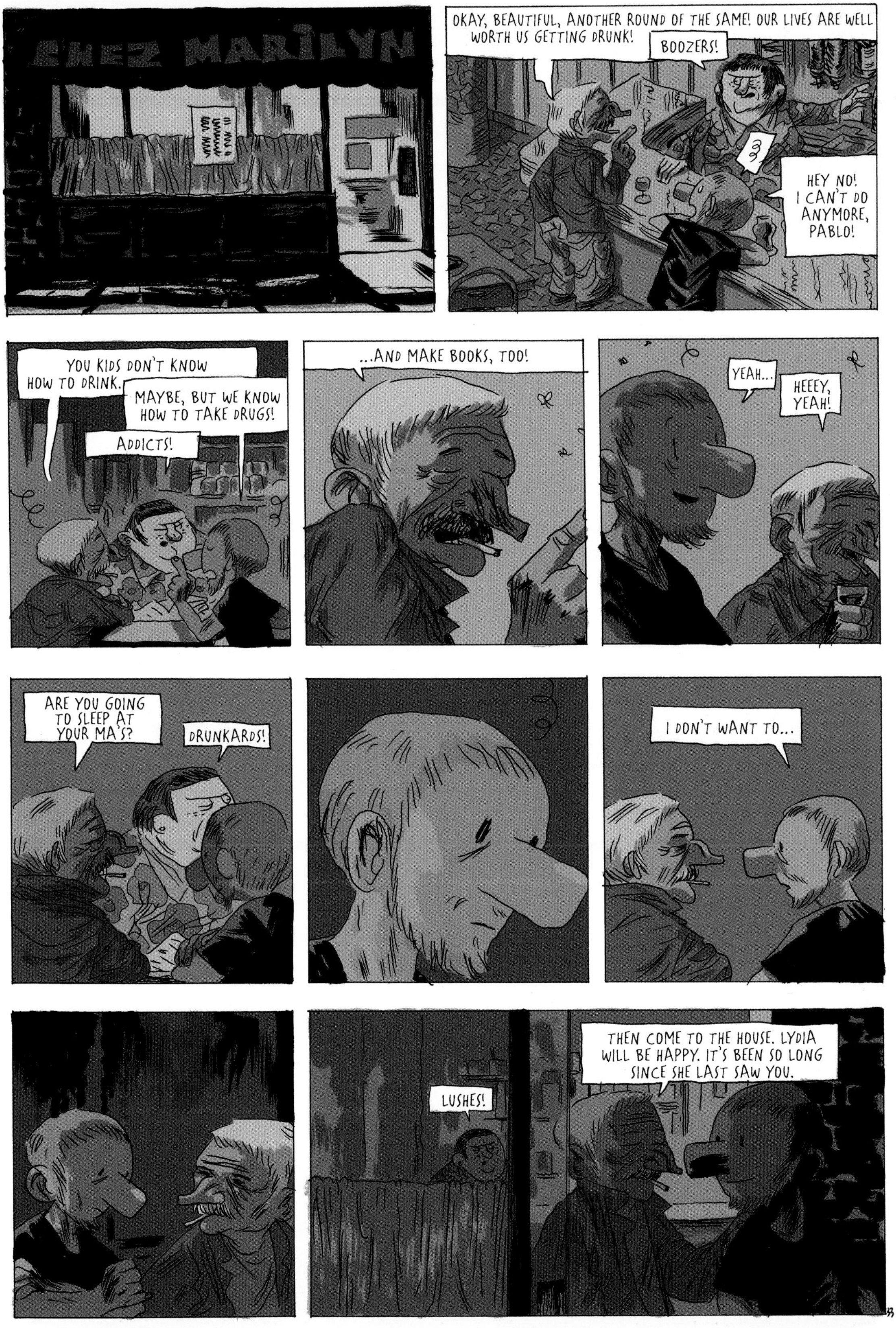
CHEZ MARILYN
OKAY, BEAUTIFUL, ANOTHER ROUND OF THE SAME! OUR LIVES ARE WELL WORTH US GETTING DRUNK!
BOOZERS!
HEY NO! I CAN'T DO ANYMORE, PABLO!
YOU KIDS DON'T KNOW HOW TO DRINK.
MAYBE, BUT WE KNOW HOW TO TAKE DRUGS!
ADDICTS!
...AND MAKE BOOKS, TOO!
YEAH...
HEEEY, YEAH!
ARE YOU GOING TO SLEEP AT YOUR MA'S?
DRUNKARDS!
I DON'T WANT TO...
LUSHES!
THEN COME TO THE HOUSE. LYDIA WILL BE HAPPY. IT'S BEEN SO LONG SINCE SHE LAST SAW YOU.

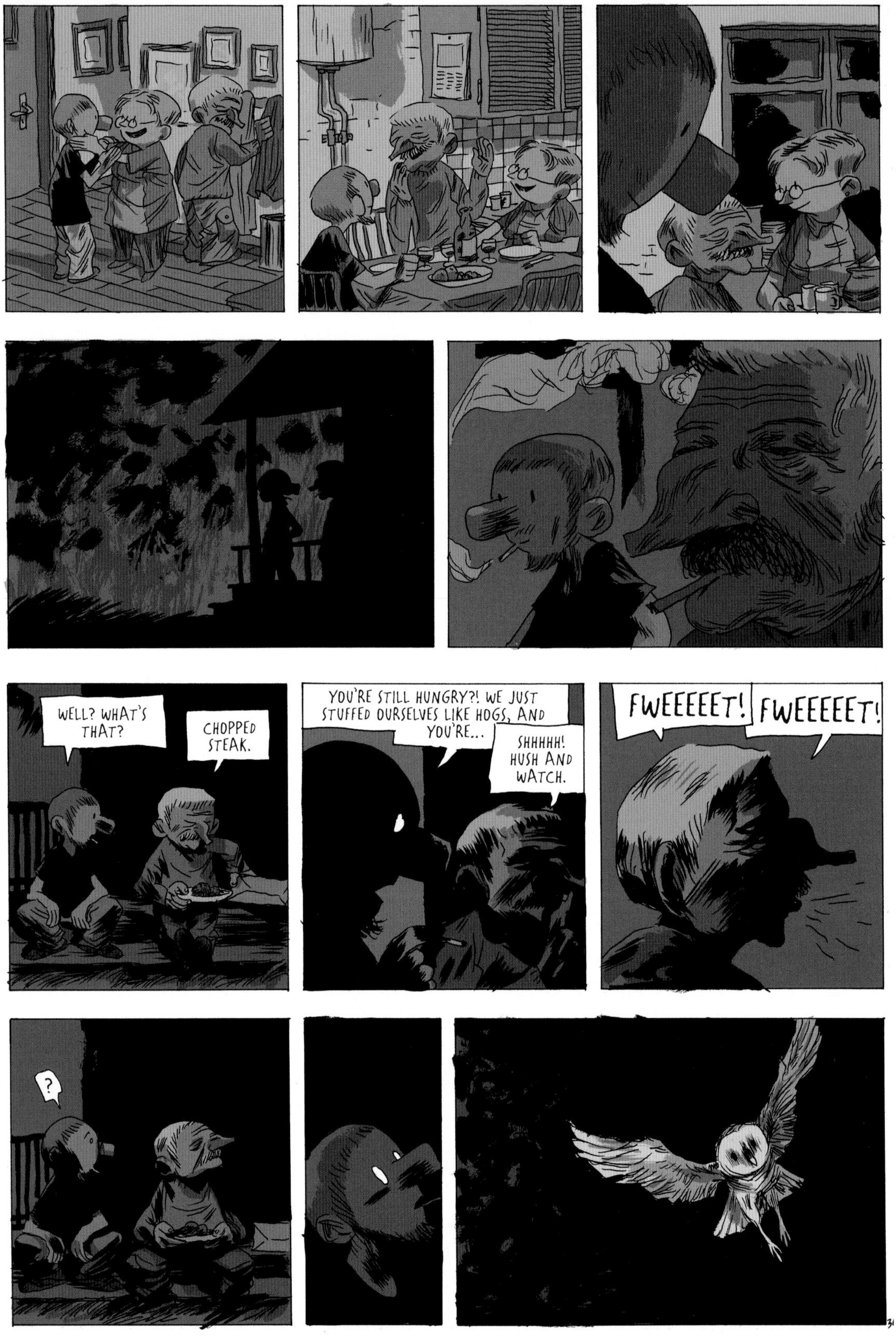
WELL? WHAT'S THAT?
CHOPPED STEAK.
YOU'RE STILL HUNGRY?! WE JUST STUFFED OURSELVES LIKE HOGS, AND YOU'RE...
SHHHHH! HUSH AND WATCH.
FWEEEEET!
FWEEEEET!
?

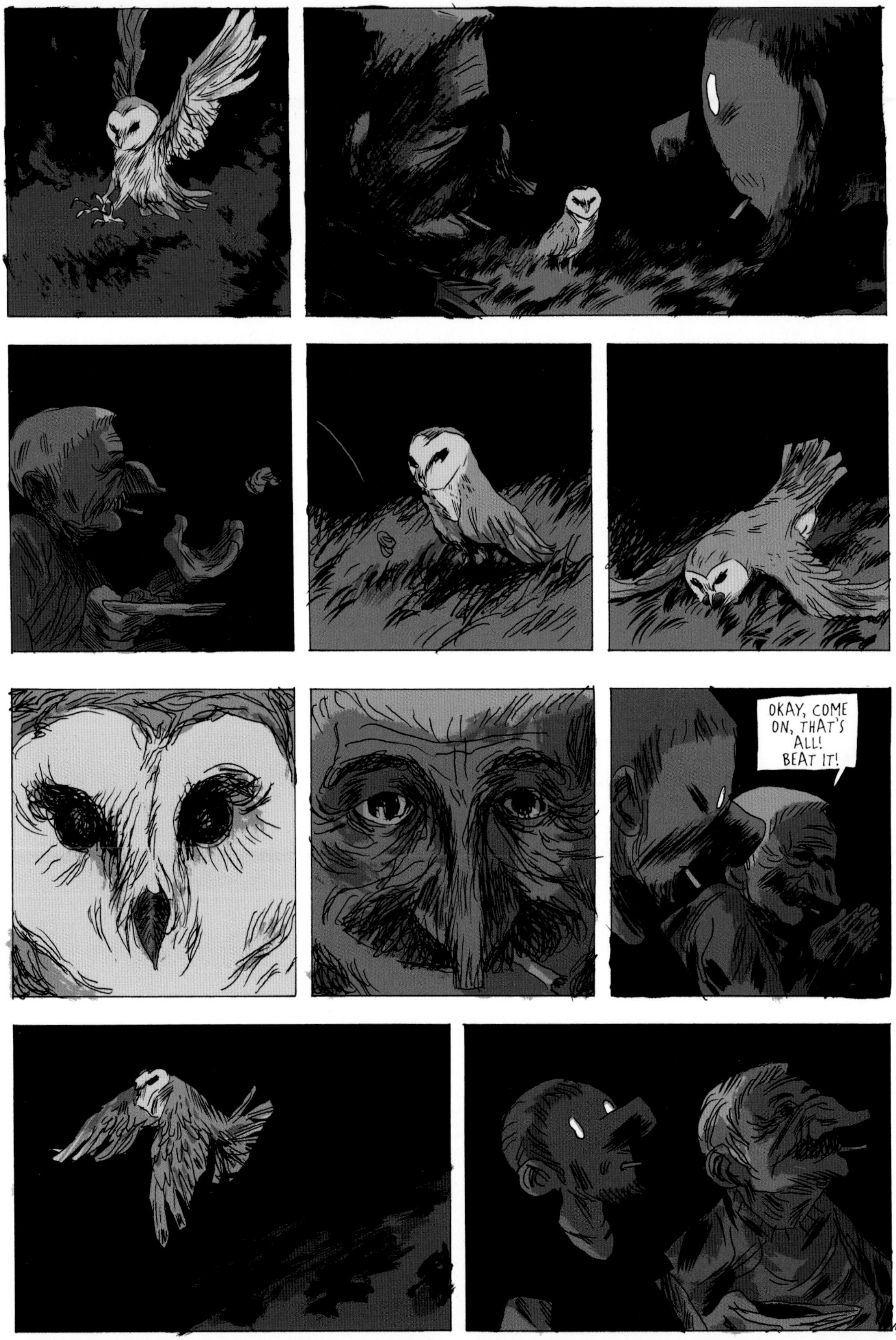
OKAY, COME ON, THAT'S ALL! BEAT IT!

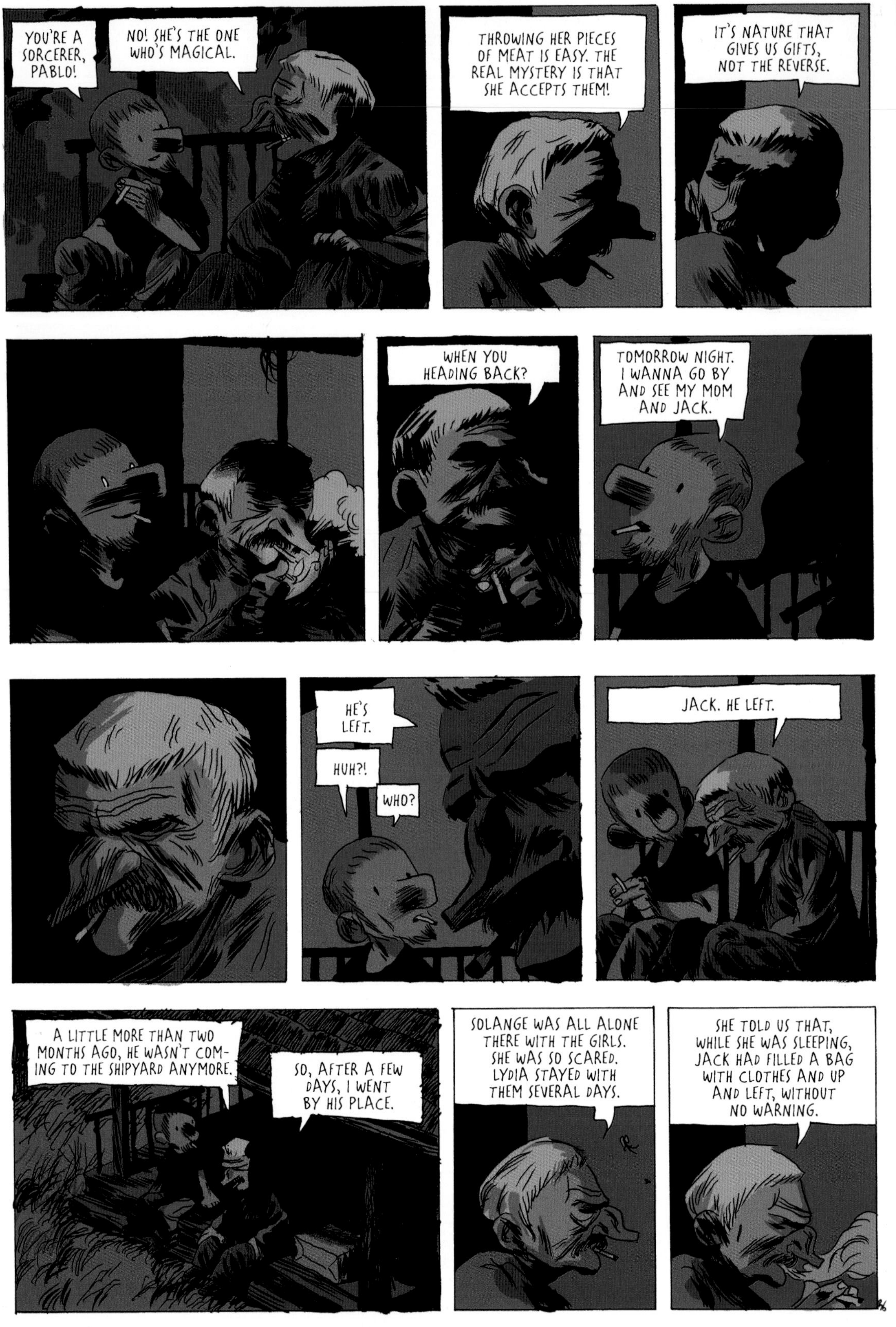
YOU'RE A SORCERER, PABLO!
NO! SHE'S THE ONE WHO'S MAGICAL.
THROWING HER PIECES OF MEAT IS EASY. THE REAL MYSTERY IS THAT SHE ACCEPTS THEM!
IT'S NATURE THAT GIVES US GIFTS, NOT THE REVERSE.
WHEN YOU HEADING BACK?
TOMORROW NIGHT. I WANNA GO BY AND SEE MY MOM AND JACK.
HE'S LEFT.
HUH?!
WHO?
JACK. HE LEFT.
A LITTLE MORE THAN TWO MONTHS AGO, HE WASN'T COMING TO THE SHIPYARD ANYMORE.
SO, AFTER A FEW DAYS, I WENT BY HIS PLACE.
SOLANGE WAS ALL ALONE THERE WITH THE GIRLS. SHE WAS SO SCARED. LYDIA STAYED WITH THEM SEVERAL DAYS.
SHE TOLD US THAT, WHILE SHE WAS SLEEPING, JACK HAD FILLED A BAG WITH CLOTHES AND UP AND LEFT, WITHOUT NO WARNING.

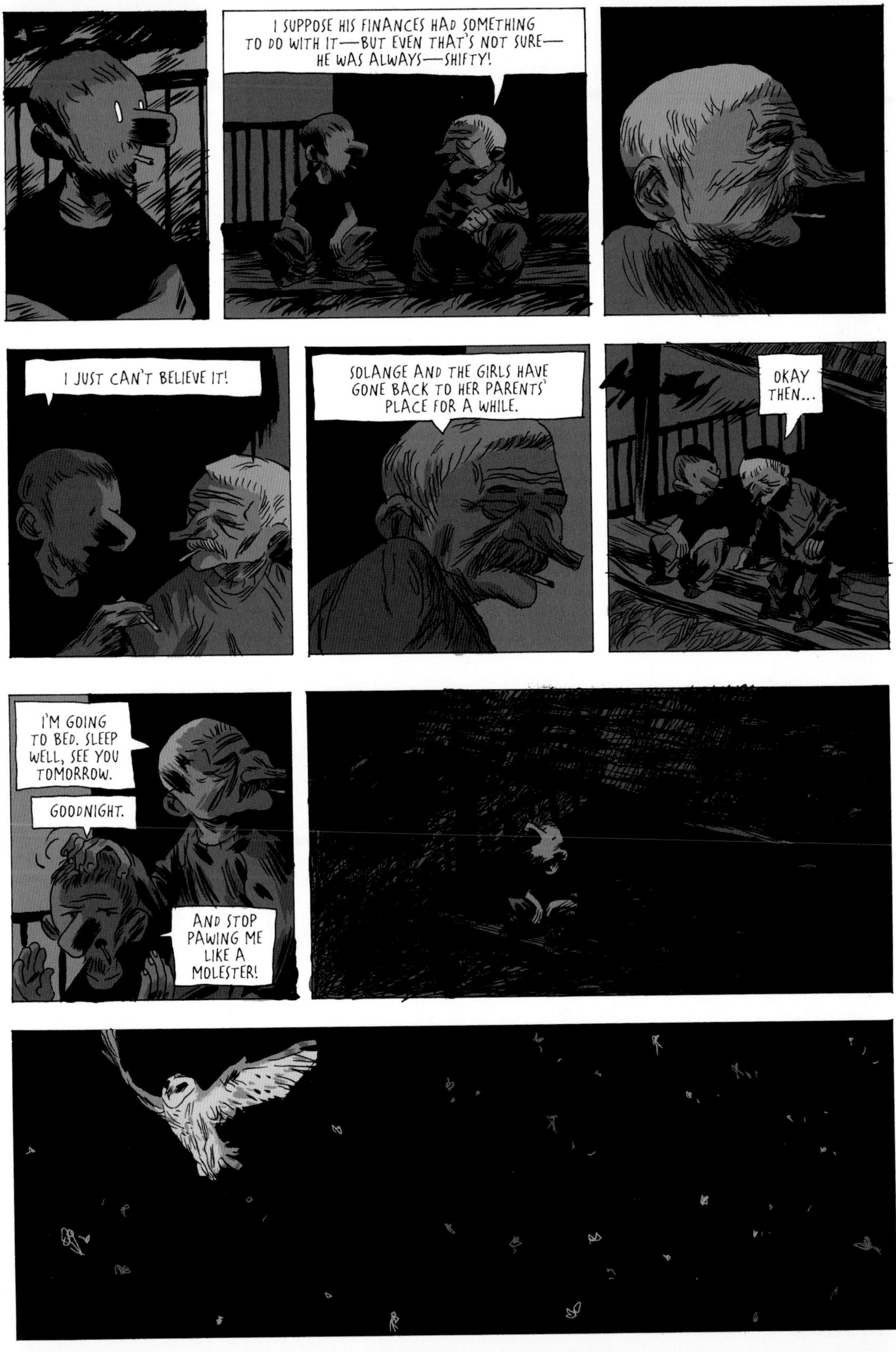
I SUPPOSE HIS FINANCES HAD SOMETHING TO DO WITH IT—BUT EVEN THAT'S NOT SURE—HE WAS ALWAYS—SHIFTY!
I JUST CAN'T BELIEVE IT!
SOLANGE AND THE GIRLS HAVE GONE BACK TO HER PARENTS' PLACE FOR A WHILE.
OKAY THEN...
I'M GOING TO BED. SLEEP WELL, SEE YOU TOMORROW.
GOODNIGHT.
AND STOP PAWING ME LIKE A MOLESTER!

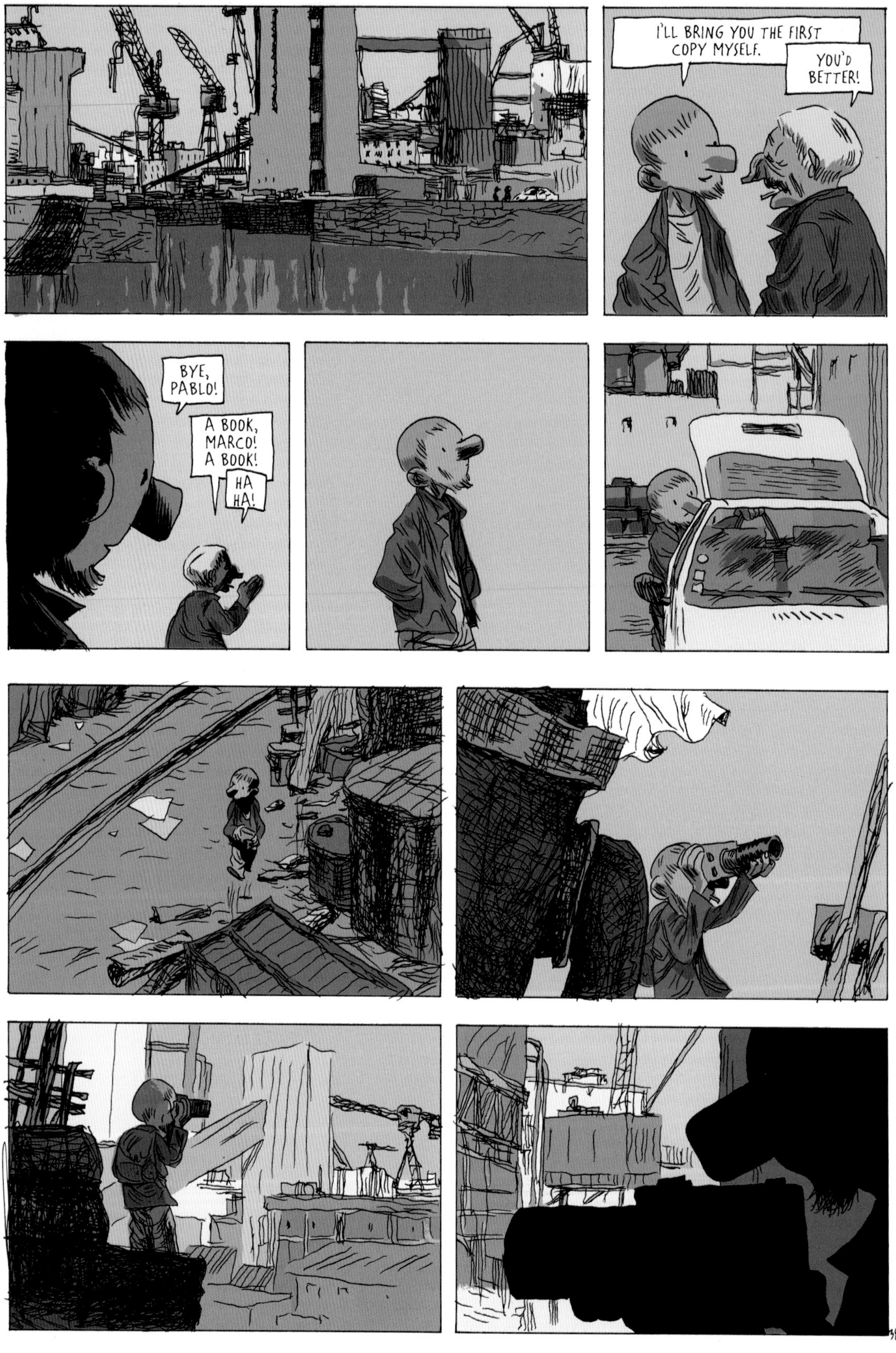
I'LL BRING YOU THE FIRST COPY MYSELF.
YOU'D BETTER!
BYE, PABLO!
A BOOK, MARCO! A BOOK!
HA HA!

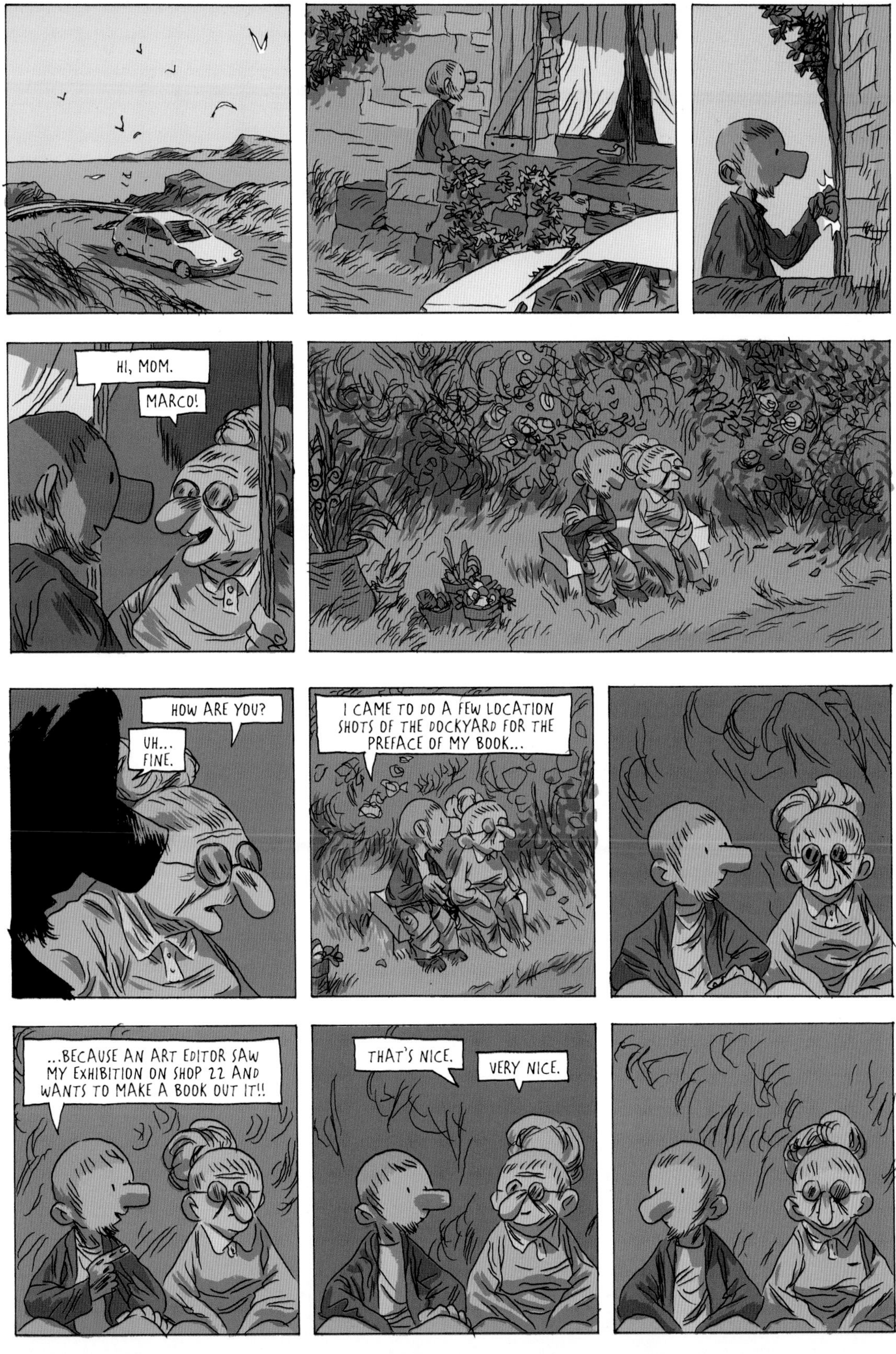
HI, MOM.
MARCO!
HOW ARE YOU?
UH... FINE.
I CAME TO DO A FEW LOCATION SHOTS OF THE DOCKYARD FOR THE PREFACE OF MY BOOK...
...BECAUSE AN ART EDITOR SAW MY EXHIBITION ON SHOP 22 AND WANTS TO MAKE A BOOK OUT IT!!
THAT'S NICE.
VERY NICE.

ARE YOU OKAY, MOM?

NOT REALLY.

TELL ME WHAT'S GOING ON.

I'M SAD, MARCO. IT'S ALL FINE TELLING MYSELF IT'S NORMAL, IT'S ALL FINE SEEING A PSYCHOLOGIST AND TAKING ALL HIS MEDICATION, IT'S ALL FINE LIVING ON STUBBORNLY, I'M SAD—ALL THE TIME.

BUT, I SUPPOSE THAT'S THE CASE WITH ALL WIDOWS OR ALMOST ALL— FRIENDS NO LONGER COME TO SEE ME. THEY SAY IT'S SO THEY WON'T BE BOTHERING ME...

...BUT I KNOW IT'S BECAUSE THIS HOUSE REEKS OF DEATH—A VIOLENT, SORDID DEATH.

IF YOUR FATHER HAD DIED IN A HOSPITAL OR IN A CAR ACCIDENT, I'M SURE THEY'D PUT FLOWERS ON HIS GRAVE FROM TIME TO TIME.

THE FACT THAT HE CHOSE TO DIE TERRIFIES THEM. IT'S AS IF IT WERE SHAMEFUL, OR NOT LIKE EVERYONE ELSE—OR COWARDLY.

I MUST BE THE ONLY ONE TO STILL BE PROUD OF HIM.

I'M PROUD, TOO.

WHEN I SAW HIS COFFIN, I THOUGHT IT WAS TOO SMALL, THAT YOUR FATHER WOULD NEVER FIT IN THERE—BUT YES HE DID. YOU SEEM BIGGER WHILE ALIVE THAN WHEN DEAD.

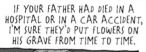

46

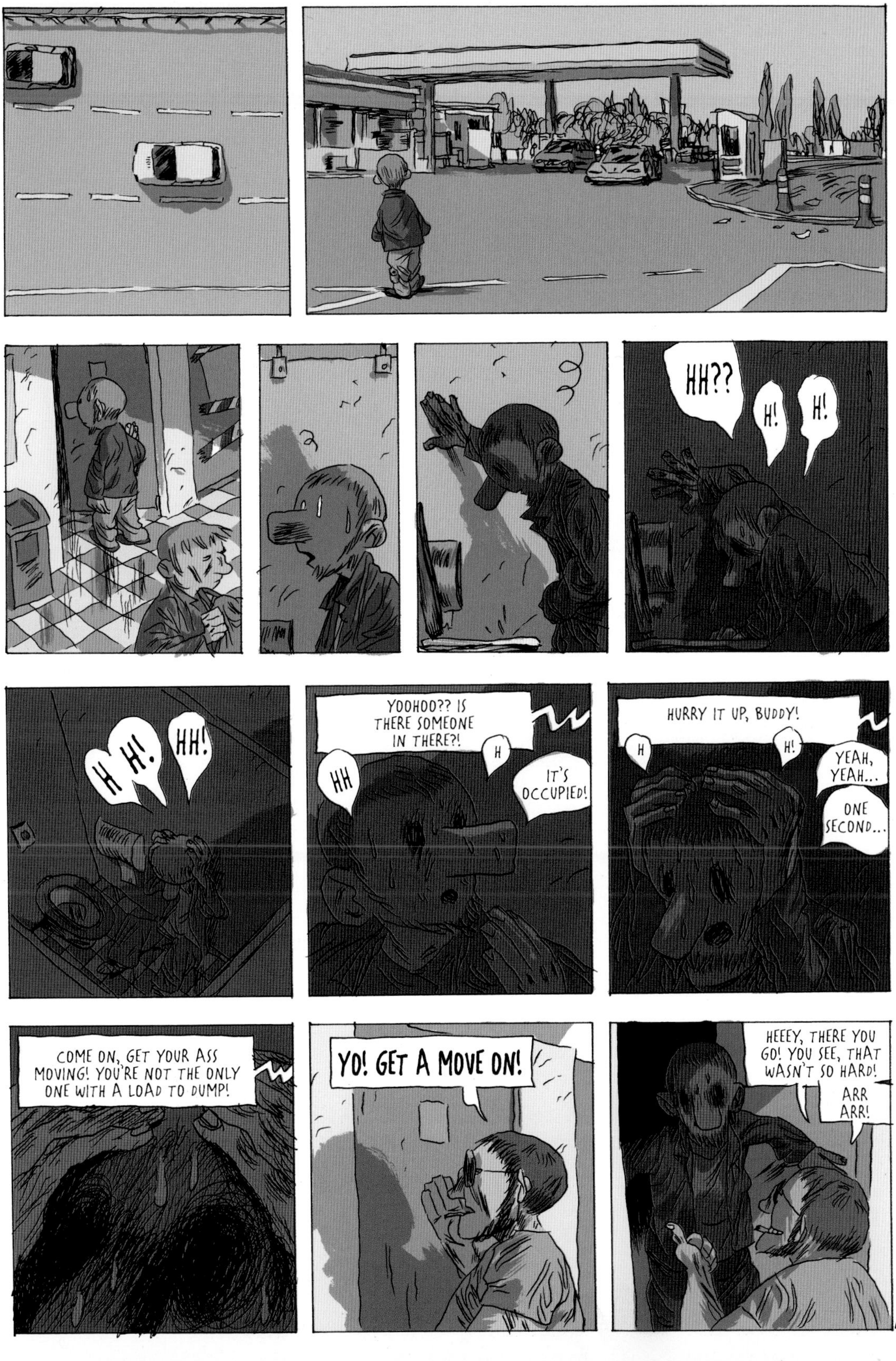
HH??
H!
H!
H H!
HH!
YOOHOO?? IS THERE SOMEONE IN THERE?!
HH
H
IT'S OCCUPIED!
HURRY IT UP, BUDDY!
H
H!
YEAH, YEAH...
ONE SECOND...
COME ON, GET YOUR ASS MOVING! YOU'RE NOT THE ONLY ONE WITH A LOAD TO DUMP!
YO! GET A MOVE ON!
HEEEY, THERE YOU GO! YOU SEE, THAT WASN'T SO HARD!
ARR ARR!

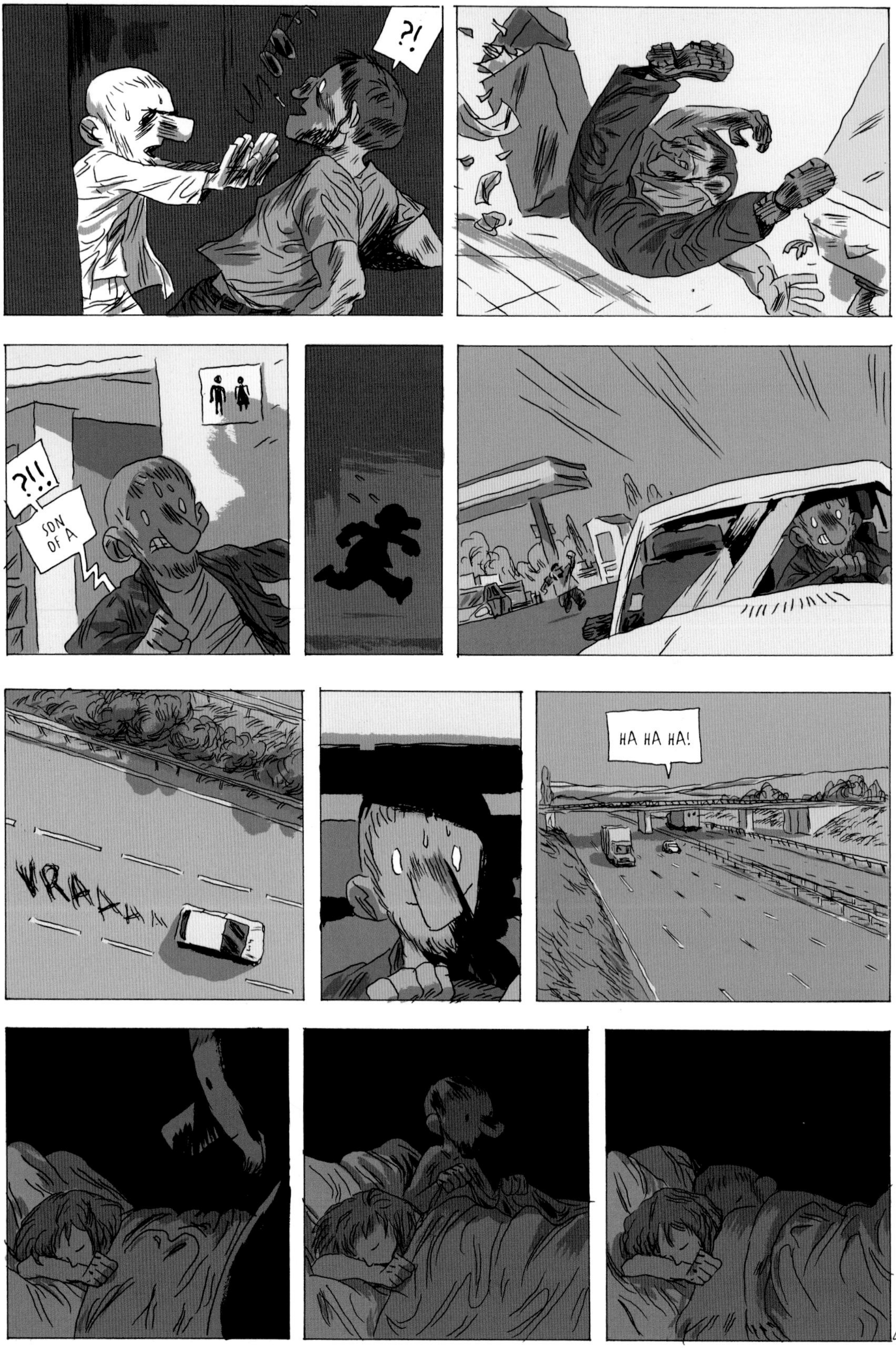
?!
?!!
SON OF A
VRAAAAAH
HA HA HA!

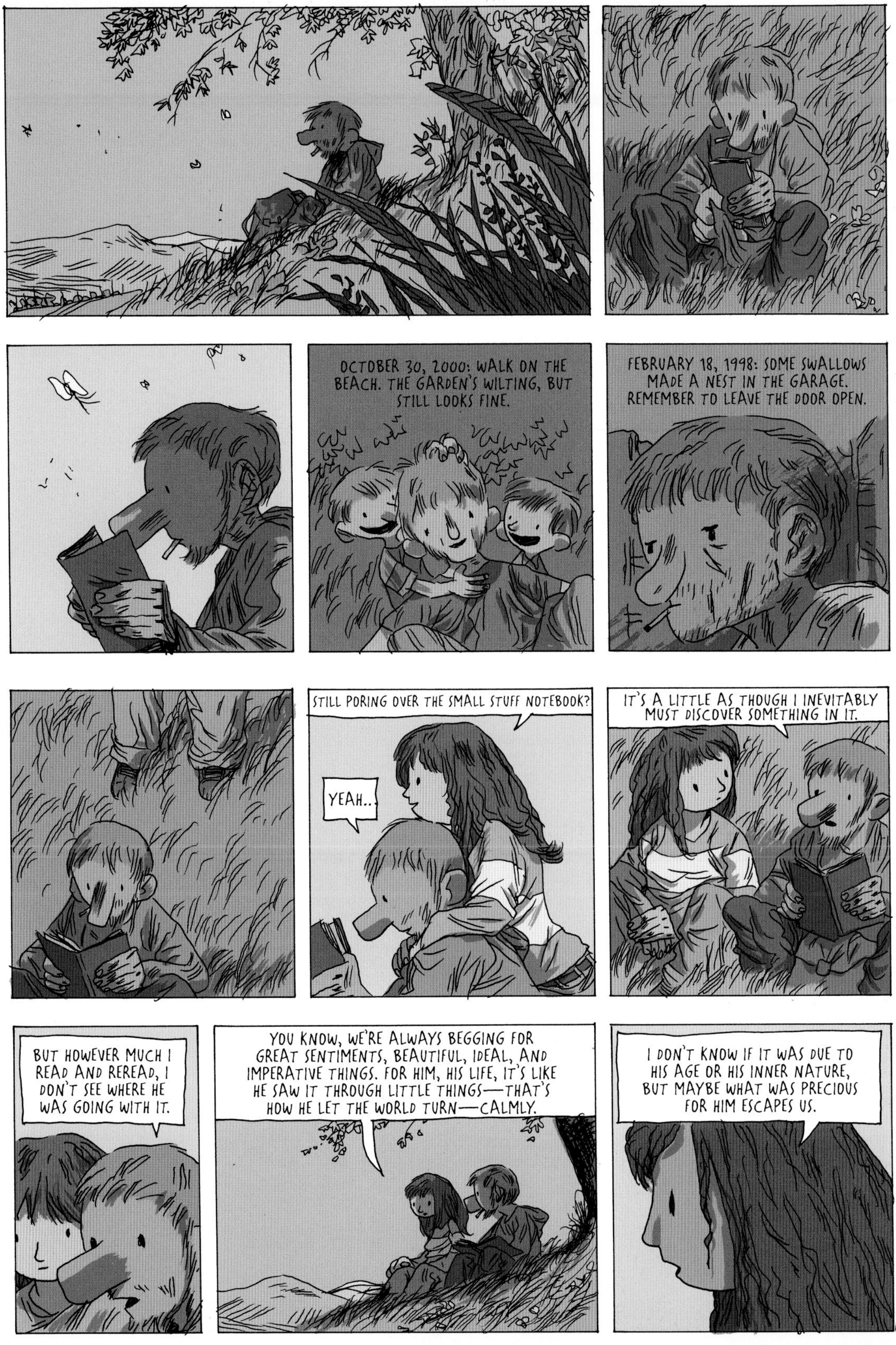

OCTOBER 30, 2000: WALK ON THE BEACH. THE GARDEN'S WILTING, BUT STILL LOOKS FINE.
FEBRUARY 18, 1998: SOME SWALLOWS MADE A NEST IN THE GARAGE. REMEMBER TO LEAVE THE DOOR OPEN.
STILL PORING OVER THE SMALL STUFF NOTEBOOK?
YEAH...
IT'S A LITTLE AS THOUGH I INEVITABLY MUST DISCOVER SOMETHING IN IT.
BUT HOWEVER MUCH I READ AND REREAD, I DON'T SEE WHERE HE WAS GOING WITH IT.
YOU KNOW, WE'RE ALWAYS BEGGING FOR GREAT SENTIMENTS, BEAUTIFUL, IDEAL, AND IMPERATIVE THINGS. FOR HIM, HIS LIFE, IT'S LIKE HE SAW IT THROUGH LITTLE THINGS—THAT'S HOW HE LET THE WORLD TURN—CALMLY.
I DON'T KNOW IF IT WAS DUE TO HIS AGE OR HIS INNER NATURE, BUT MAYBE WHAT WAS PRECIOUS FOR HIM ESCAPES US.

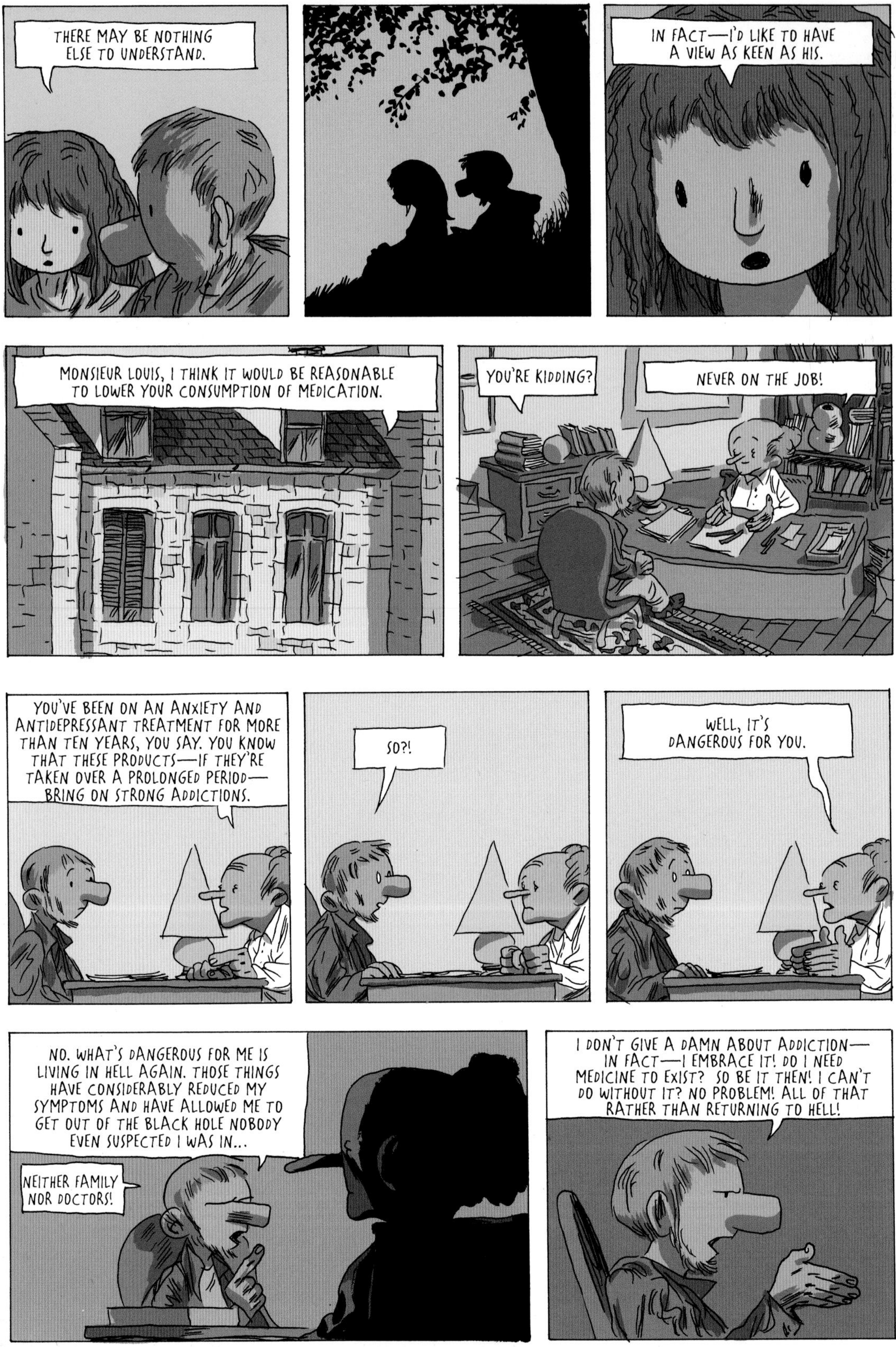
THERE MAY BE NOTHING ELSE TO UNDERSTAND.
IN FACT—I'D LIKE TO HAVE A VIEW AS KEEN AS HIS.
MONSIEUR LOUIS, I THINK IT WOULD BE REASONABLE TO LOWER YOUR CONSUMPTION OF MEDICATION.
YOU'RE KIDDING?
NEVER ON THE JOB!
YOU'VE BEEN ON AN ANXIETY AND ANTIDEPRESSANT TREATMENT FOR MORE THAN TEN YEARS, YOU SAY. YOU KNOW THAT THESE PRODUCTS—IF THEY'RE TAKEN OVER A PROLONGED PERIOD—BRING ON STRONG ADDICTIONS.
SO?!
WELL, IT'S DANGEROUS FOR YOU.
NO. WHAT'S DANGEROUS FOR ME IS LIVING IN HELL AGAIN. THOSE THINGS HAVE CONSIDERABLY REDUCED MY SYMPTOMS AND HAVE ALLOWED ME TO GET OUT OF THE BLACK HOLE NOBODY EVEN SUSPECTED I WAS IN...
NEITHER FAMILY NOR DOCTORS!
I DON'T GIVE A DAMN ABOUT ADDICTION—IN FACT—I EMBRACE IT! DO I NEED MEDICINE TO EXIST? SO BE IT THEN! I CAN'T DO WITHOUT IT? NO PROBLEM! ALL OF THAT RATHER THAN RETURNING TO HELL!

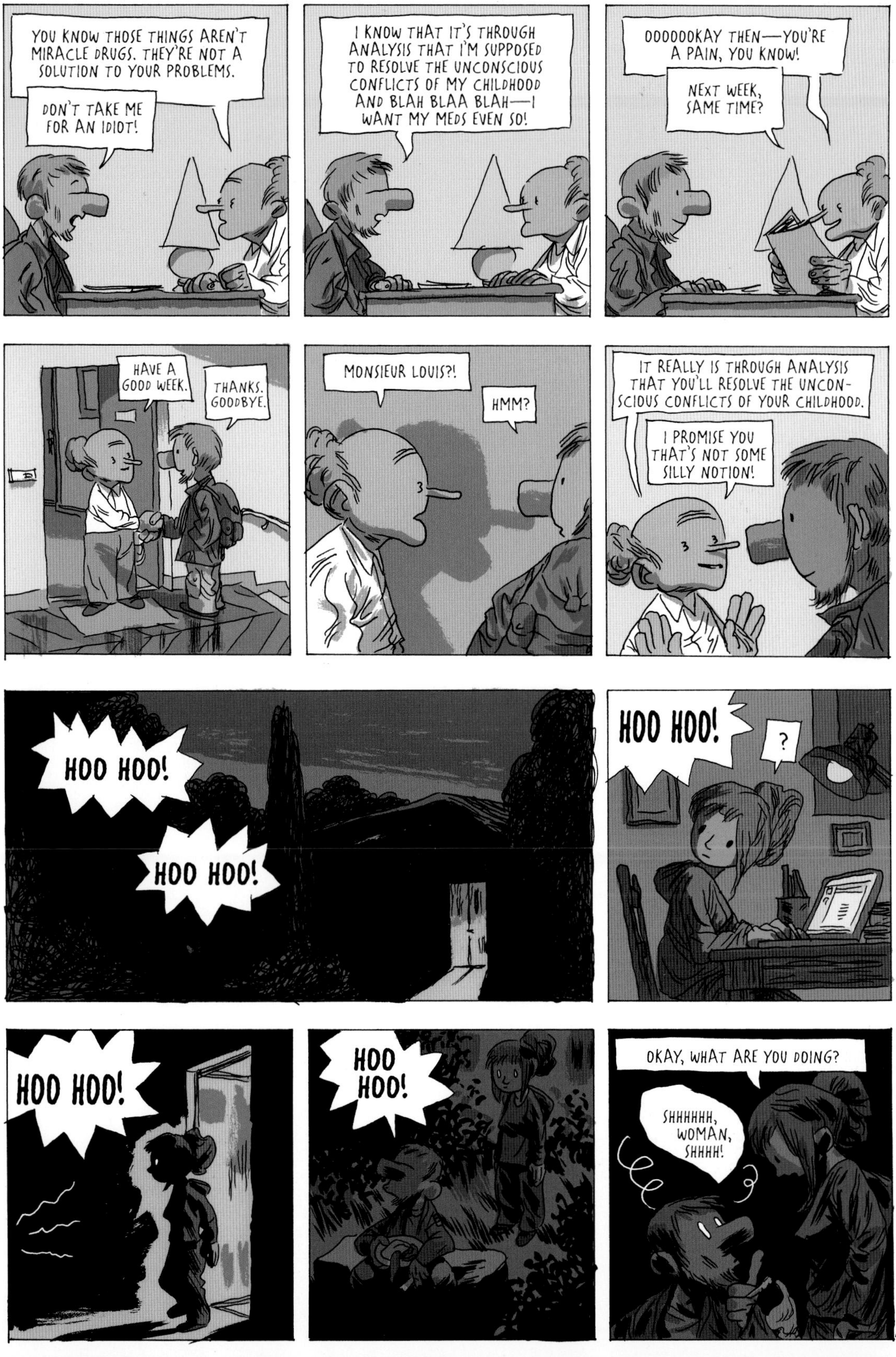
YOU KNOW THOSE THINGS AREN'T MIRACLE DRUGS. THEY'RE NOT A SOLUTION TO YOUR PROBLEMS.
DON'T TAKE ME FOR AN IDIOT!
I KNOW THAT IT'S THROUGH ANALYSIS THAT I'M SUPPOSED TO RESOLVE THE UNCONSCIOUS CONFLICTS OF MY CHILDHOOD AND BLAH BLAA BLAH—I WANT MY MEDS EVEN SO!
OOOOOOKAY THEN—YOU'RE A PAIN, YOU KNOW!
NEXT WEEK, SAME TIME?
HAVE A GOOD WEEK.
THANKS. GOODBYE.
MONSIEUR LOUIS?!
HMM?
IT REALLY IS THROUGH ANALYSIS THAT YOU'LL RESOLVE THE UNCONSCIOUS CONFLICTS OF YOUR CHILDHOOD.
I PROMISE YOU THAT'S NOT SOME SILLY NOTION!
HOO HOO!
HOO HOO!
HOO HOO!
?
HOO HOO!
HOO HOO!
OKAY, WHAT ARE YOU DOING?
SHHHHHH, WOMAN, SHHHH!

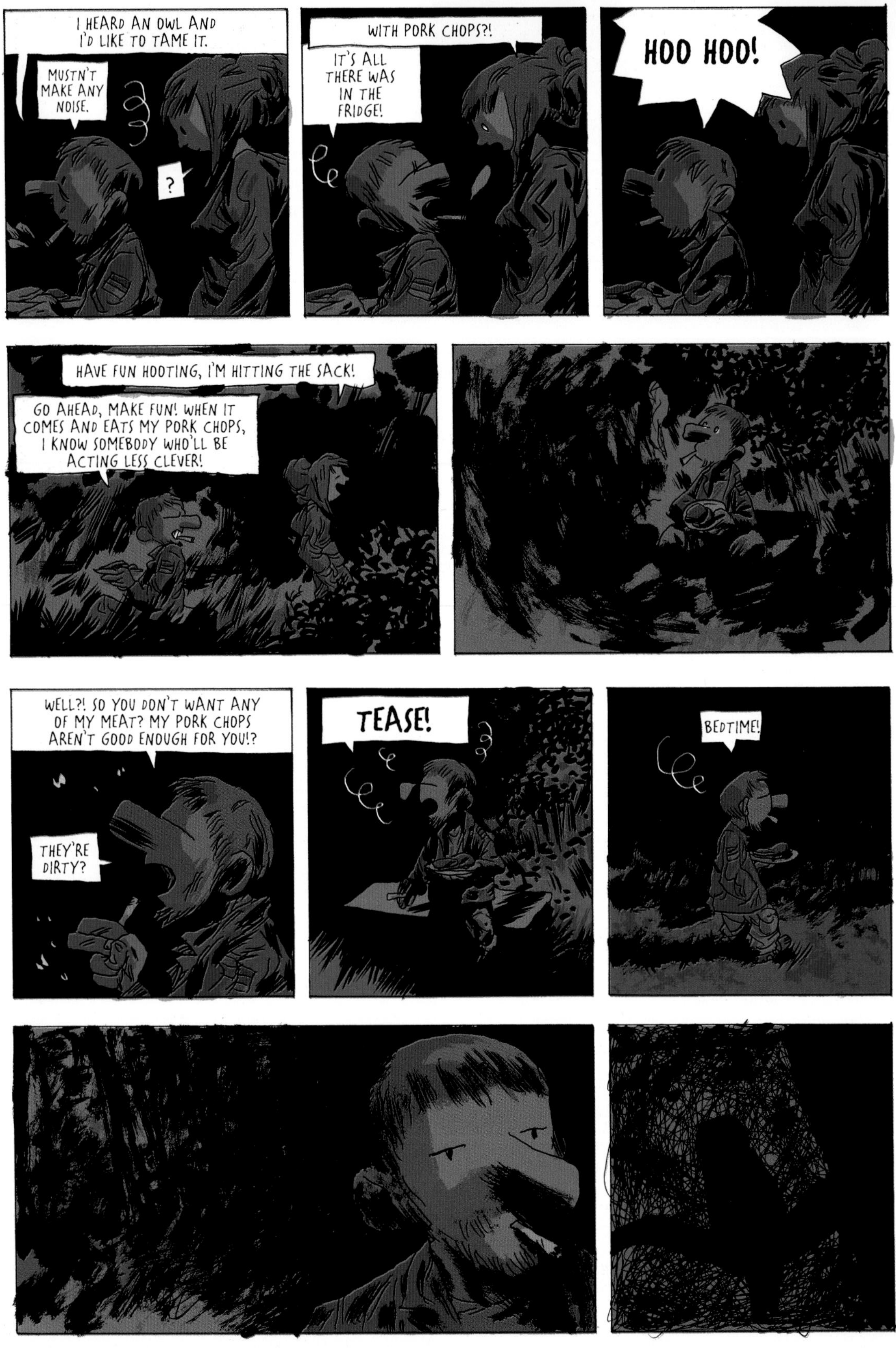
I HEARD AN OWL AND I'D LIKE TO TAME IT.
MUSTN'T MAKE ANY NOISE.
?
WITH PORK CHOPS?!
IT'S ALL THERE WAS IN THE FRIDGE!
HOO HOO!
HAVE FUN HOOTING, I'M HITTING THE SACK!
GO AHEAD, MAKE FUN! WHEN IT COMES AND EATS MY PORK CHOPS, I KNOW SOMEBODY WHO'LL BE ACTING LESS CLEVER!
WELL?! SO YOU DON'T WANT ANY OF MY MEAT? MY PORK CHOPS AREN'T GOOD ENOUGH FOR YOU!?
THEY'RE DIRTY?
TEASE!
BEDTIME!

IN A REASSURING WAY OR, ON THE CONTRARY, A TERRIFYING WAY, EVERYTHING I DO BEARS TRACES OF MY FATHER.

WHAT HE TAUGHT ME CAN'T BE SUMMED UP IN WHAT I'M LIVING—I'M INTIMATELY PART OF HIM.

I SOMETIMES BELIEVE, IN RARE MOMENTS OF EUPHORIA, THAT I'VE FREED MYSELF OF HIM...

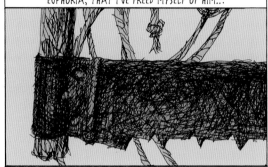

...BUT IT NEVER LASTS VERY LONG.

AN HOUR DOESN'T GO BY WITHOUT HIM COMING BACK TO THE SURFACE, FOR BETTER OR WORSE.

I DON'T HAVE ANY CERTAINTY THAT WE'RE REALLY SEPARATE.

I'M IN HIM, HE'S IN ME. I'M DEAD, HE'S ALIVE— IT'S A MYSTERY.

TO FINALLY KNOW WHAT I AM SURELY MUST COME THROUGH KNOWING WHO HE WAS.

47

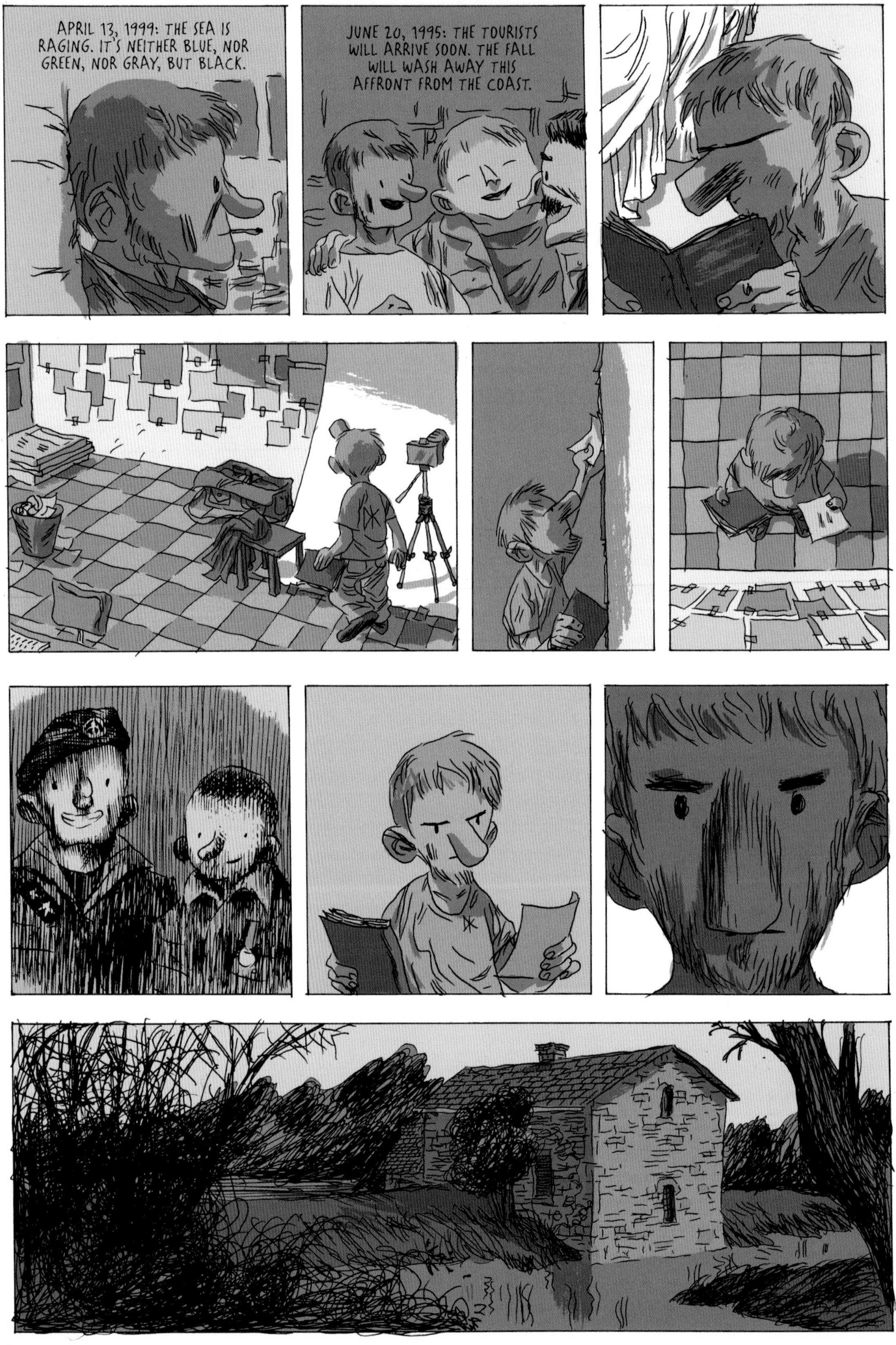
APRIL 13, 1999: THE SEA IS RAGING. IT'S NEITHER BLUE, NOR GREEN, NOR GRAY, BUT BLACK.
JUNE 20, 1995: THE TOURISTS WILL ARRIVE SOON. THE FALL WILL WASH AWAY THIS AFFRONT FROM THE COAST.

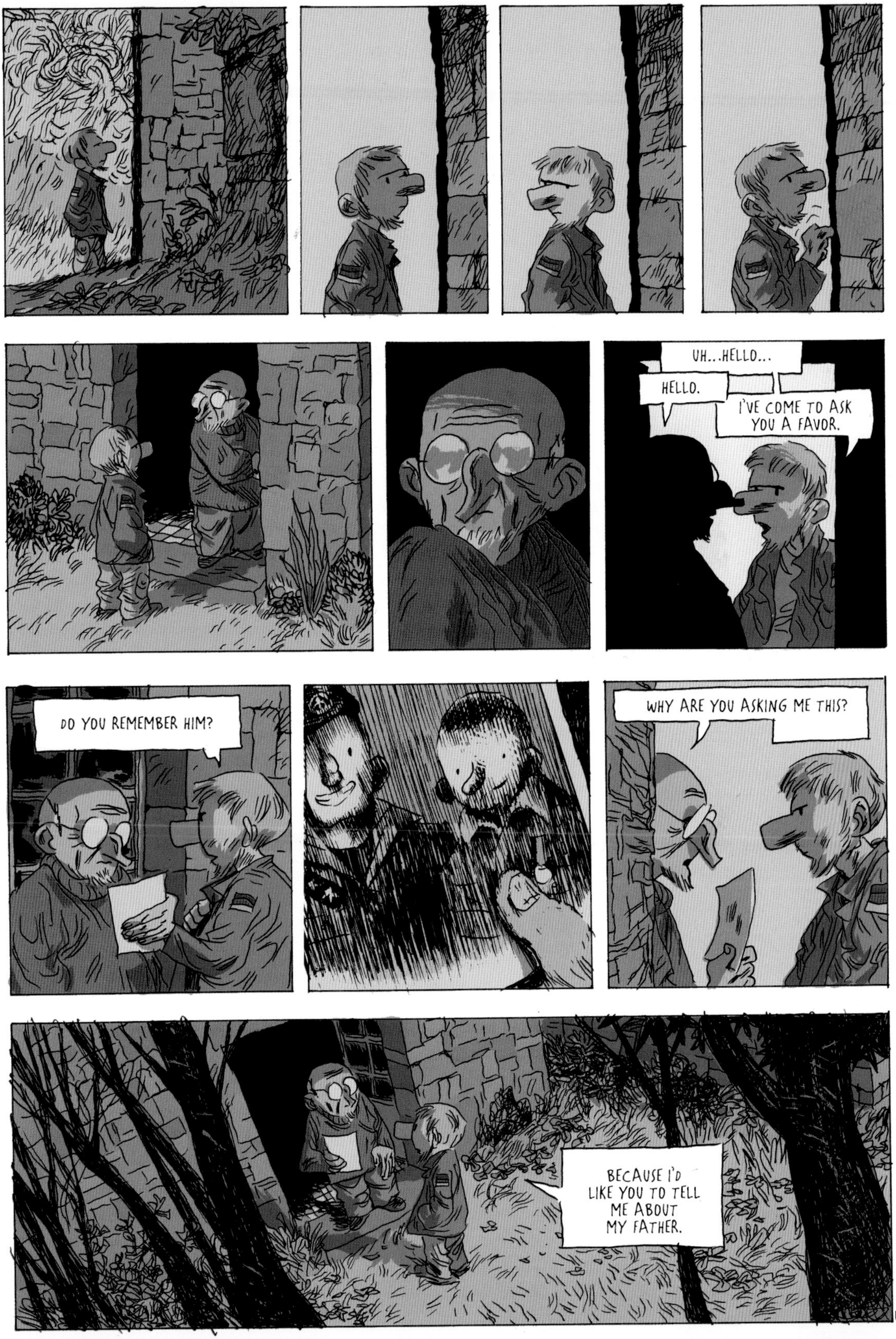
UH...HELLO...
HELLO.
I'VE COME TO ASK YOU A FAVOR.
DO YOU REMEMBER HIM?
WHY ARE YOU ASKING ME THIS?
BECAUSE I'D LIKE YOU TO TELL ME ABOUT MY FATHER.

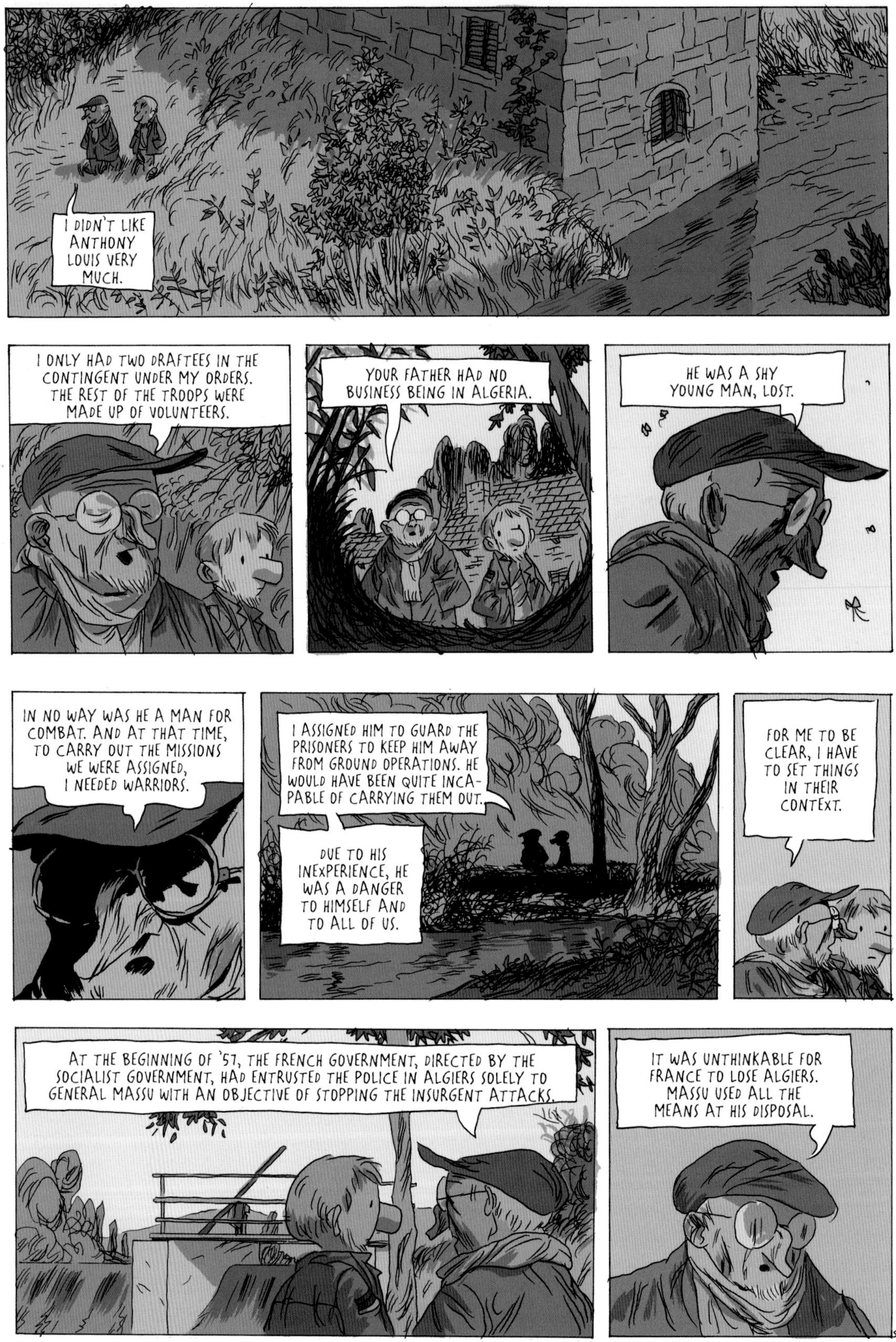
I DIDN'T LIKE ANTHONY LOUIS VERY MUCH.
I ONLY HAD TWO DRAFTEES IN THE CONTINGENT UNDER MY ORDERS. THE REST OF THE TROOPS WERE MADE UP OF VOLUNTEERS.
YOUR FATHER HAD NO BUSINESS BEING IN ALGERIA.
HE WAS A SHY YOUNG MAN, LOST.
IN NO WAY WAS HE A MAN FOR COMBAT. AND AT THAT TIME, TO CARRY OUT THE MISSIONS WE WERE ASSIGNED, I NEEDED WARRIORS.
I ASSIGNED HIM TO GUARD THE PRISONERS TO KEEP HIM AWAY FROM GROUND OPERATIONS. HE WOULD HAVE BEEN QUITE INCAPABLE OF CARRYING THEM OUT.
DUE TO HIS INEXPERIENCE, HE WAS A DANGER TO HIMSELF AND TO ALL OF US.
FOR ME TO BE CLEAR, I HAVE TO SET THINGS IN THEIR CONTEXT.
AT THE BEGINNING OF '57, THE FRENCH GOVERNMENT, DIRECTED BY THE SOCIALIST GOVERNMENT, HAD ENTRUSTED THE POLICE IN ALGIERS SOLELY TO GENERAL MASSU WITH AN OBJECTIVE OF STOPPING THE INSURGENT ATTACKS.
IT WAS UNTHINKABLE FOR FRANCE TO LOSE ALGIERS. MASSU USED ALL THE MEANS AT HIS DISPOSAL.

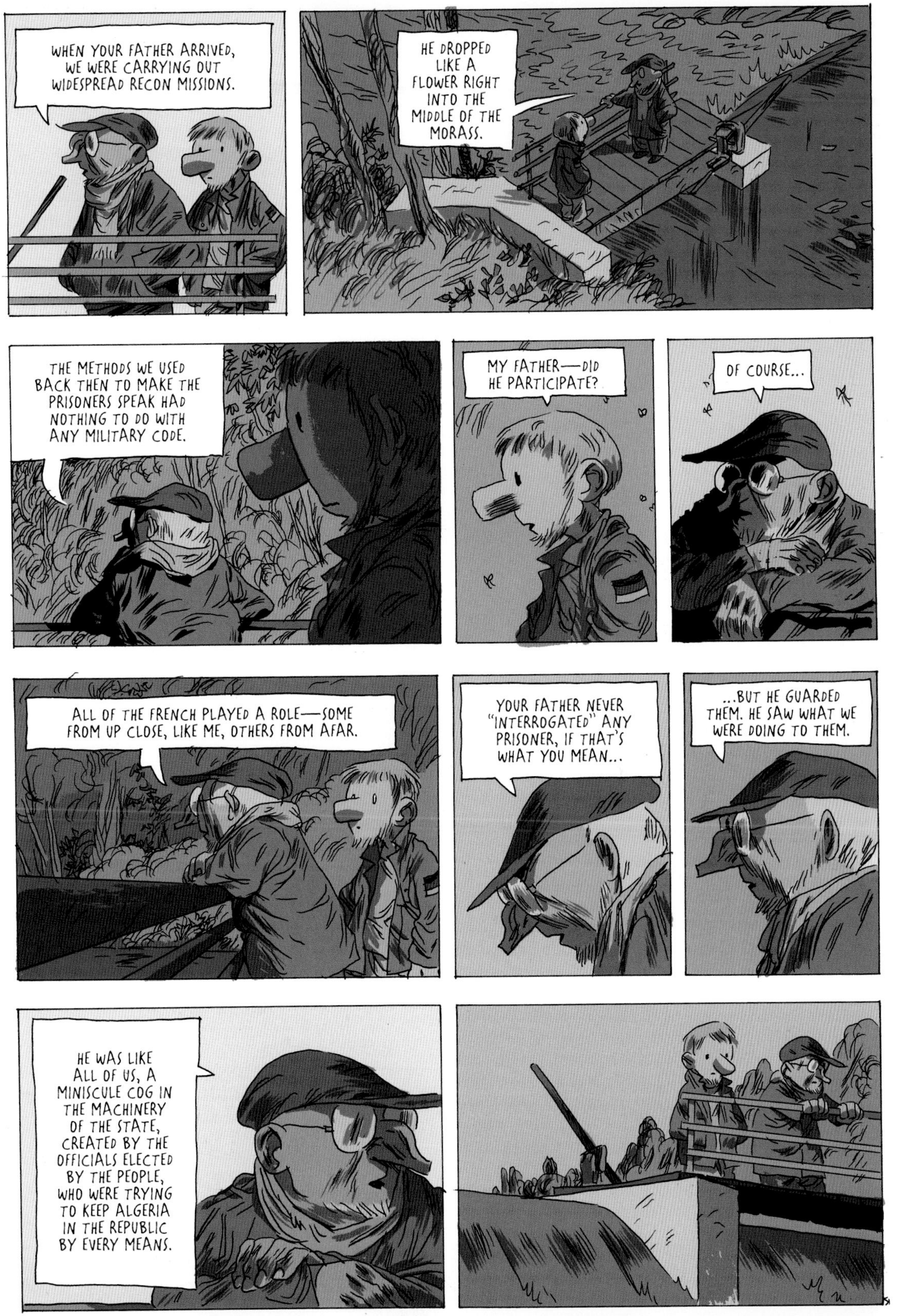

WHEN YOUR FATHER ARRIVED, WE WERE CARRYING OUT WIDESPREAD RECON MISSIONS.
HE DROPPED LIKE A FLOWER RIGHT INTO THE MIDDLE OF THE MORASS.
THE METHODS WE USED BACK THEN TO MAKE THE PRISONERS SPEAK HAD NOTHING TO DO WITH ANY MILITARY CODE.
MY FATHER—DID HE PARTICIPATE?
OF COURSE...
ALL OF THE FRENCH PLAYED A ROLE—SOME FROM UP CLOSE, LIKE ME, OTHERS FROM AFAR.
YOUR FATHER NEVER "INTERROGATED" ANY PRISONER, IF THAT'S WHAT YOU MEAN...
...BUT HE GUARDED THEM. HE SAW WHAT WE WERE DOING TO THEM.
HE WAS LIKE ALL OF US, A MINISCULE COG IN THE MACHINERY OF THE STATE, CREATED BY THE OFFICIALS ELECTED BY THE PEOPLE, WHO WERE TRYING TO KEEP ALGERIA IN THE REPUBLIC BY EVERY MEANS.

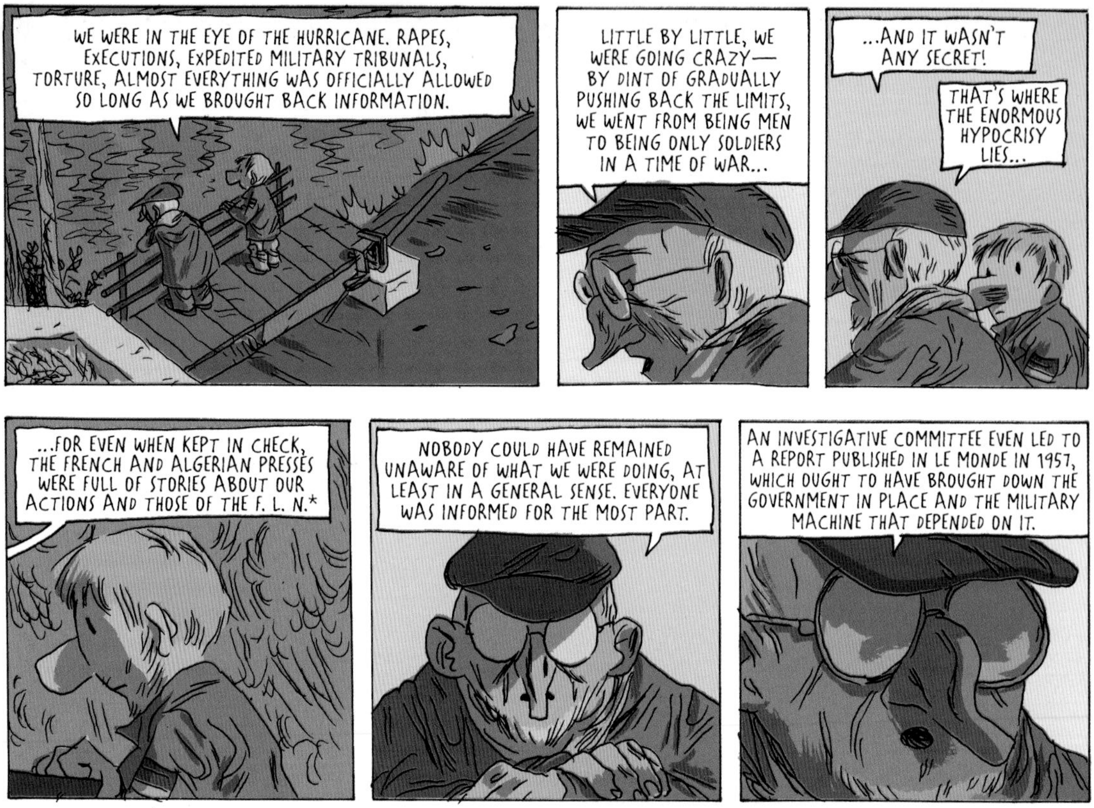
WE WERE IN THE EYE OF THE HURRICANE. RAPES, EXECUTIONS, EXPEDITED MILITARY TRIBUNALS, TORTURE, ALMOST EVERYTHING WAS OFFICIALLY ALLOWED SO LONG AS WE BROUGHT BACK INFORMATION.
LITTLE BY LITTLE, WE WERE GOING CRAZY— BY DINT OF GRADUALLY PUSHING BACK THE LIMITS, WE WENT FROM BEING MEN TO BEING ONLY SOLDIERS IN A TIME OF WAR...
...AND IT WASN'T ANY SECRET!
THAT'S WHERE THE ENORMOUS HYPOCRISY LIES...
...FOR EVEN WHEN KEPT IN CHECK, THE FRENCH AND ALGERIAN PRESSES WERE FULL OF STORIES ABOUT OUR ACTIONS AND THOSE OF THE F. L. N.*
NOBODY COULD HAVE REMAINED UNAWARE OF WHAT WE WERE DOING, AT LEAST IN A GENERAL SENSE. EVERYONE WAS INFORMED FOR THE MOST PART.
AN INVESTIGATIVE COMMITTEE EVEN LED TO A REPORT PUBLISHED IN LE MONDE IN 1957, WHICH OUGHT TO HAVE BROUGHT DOWN THE GOVERNMENT IN PLACE AND THE MILITARY MACHINE THAT DEPENDED ON IT.

* THE FRONT DE LIBÉRATION NATIONALE, THE REVOLUTIONARY MOVEMENT IN ALGERIA SEEKING INDEPENDENCE FROM FRANCE IN THE 1950S AND '60S.

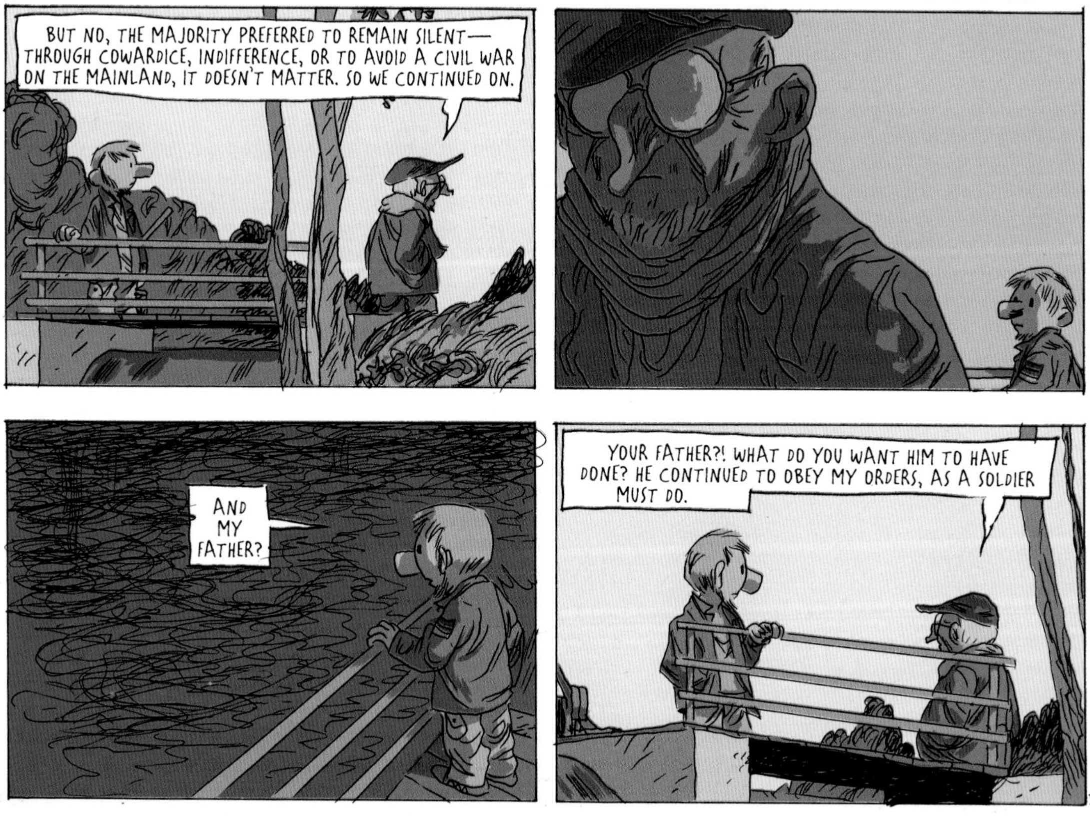
BUT NO, THE MAJORITY PREFERRED TO REMAIN SILENT— THROUGH COWARDICE, INDIFFERENCE, OR TO AVOID A CIVIL WAR ON THE MAINLAND, IT DOESN'T MATTER. SO WE CONTINUED ON.
AND MY FATHER?
YOUR FATHER?! WHAT DO YOU WANT HIM TO HAVE DONE? HE CONTINUED TO OBEY MY ORDERS, AS A SOLDIER MUST DO.

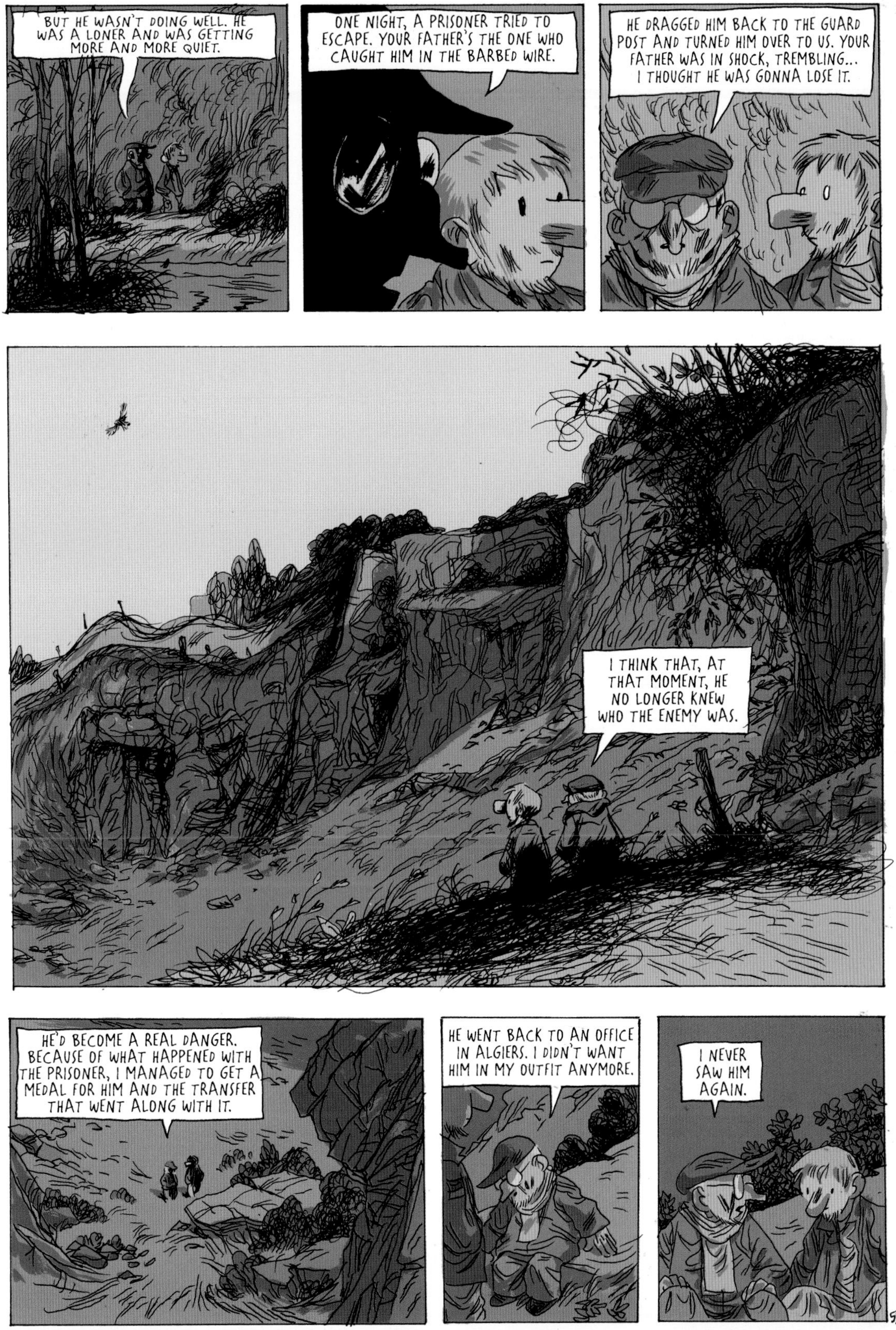
BUT HE WASN'T DOING WELL. HE WAS A LONER AND WAS GETTING MORE AND MORE QUIET.
ONE NIGHT, A PRISONER TRIED TO ESCAPE. YOUR FATHER'S THE ONE WHO CAUGHT HIM IN THE BARBED WIRE.
HE DRAGGED HIM BACK TO THE GUARD POST AND TURNED HIM OVER TO US. YOUR FATHER WAS IN SHOCK, TREMBLING... I THOUGHT HE WAS GONNA LOSE IT.
I THINK THAT, AT THAT MOMENT, HE NO LONGER KNEW WHO THE ENEMY WAS.
HE'D BECOME A REAL DANGER. BECAUSE OF WHAT HAPPENED WITH THE PRISONER, I MANAGED TO GET A MEDAL FOR HIM AND THE TRANSFER THAT WENT ALONG WITH IT.
HE WENT BACK TO AN OFFICE IN ALGIERS. I DIDN'T WANT HIM IN MY OUTFIT ANYMORE.
I NEVER SAW HIM AGAIN.

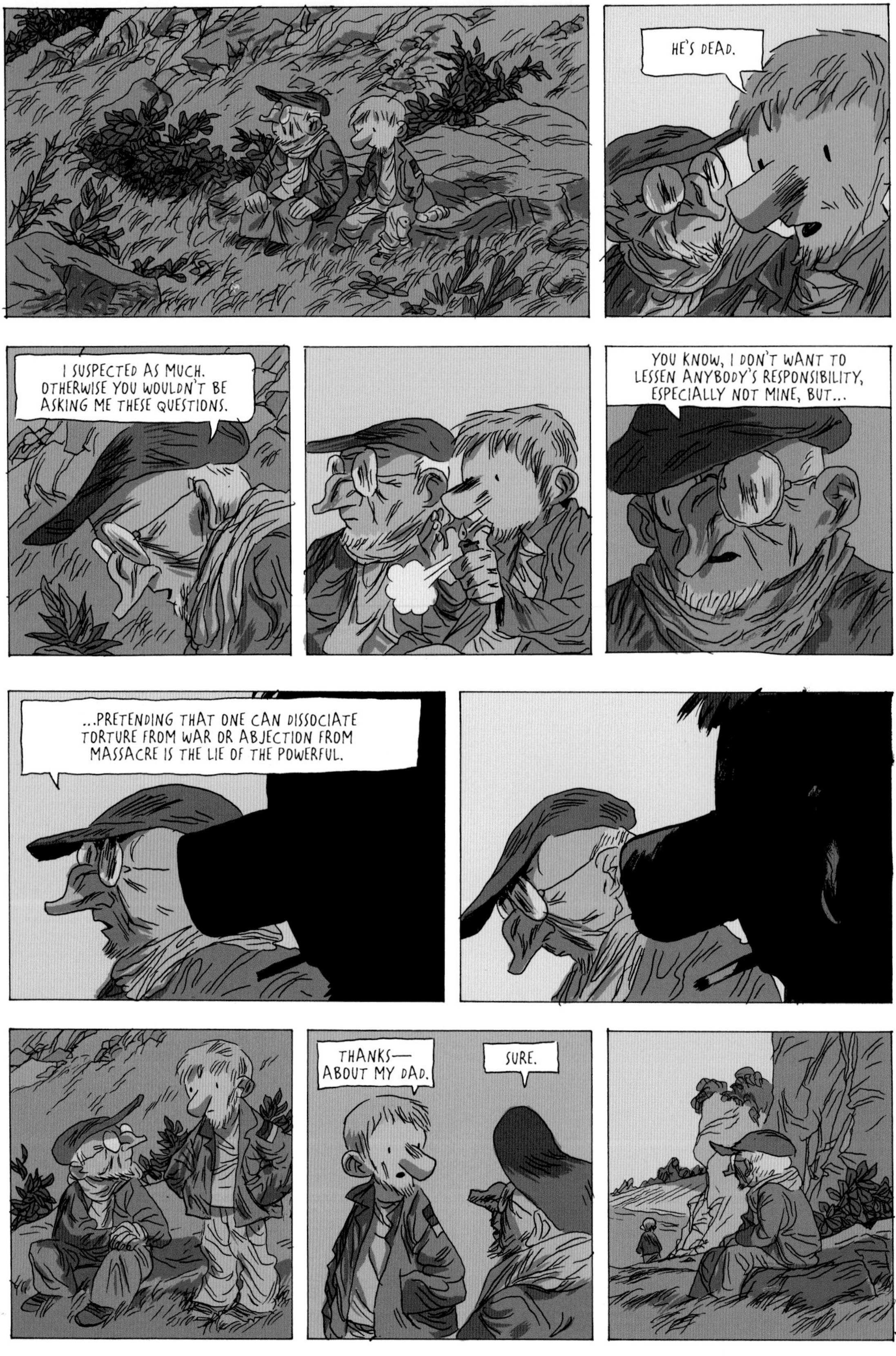
HE'S DEAD.
I SUSPECTED AS MUCH. OTHERWISE YOU WOULDN'T BE ASKING ME THESE QUESTIONS.
YOU KNOW, I DON'T WANT TO LESSEN ANYBODY'S RESPONSIBILITY, ESPECIALLY NOT MINE, BUT...
...PRETENDING THAT ONE CAN DISSOCIATE TORTURE FROM WAR OR ABJECTION FROM MASSACRE IS THE LIE OF THE POWERFUL.
THANKS— ABOUT MY DAD.
SURE.

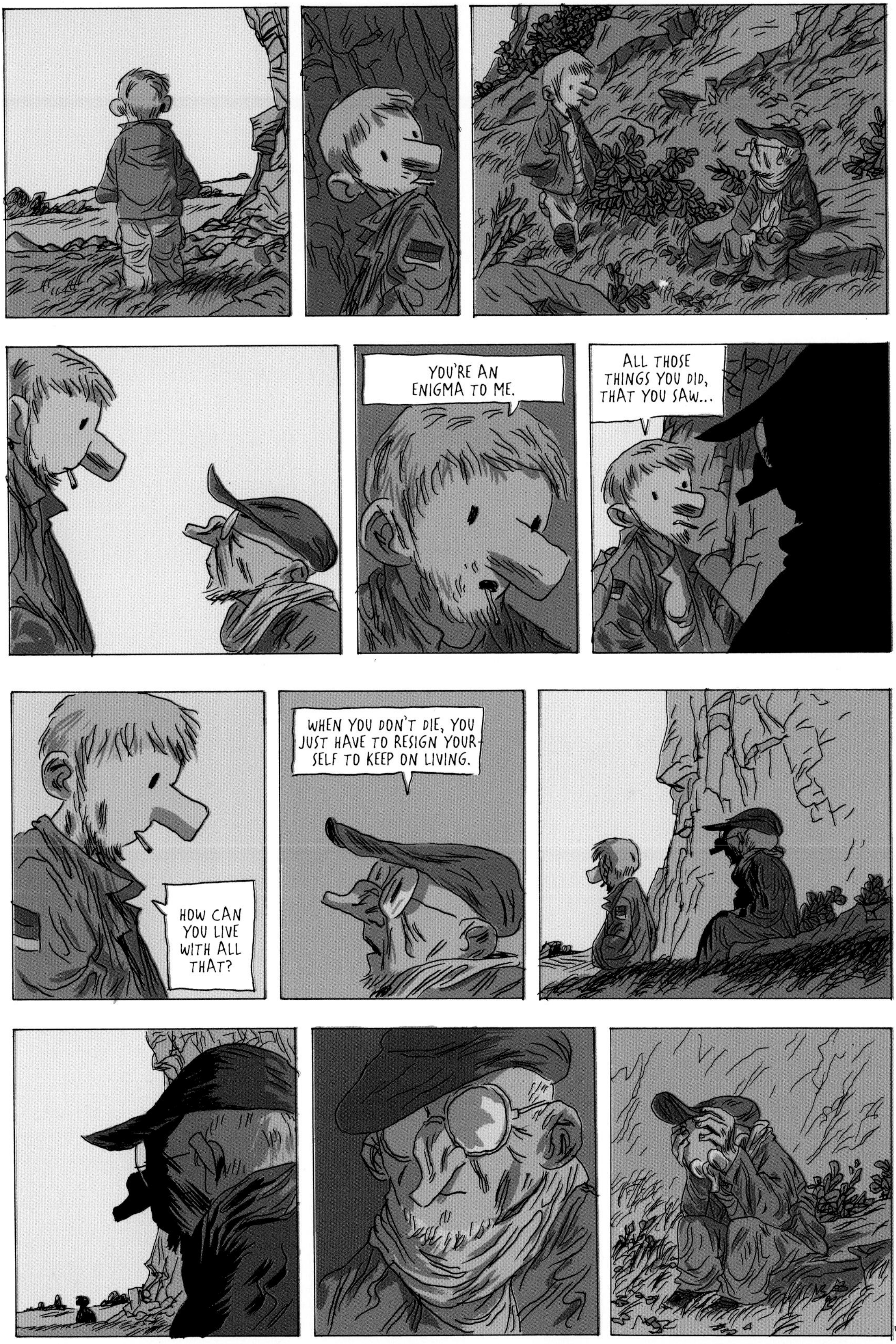
YOU'RE AN ENIGMA TO ME.
ALL THOSE THINGS YOU DID, THAT YOU SAW...
HOW CAN YOU LIVE WITH ALL THAT?
WHEN YOU DON'T DIE, YOU JUST HAVE TO RESIGN YOURSELF TO KEEP ON LIVING.

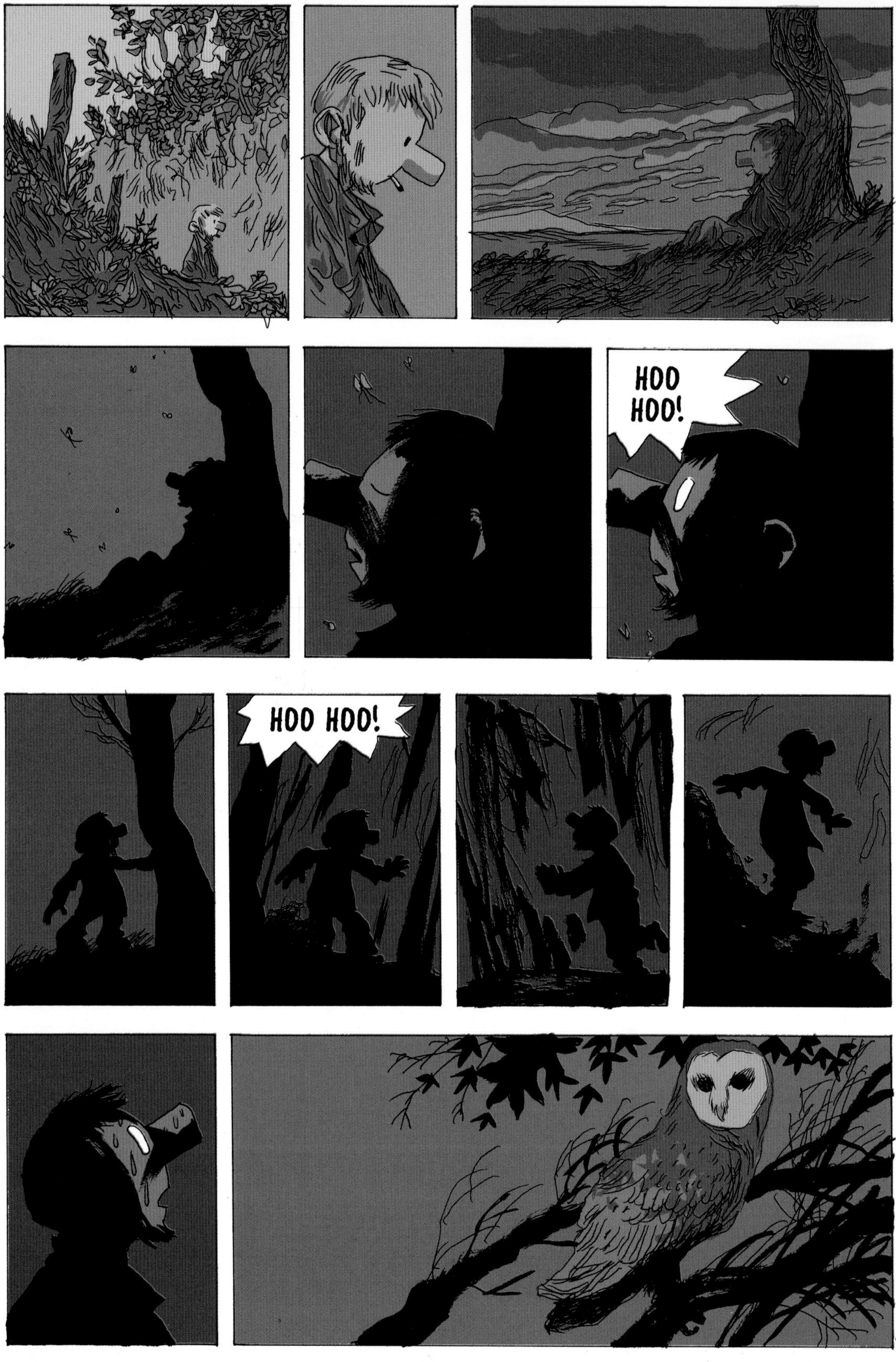
HOO HOO!
HOO HOO!

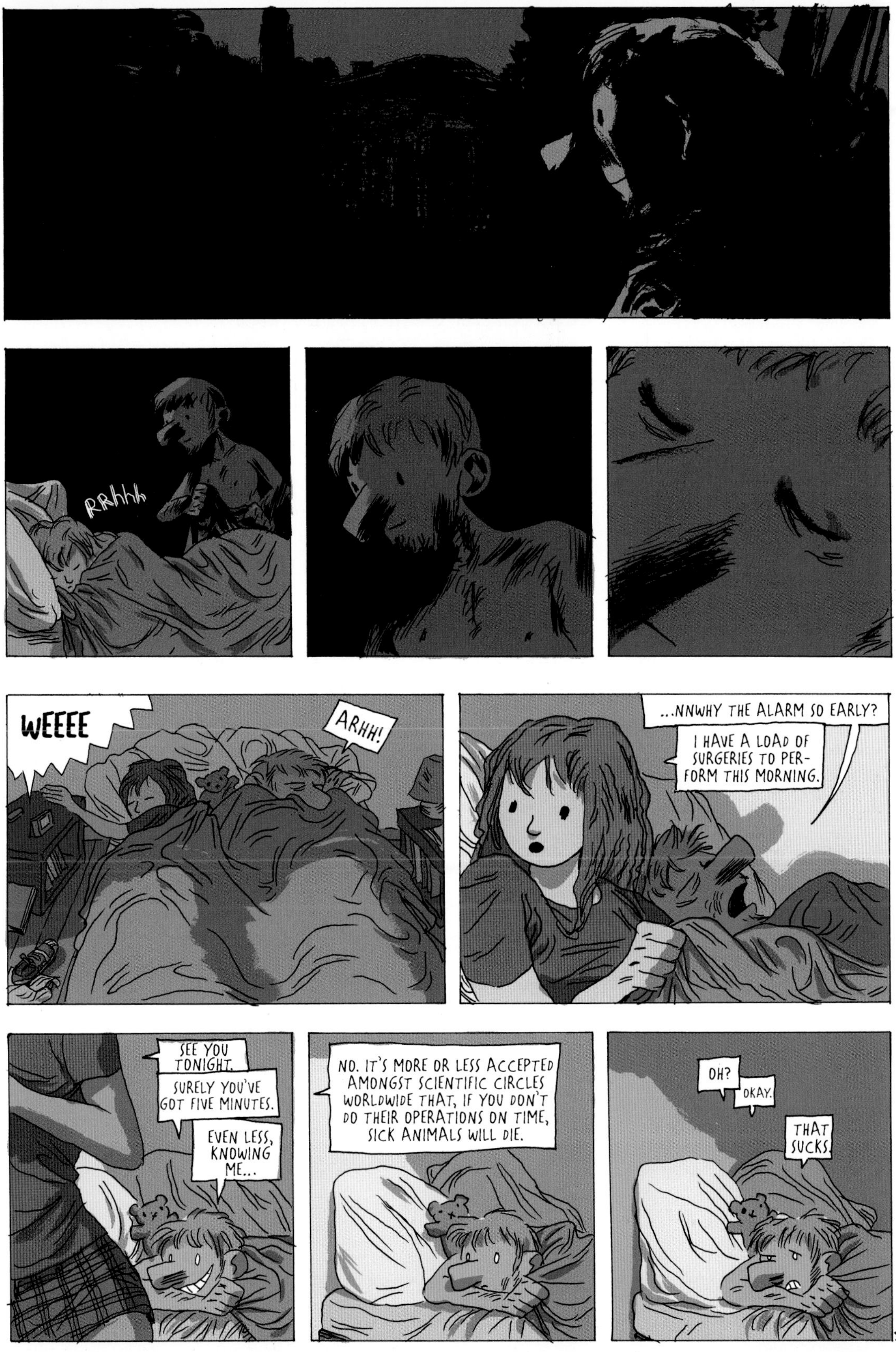
RRhhh
WEEEE
ARHH!
...NNWHY THE ALARM SO EARLY?
I HAVE A LOAD OF SURGERIES TO PER-FORM THIS MORNING.
SEE YOU TONIGHT.
SURELY YOU'VE GOT FIVE MINUTES.
EVEN LESS, KNOWING ME...
NO. IT'S MORE OR LESS ACCEPTED AMONGST SCIENTIFIC CIRCLES WORLDWIDE THAT, IF YOU DON'T DO THEIR OPERATIONS ON TIME, SICK ANIMALS WILL DIE.
OH?
OKAY.
THAT SUCKS.

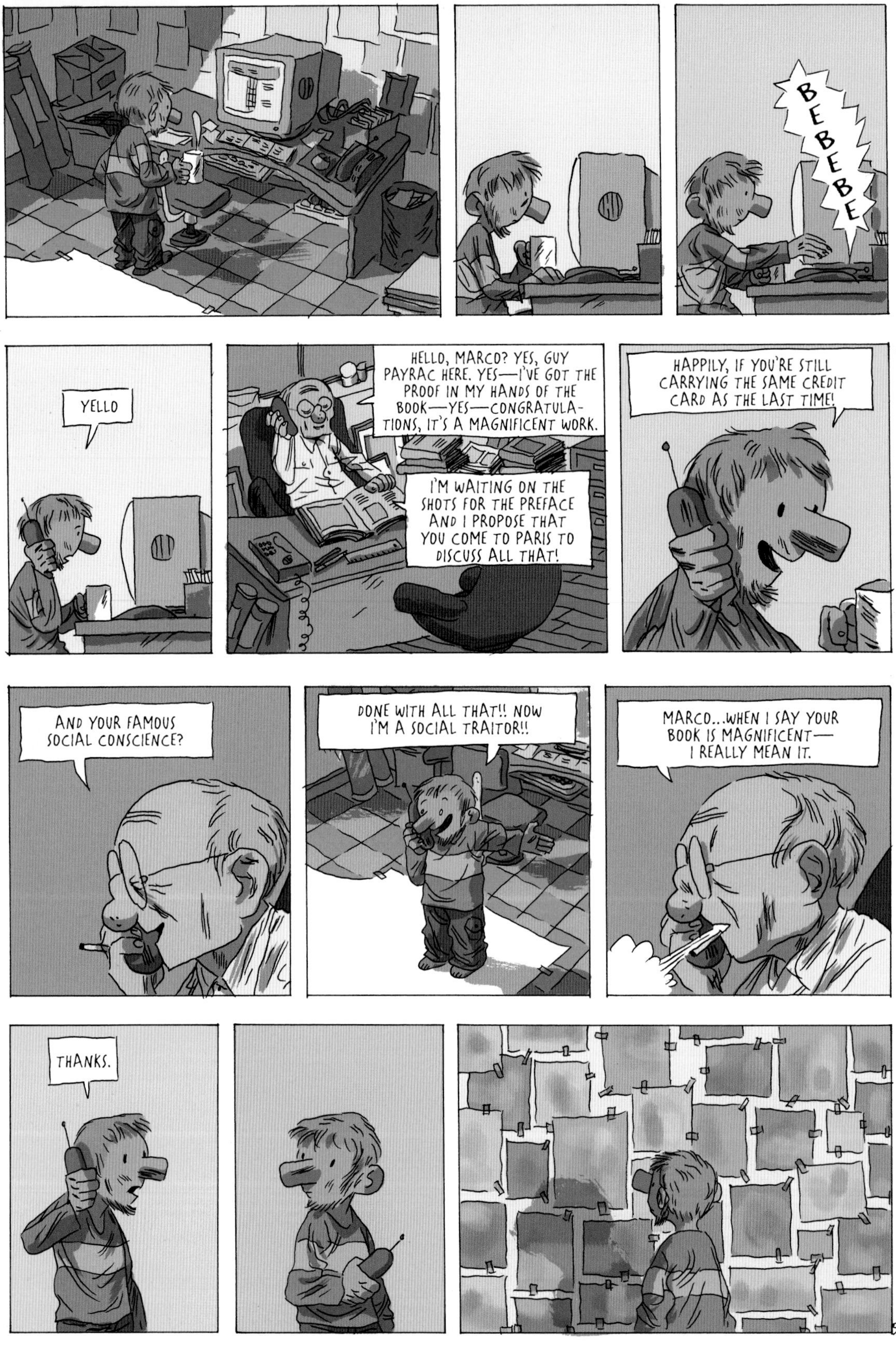
BEBEBEBE
YELLO
HELLO, MARCO? YES, GUY PAYRAC HERE. YES—I'VE GOT THE PROOF IN MY HANDS OF THE BOOK—YES—CONGRATULA-TIONS, IT'S A MAGNIFICENT WORK.
I'M WAITING ON THE SHOTS FOR THE PREFACE AND I PROPOSE THAT YOU COME TO PARIS TO DISCUSS ALL THAT!
HAPPILY, IF YOU'RE STILL CARRYING THE SAME CREDIT CARD AS THE LAST TIME!
AND YOUR FAMOUS SOCIAL CONSCIENCE?
DONE WITH ALL THAT!! NOW I'M A SOCIAL TRAITOR!!
MARCO...WHEN I SAY YOUR BOOK IS MAGNIFICENT—I REALLY MEAN IT.
THANKS.

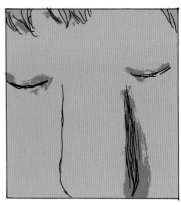

AUGUST 16, 1997. I'M NO LONGER ALTOGETHER PRESENT IN THE MODERN WORLD.

JUNE 27, 1999: A BARN OWL HAS MADE HER NEST IN THE ATTIC IN A BOX OF THE CHILDREN'S OLD TOYS.

MARCH 2, 1997: YOU HAVE TO LET BEAUTY GO AND PRESERVE WHAT'S PRECIOUS.

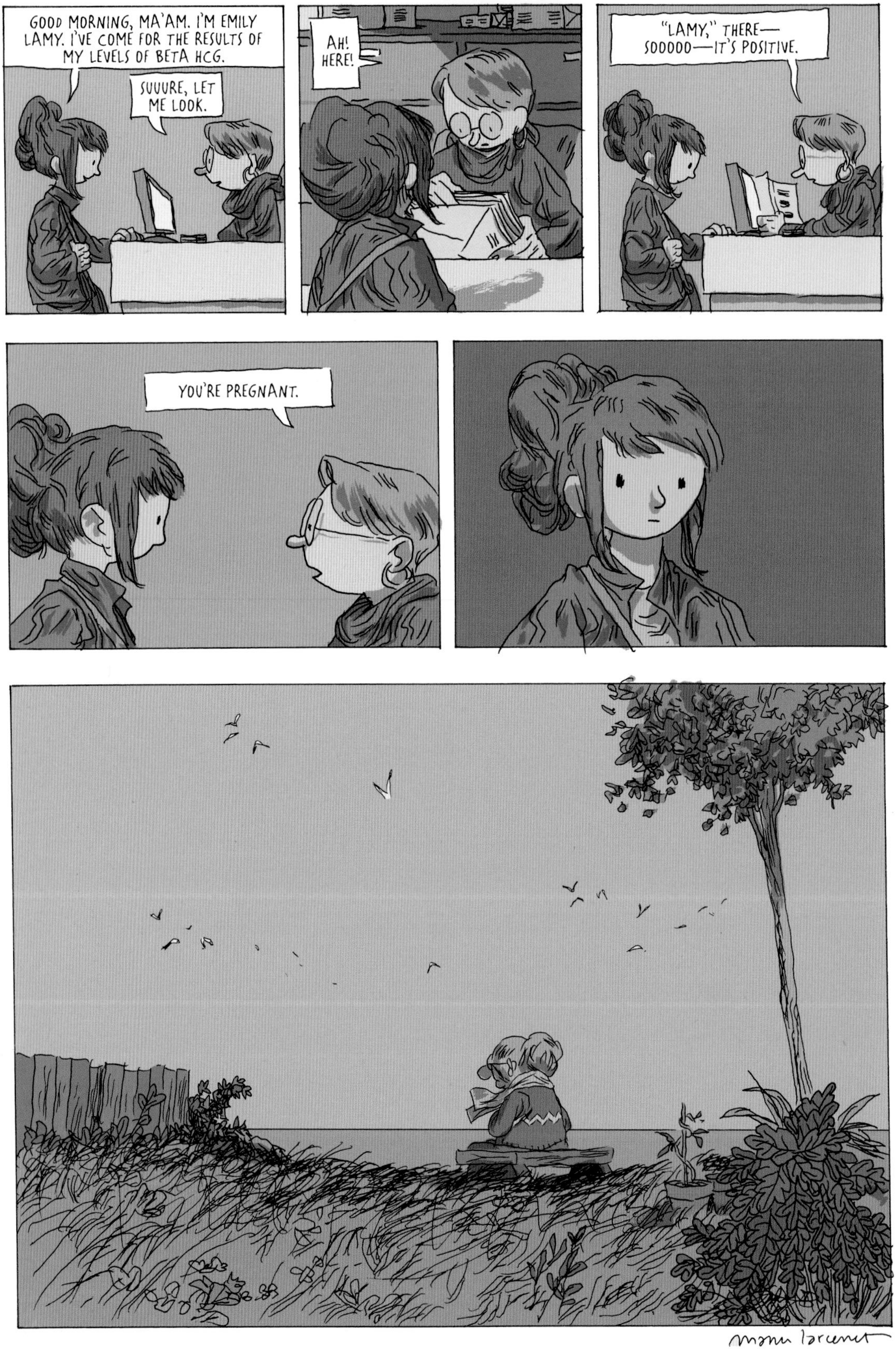
GOOD MORNING, MA'AM. I'M EMILY LAMY. I'VE COME FOR THE RESULTS OF MY LEVELS OF BETA HCG.
SUUURE, LET ME LOOK.
AH! HERE!
"LAMY," THERE— SOOOOO—IT'S POSITIVE.
YOU'RE PREGNANT.
manu larcenet

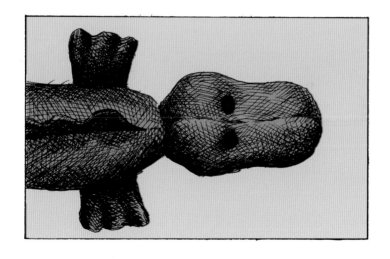

Ordinary Victories
4. Hammering nails

"I am disturbance
When the crowd is quiet."
Magyd Cherfi

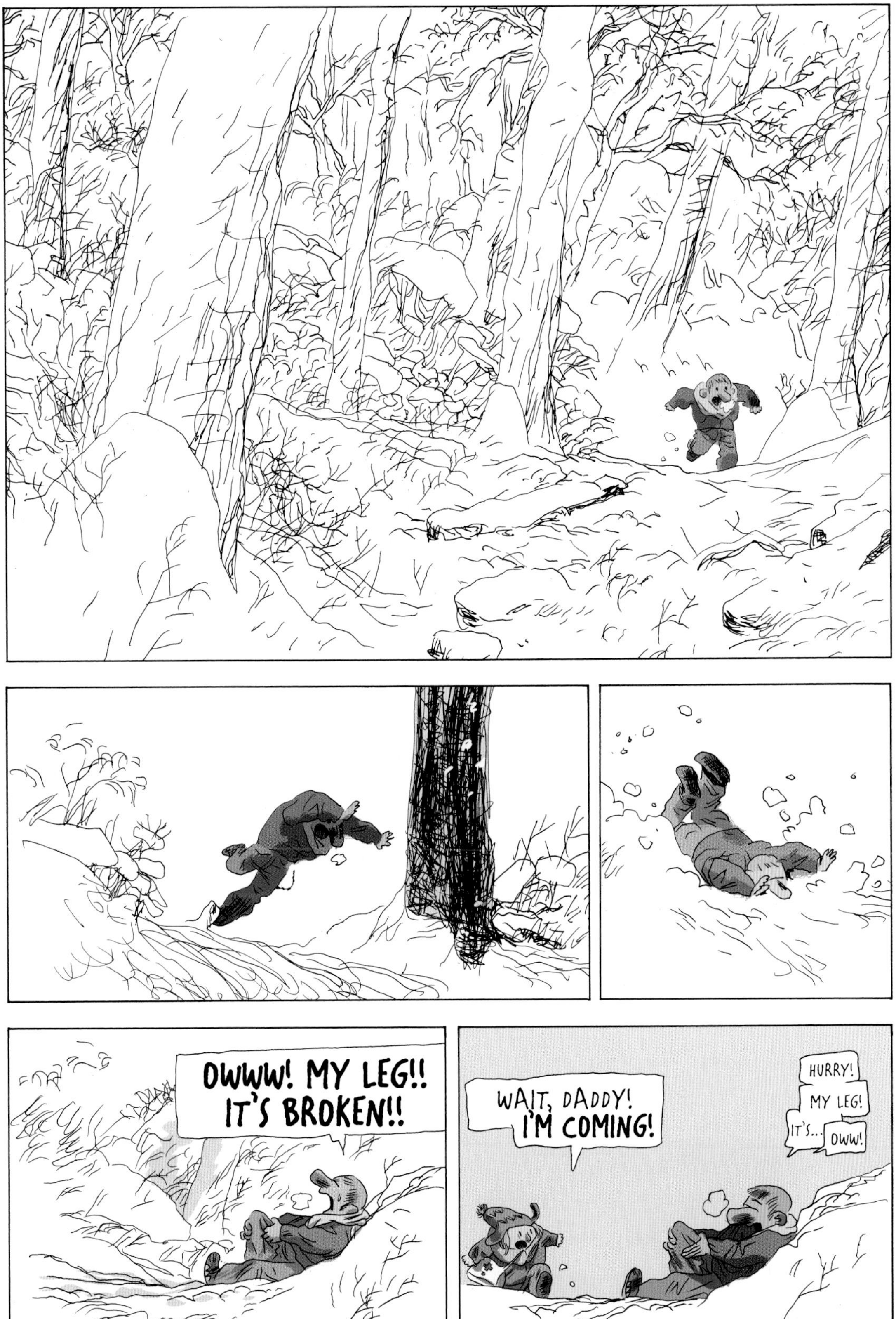
OWWW! MY LEG!! IT'S BROKEN!!
WAIT, DADDY! I'M COMING!
HURRY!
MY LEG!
IT'S...
OWW!

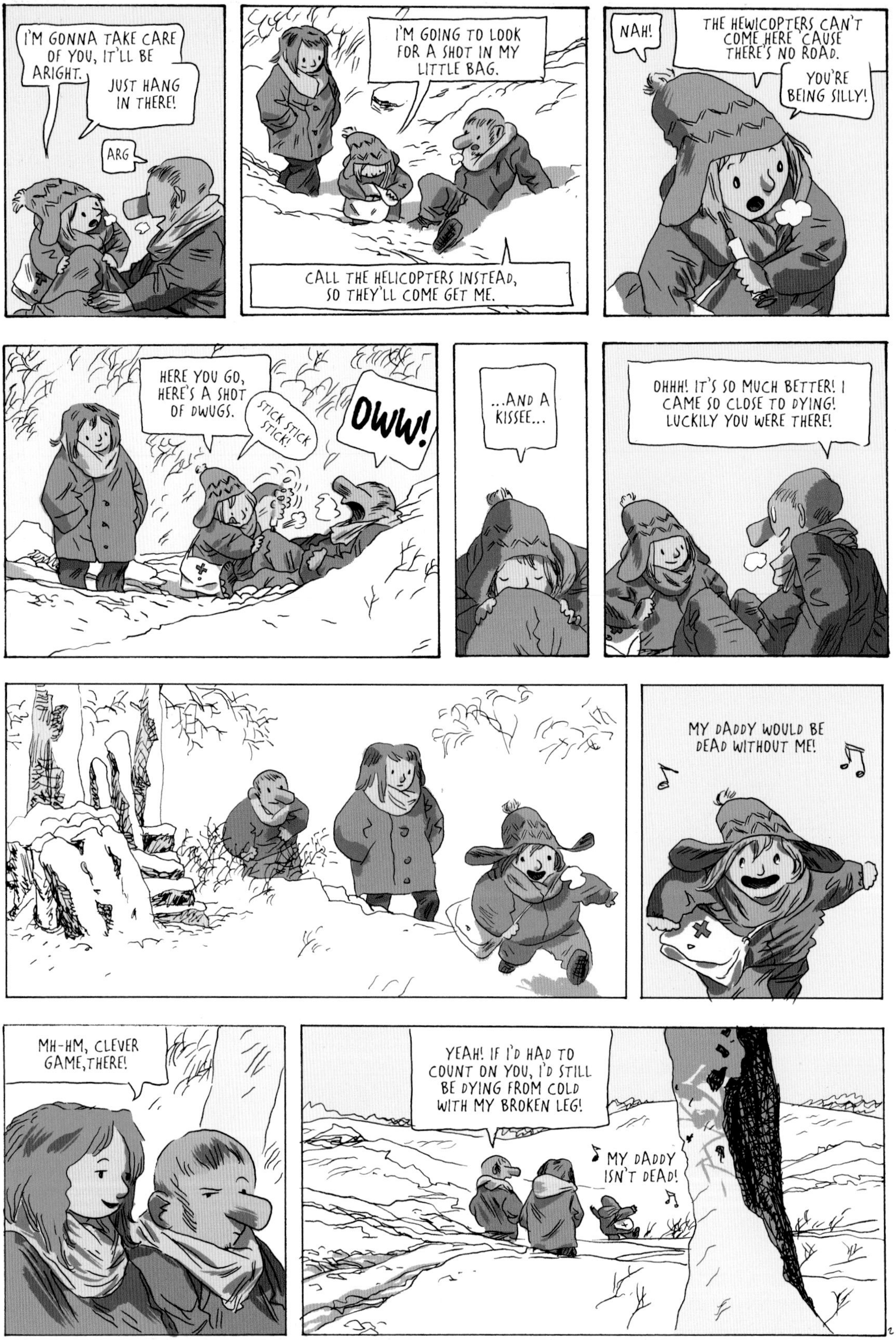
I'M GONNA TAKE CARE OF YOU, IT'LL BE ARIGHT.
JUST HANG IN THERE!
ARG
I'M GOING TO LOOK FOR A SHOT IN MY LITTLE BAG.
CALL THE HELICOPTERS INSTEAD, SO THEY'LL COME GET ME.
NAH!
THE HEWICOPTERS CAN'T COME HERE 'CAUSE THERE'S NO ROAD.
YOU'RE BEING SILLY!
HERE YOU GO, HERE'S A SHOT OF DWUGS.
STICK STICK STICK!
OWW!
...AND A KISSEE...
OHHH! IT'S SO MUCH BETTER! I CAME SO CLOSE TO DYING! LUCKILY YOU WERE THERE!
MY DADDY WOULD BE DEAD WITHOUT ME!
MH-HM, CLEVER GAME, THERE!
YEAH! IF I'D HAD TO COUNT ON YOU, I'D STILL BE DYING FROM COLD WITH MY BROKEN LEG!
MY DADDY ISN'T DEAD!

MY DAUGHTER IS WONDERFUL.

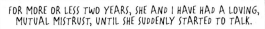

FOR MORE OR LESS TWO YEARS, SHE AND I HAVE HAD A LOVING, MUTUAL MISTRUST, UNTIL SHE SUDDENLY STARTED TO TALK.

I THEN DISCOVERED THE DIZZYING BREADTH OF HER THIRST FOR INFORMATION AND HER OBSTINATE WILL TO ADAPT.

IF I HAD TO TAKE IN SO MANY REVOLUTIONARY DISCOVERIES IN SO LITTLE TIME, I'D GO CRAZY.

FOR THERE'S NOTHING LOGICAL ABOUT THE WORLD! IT'S RIDDLED WITH SUBTLETIES, TRAPS, FALSE LEADS, SO MUCH SO THAT ONE MUST BE TENACIOUS AND ON CONSTANT ALERT JUST TO KEEP UP WITH THE FLOW.

IN HER WAKE, MY DAUGHTER IS FORCING ME TO RETHINK EVERYTHING FROM ANGLES THAT ARE INEVITABLY DIFFERENT.

SELF-ASSURED BY HER TINY LIFE, SHE'S EDUCATING ME.

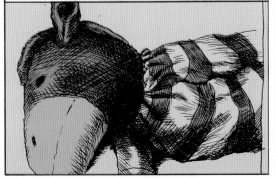

I FEEL AN AUTHENTIC RESPECT FOR HER, QUITE DISTINCT FROM THE INSTINCTIVE AFFECTION SHE INSPIRES IN ME.

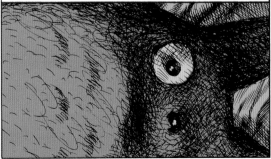

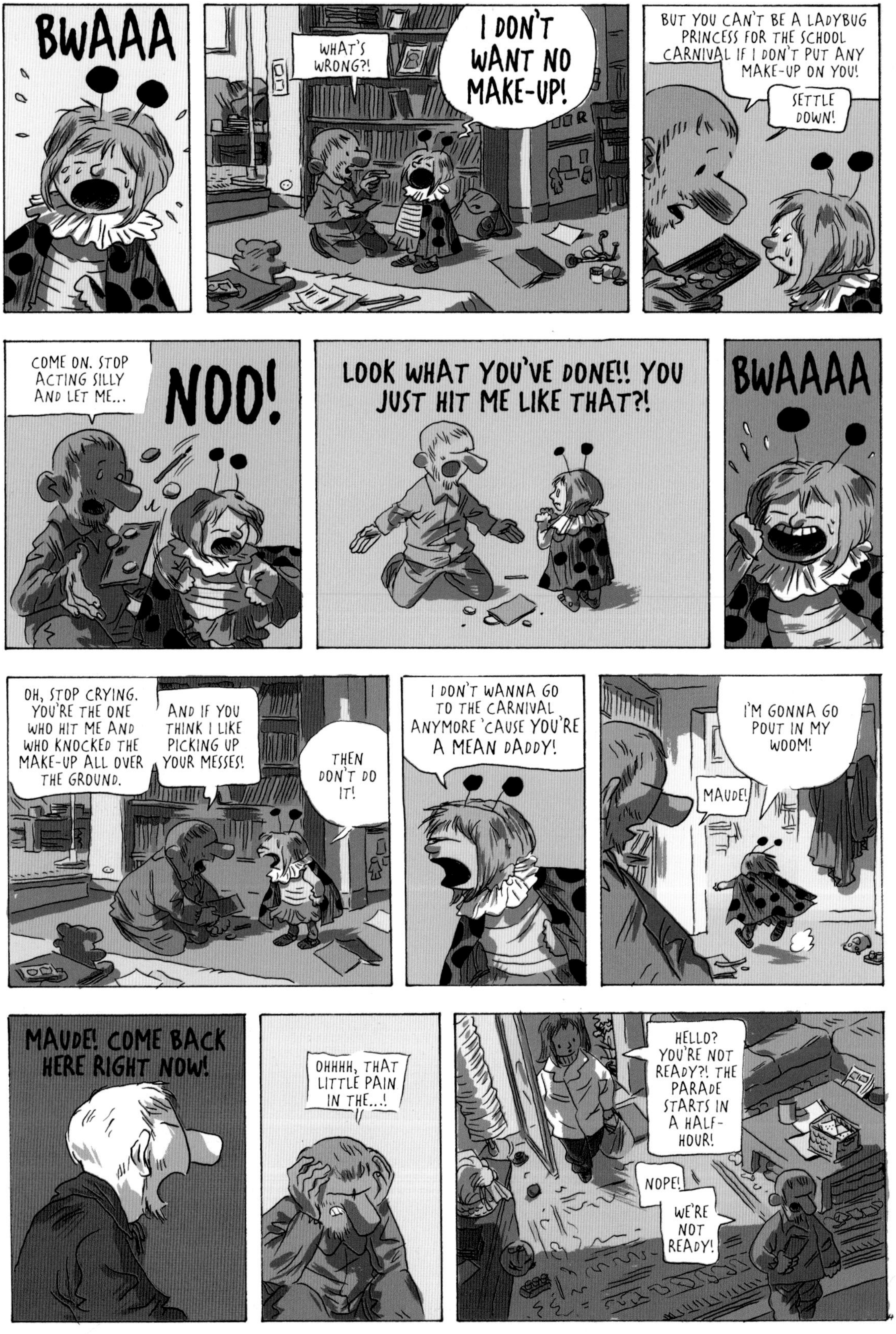

BWAAA
WHAT'S WRONG?!
I DON'T WANT NO MAKE-UP!
BUT YOU CAN'T BE A LADYBUG PRINCESS FOR THE SCHOOL CARNIVAL IF I DON'T PUT ANY MAKE-UP ON YOU!
SETTLE DOWN!
COME ON. STOP ACTING SILLY AND LET ME...
NOO!
LOOK WHAT YOU'VE DONE!! YOU JUST HIT ME LIKE THAT?!
BWAAAA
OH, STOP CRYING. YOU'RE THE ONE WHO HIT ME AND WHO KNOCKED THE MAKE-UP ALL OVER THE GROUND.
AND IF YOU THINK I LIKE PICKING UP YOUR MESSES!
THEN DON'T DO IT!
I DON'T WANNA GO TO THE CARNIVAL ANYMORE 'CAUSE YOU'RE A MEAN DADDY!
I'M GONNA GO POUT IN MY WOOM!
MAUDE!
MAUDE! COME BACK HERE RIGHT NOW!
OHHHH, THAT LITTLE PAIN IN THE...!
HELLO? YOU'RE NOT READY?! THE PARADE STARTS IN A HALF-HOUR!
NOPE!
WE'RE NOT READY!

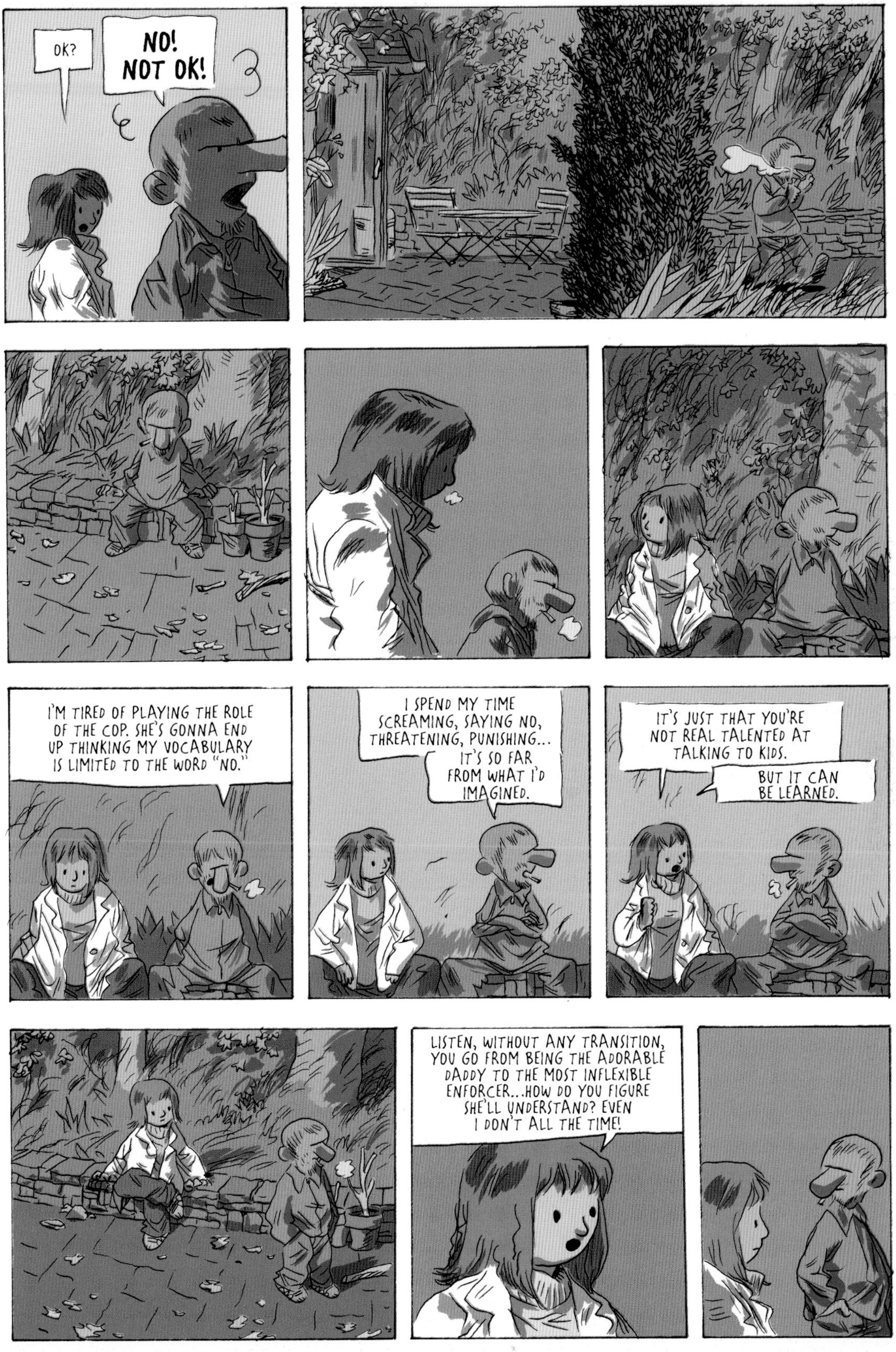
OK?
NO! NOT OK!
I'M TIRED OF PLAYING THE ROLE OF THE COP. SHE'S GONNA END UP THINKING MY VOCABULARY IS LIMITED TO THE WORD "NO."
I SPEND MY TIME SCREAMING, SAYING NO, THREATENING, PUNISHING...
IT'S SO FAR FROM WHAT I'D IMAGINED.
IT'S JUST THAT YOU'RE NOT REAL TALENTED AT TALKING TO KIDS.
BUT IT CAN BE LEARNED.
LISTEN, WITHOUT ANY TRANSITION, YOU GO FROM BEING THE ADORABLE DADDY TO THE MOST INFLEXIBLE ENFORCER...HOW DO YOU FIGURE SHE'LL UNDERSTAND? EVEN I DON'T ALL THE TIME!

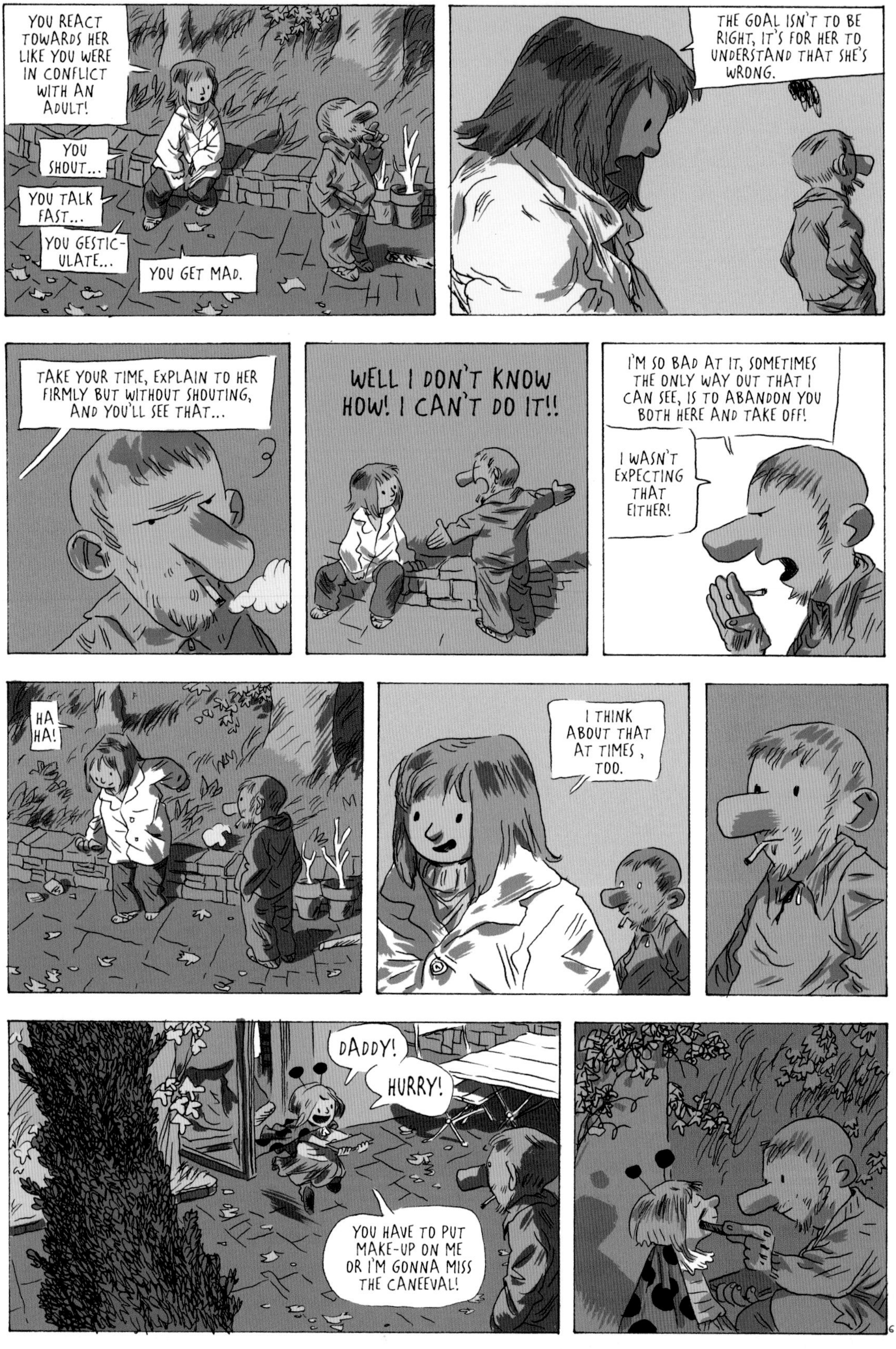

YOU REACT TOWARDS HER LIKE YOU WERE IN CONFLICT WITH AN ADULT!
YOU SHOUT...
YOU TALK FAST...
YOU GESTICULATE...
YOU GET MAD.
THE GOAL ISN'T TO BE RIGHT, IT'S FOR HER TO UNDERSTAND THAT SHE'S WRONG.
TAKE YOUR TIME, EXPLAIN TO HER FIRMLY BUT WITHOUT SHOUTING, AND YOU'LL SEE THAT...
WELL I DON'T KNOW HOW! I CAN'T DO IT!!
I'M SO BAD AT IT, SOMETIMES THE ONLY WAY OUT THAT I CAN SEE, IS TO ABANDON YOU BOTH HERE AND TAKE OFF!
I WASN'T EXPECTING THAT EITHER!
HA HA!
I THINK ABOUT THAT AT TIMES, TOO.
DADDY!
HURRY!
YOU HAVE TO PUT MAKE-UP ON ME OR I'M GONNA MISS THE CANEEVAL!

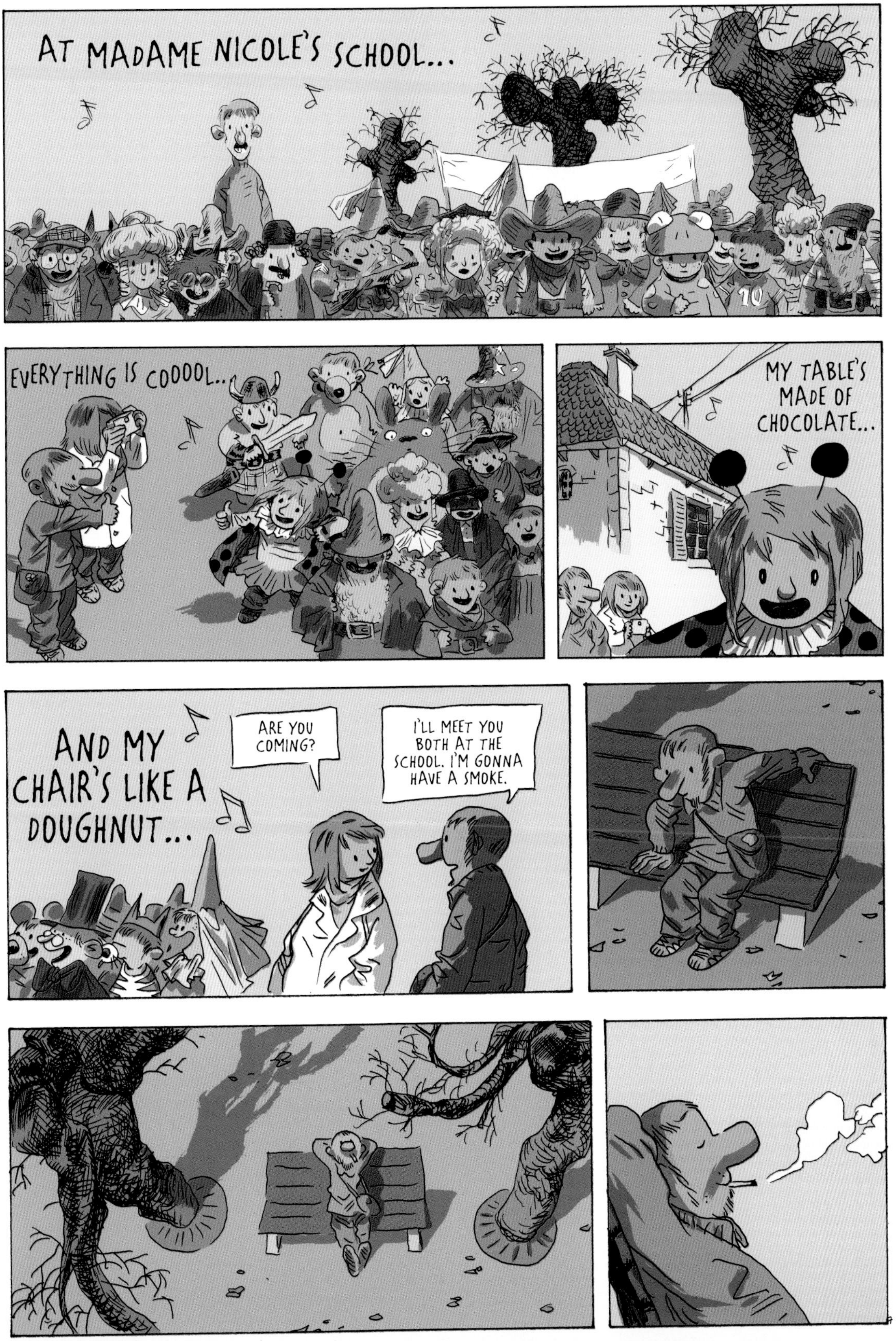
AT MADAME NICOLE'S SCHOOL...
EVERYTHING IS COOOOL...
MY TABLE'S MADE OF CHOCOLATE...
AND MY CHAIR'S LIKE A DOUGHNUT...
ARE YOU COMING?
I'LL MEET YOU BOTH AT THE SCHOOL. I'M GONNA HAVE A SMOKE.

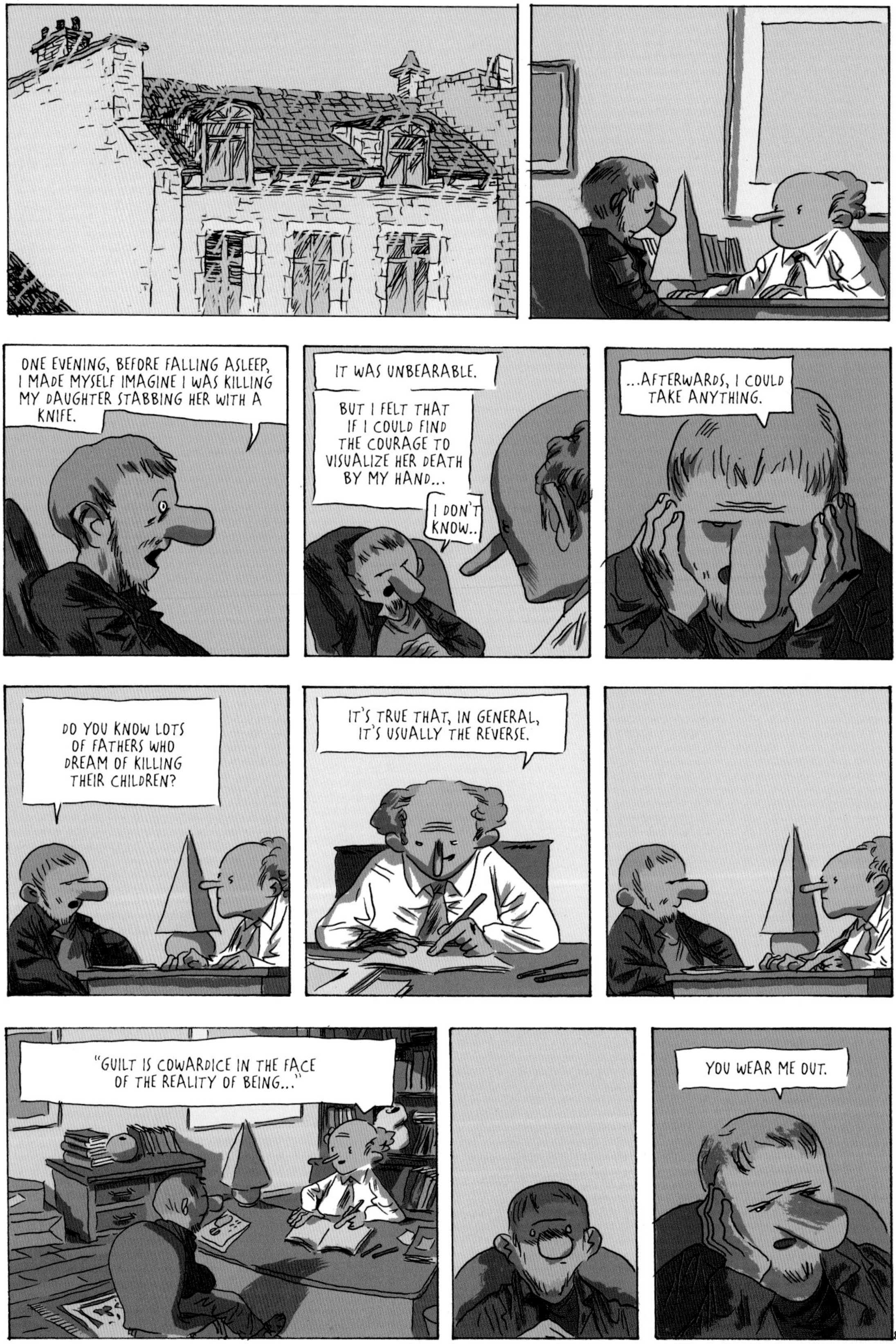

ONE EVENING, BEFORE FALLING ASLEEP, I MADE MYSELF IMAGINE I WAS KILLING MY DAUGHTER STABBING HER WITH A KNIFE.
IT WAS UNBEARABLE.
BUT I FELT THAT IF I COULD FIND THE COURAGE TO VISUALIZE HER DEATH BY MY HAND...
I DON'T KNOW..
...AFTERWARDS, I COULD TAKE ANYTHING.
DO YOU KNOW LOTS OF FATHERS WHO DREAM OF KILLING THEIR CHILDREN?
IT'S TRUE THAT, IN GENERAL, IT'S USUALLY THE REVERSE.
"GUILT IS COWARDICE IN THE FACE OF THE REALITY OF BEING..."
YOU WEAR ME OUT.

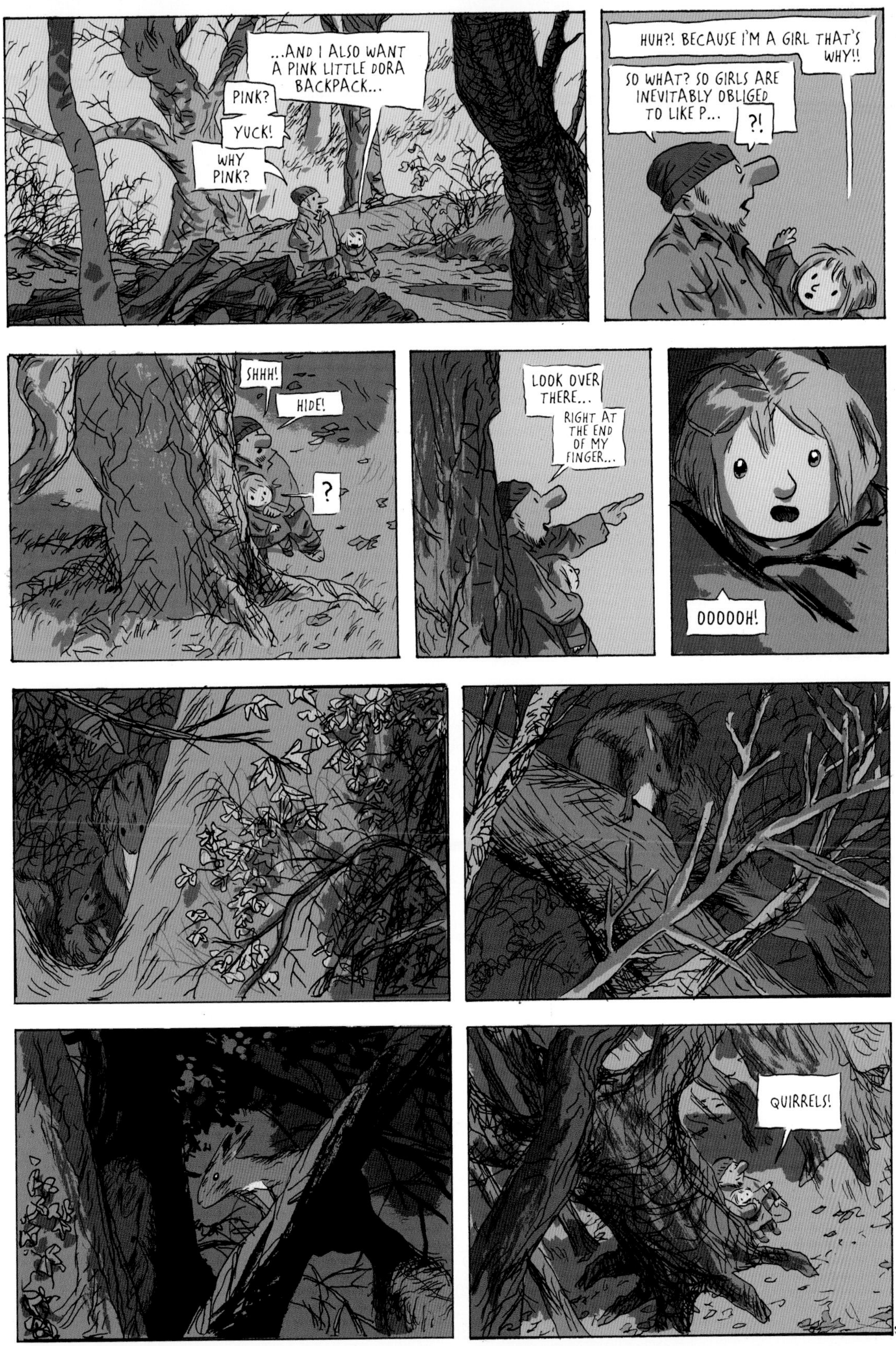
...AND I ALSO WANT A PINK LITTLE DORA BACKPACK...
PINK?
YUCK!
WHY PINK?
HUH?! BECAUSE I'M A GIRL THAT'S WHY!!
SO WHAT? SO GIRLS ARE INEVITABLY OBLIGED TO LIKE P...
?!
SHHH!
HIDE!
?
LOOK OVER THERE...
RIGHT AT THE END OF MY FINGER...
OOOOOH!
QUIRRELS!

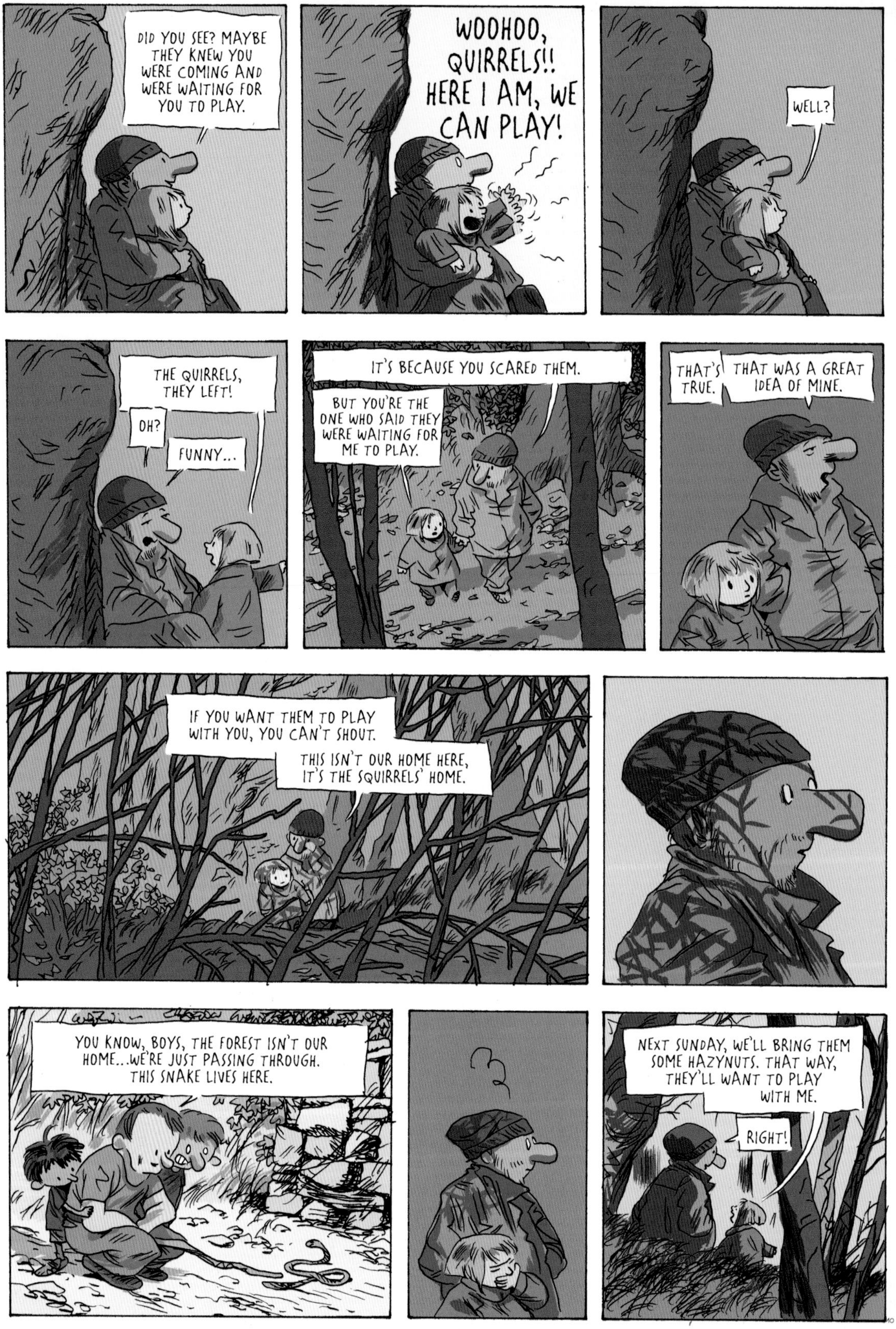

DID YOU SEE? MAYBE THEY KNEW YOU WERE COMING AND WERE WAITING FOR YOU TO PLAY.
WOOHOO, QUIRRELS!! HERE I AM, WE CAN PLAY!
WELL?
THE QUIRRELS, THEY LEFT!
OH?
FUNNY...
IT'S BECAUSE YOU SCARED THEM.
BUT YOU'RE THE ONE WHO SAID THEY WERE WAITING FOR ME TO PLAY.
THAT'S TRUE.
THAT WAS A GREAT IDEA OF MINE.
IF YOU WANT THEM TO PLAY WITH YOU, YOU CAN'T SHOUT.
THIS ISN'T OUR HOME HERE, IT'S THE SQUIRRELS' HOME.
YOU KNOW, BOYS, THE FOREST ISN'T OUR HOME...WE'RE JUST PASSING THROUGH. THIS SNAKE LIVES HERE.
NEXT SUNDAY, WE'LL BRING THEM SOME HAZYNUTS. THAT WAY, THEY'LL WANT TO PLAY WITH ME.
RIGHT!

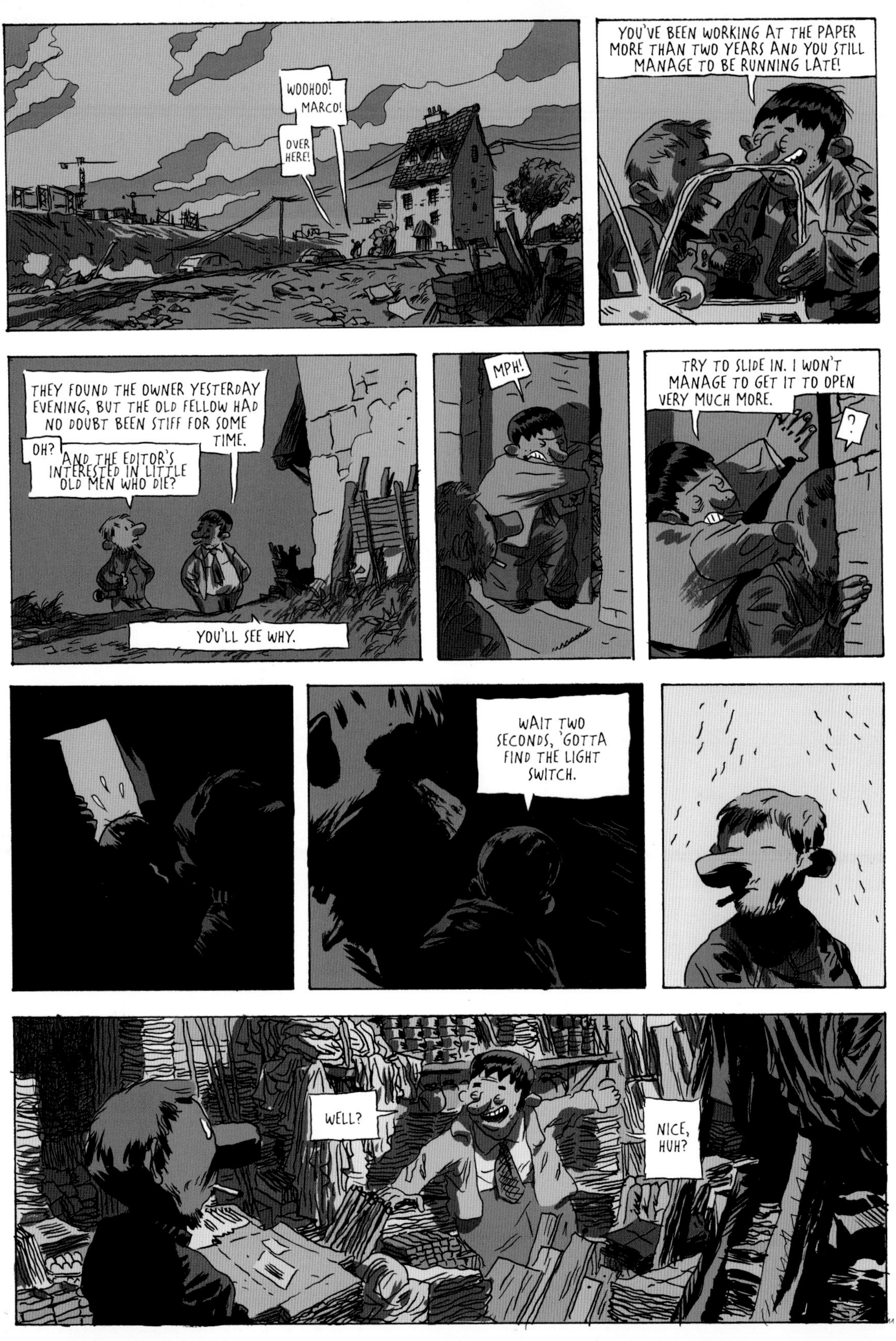
WOODHOO! MARCO!
OVER HERE!
YOU'VE BEEN WORKING AT THE PAPER MORE THAN TWO YEARS AND YOU STILL MANAGE TO BE RUNNING LATE!
THEY FOUND THE OWNER YESTERDAY EVENING, BUT THE OLD FELLOW HAD NO DOUBT BEEN STIFF FOR SOME TIME.
OH?
AND THE EDITOR'S INTERESTED IN LITTLE OLD MEN WHO DIE?
YOU'LL SEE WHY.
MPH!
TRY TO SLIDE IN. I WON'T MANAGE TO GET IT TO OPEN VERY MUCH MORE.
?
WAIT TWO SECONDS, 'GOTTA FIND THE LIGHT SWITCH.
WELL?
NICE, HUH?

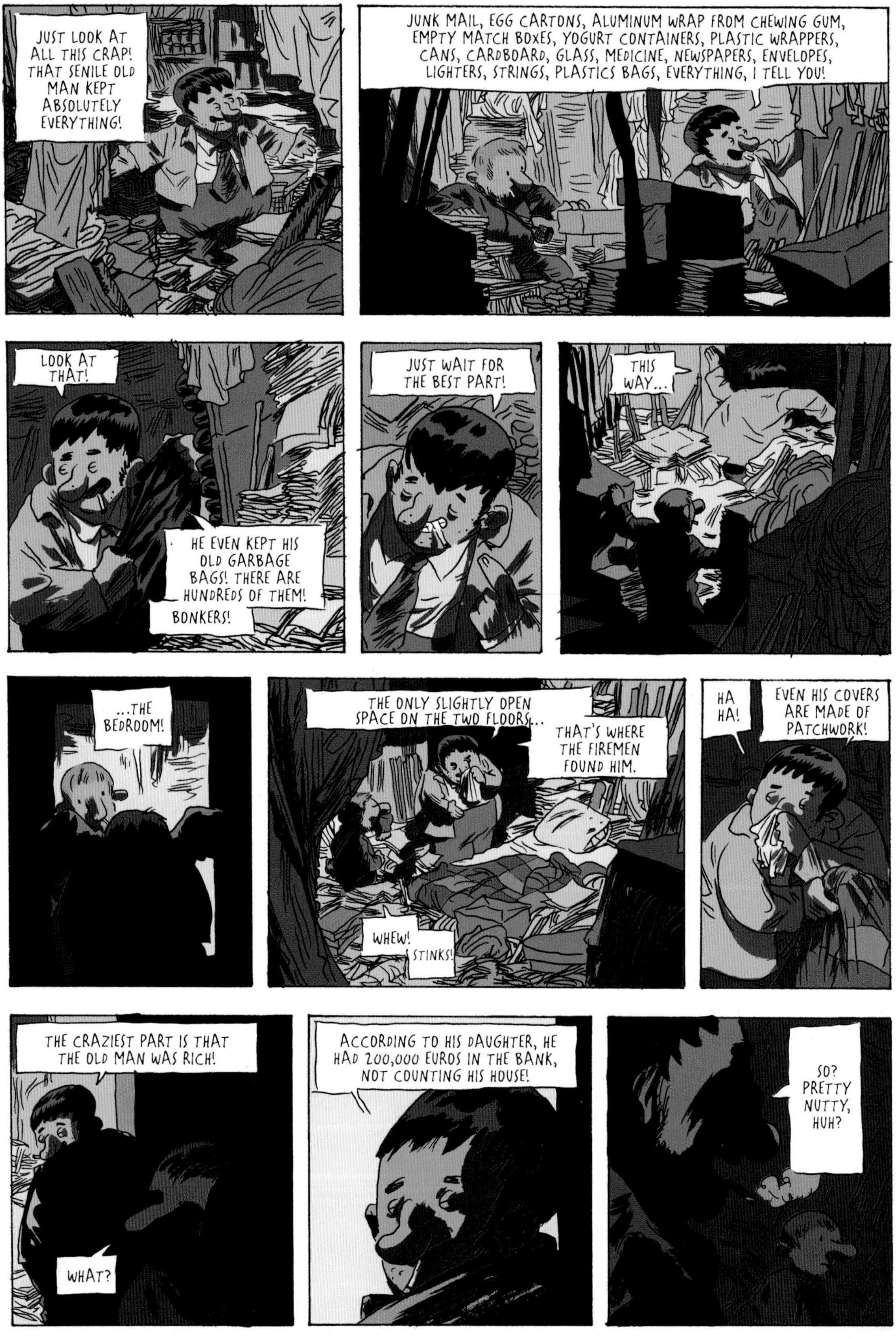
JUST LOOK AT ALL THIS CRAP! THAT SENILE OLD MAN KEPT ABSOLUTELY EVERYTHING!
JUNK MAIL, EGG CARTONS, ALUMINUM WRAP FROM CHEWING GUM, EMPTY MATCH BOXES, YOGURT CONTAINERS, PLASTIC WRAPPERS, CANS, CARDBOARD, GLASS, MEDICINE, NEWSPAPERS, ENVELOPES, LIGHTERS, STRINGS, PLASTICS BAGS, EVERYTHING, I TELL YOU!
LOOK AT THAT!
HE EVEN KEPT HIS OLD GARBAGE BAGS! THERE ARE HUNDREDS OF THEM!
BONKERS!
JUST WAIT FOR THE BEST PART!
THIS WAY...
...THE BEDROOM!
THE ONLY SLIGHTLY OPEN SPACE ON THE TWO FLOORS...
THAT'S WHERE THE FIREMEN FOUND HIM.
WHEW!
STINKS!
HA HA!
EVEN HIS COVERS ARE MADE OF PATCHWORK!
THE CRAZIEST PART IS THAT THE OLD MAN WAS RICH!
WHAT?
ACCORDING TO HIS DAUGHTER, HE HAD 200,000 EUROS IN THE BANK, NOT COUNTING HIS HOUSE!
SO? PRETTY NUTTY, HUH?

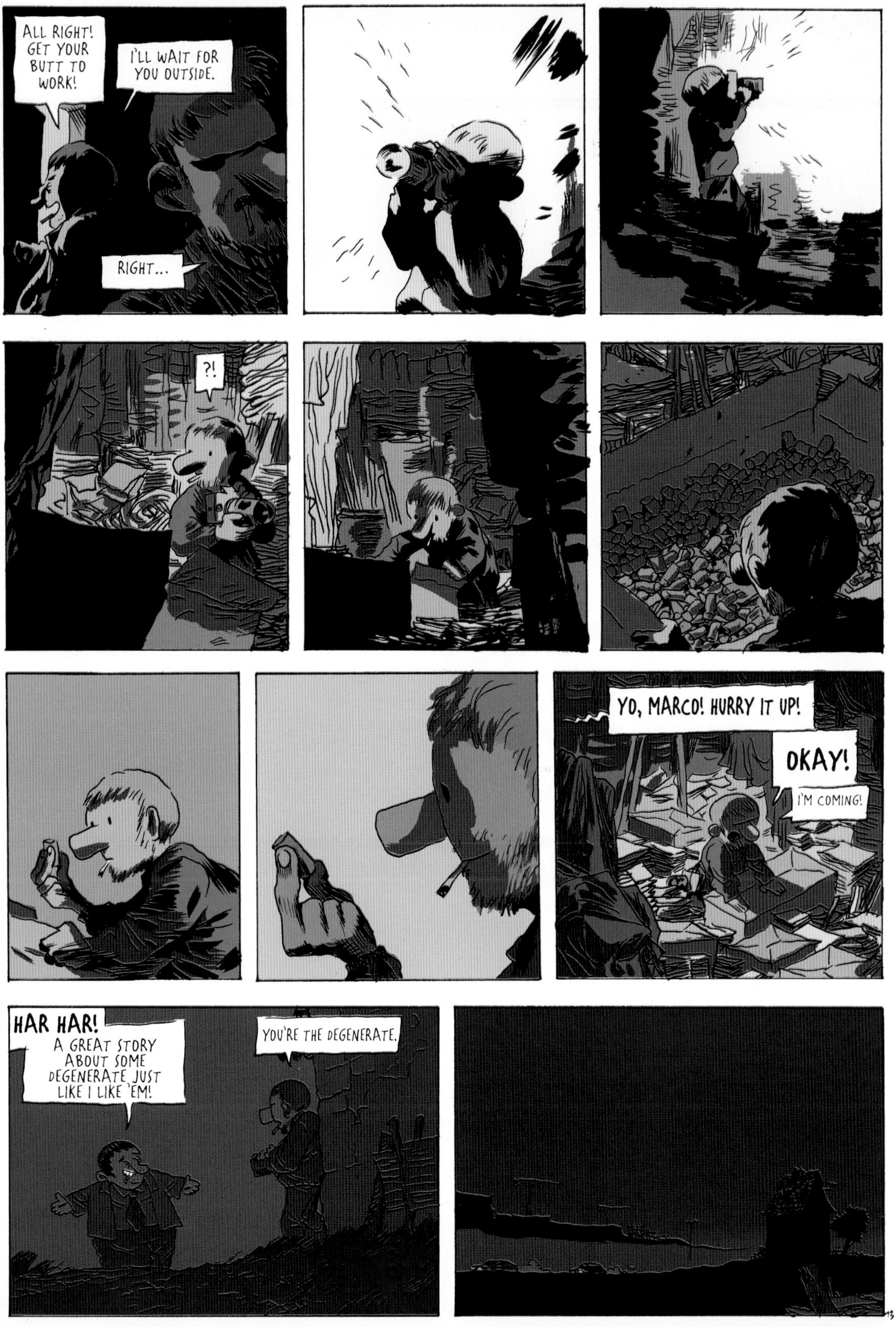
ALL RIGHT! GET YOUR BUTT TO WORK!
I'LL WAIT FOR YOU OUTSIDE.
RIGHT...
?!
YO, MARCO! HURRY IT UP!
OKAY!
I'M COMING!
HAR HAR! A GREAT STORY ABOUT SOME DEGENERATE JUST LIKE I LIKE 'EM!
YOU'RE THE DEGENERATE.

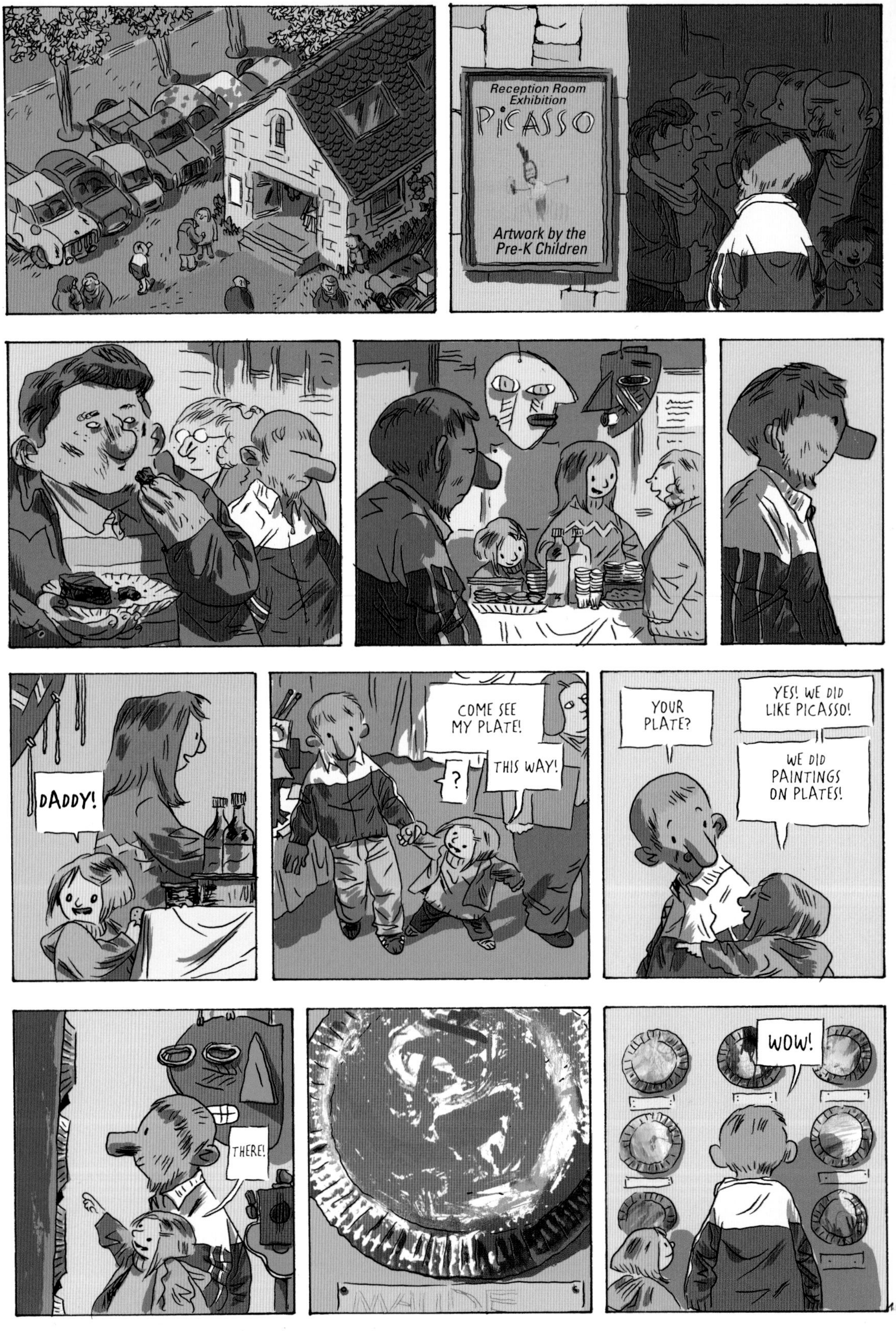
Reception Room Exhibition
PICASSO
Artwork by the Pre-K Children
DADDY!
COME SEE MY PLATE!
?
THIS WAY!
YOUR PLATE?
YES! WE DID LIKE PICASSO!
WE DID PAINTINGS ON PLATES!
THERE!
WOW!

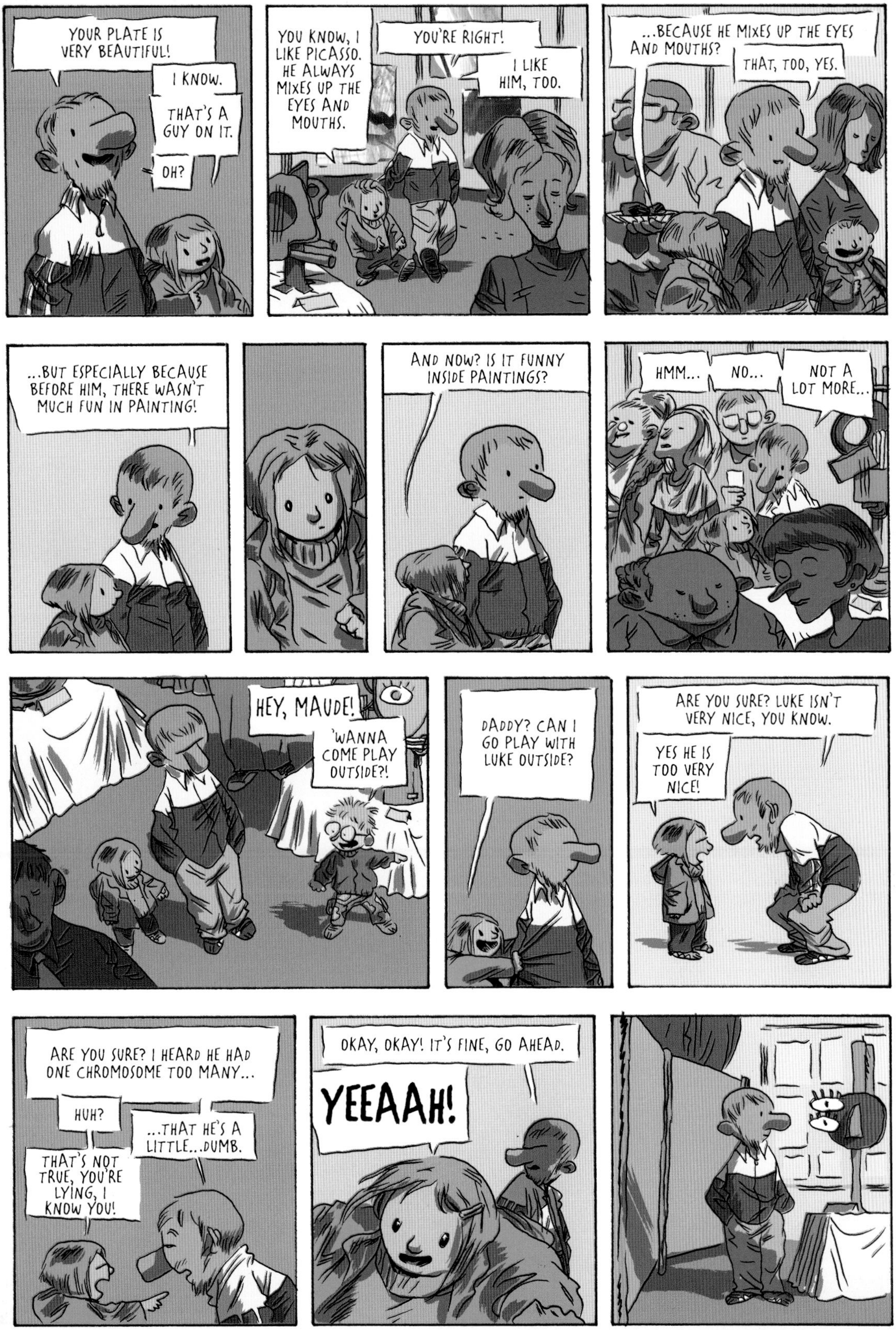
YOUR PLATE IS VERY BEAUTIFUL!
I KNOW.
THAT'S A GUY ON IT.
OH?
YOU KNOW, I LIKE PICASSO. HE ALWAYS MIXES UP THE EYES AND MOUTHS.
YOU'RE RIGHT!
I LIKE HIM, TOO.
...BECAUSE HE MIXES UP THE EYES AND MOUTHS?
THAT, TOO, YES.
...BUT ESPECIALLY BECAUSE BEFORE HIM, THERE WASN'T MUCH FUN IN PAINTING!
AND NOW? IS IT FUNNY INSIDE PAINTINGS?
HMM...
NO...
NOT A LOT MORE...
HEY, MAUDE!
'WANNA COME PLAY OUTSIDE?!
DADDY? CAN I GO PLAY WITH LUKE OUTSIDE?
ARE YOU SURE? LUKE ISN'T VERY NICE, YOU KNOW.
YES HE IS TOO VERY NICE!
ARE YOU SURE? I HEARD HE HAD ONE CHROMOSOME TOO MANY...
HUH?
...THAT HE'S A LITTLE...DUMB.
THAT'S NOT TRUE, YOU'RE LYING, I KNOW YOU!
OKAY, OKAY! IT'S FINE, GO AHEAD.
YEEAAH!

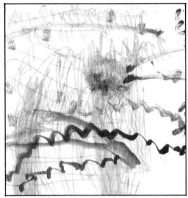

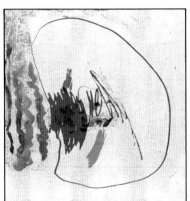

YELLO?

PABLO!

WOW!

HOW ARE THINGS?

WE'RE GONNA BE NEEDING YOU, BOY...

?

OH?

WHY?

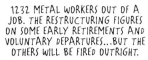

IT WON'T BE OFFICIAL FOR SEVERAL DAYS, BUT...THEY'RE GONNA BE SHUTTING DOWN THE METAL SHOPS.

1232 METAL WORKERS OUT OF A JOB. THE RESTRUCTURING FIGURES ON SOME EARLY RETIREMENTS AND VOLUNTARY DEPARTURES...BUT THE OTHERS WILL BE FIRED OUTRIGHT.

SO THE GUYS ASKED ME TO CALL YOU. THEY'RE GONNA BE NEEDING JOURNALISTS.

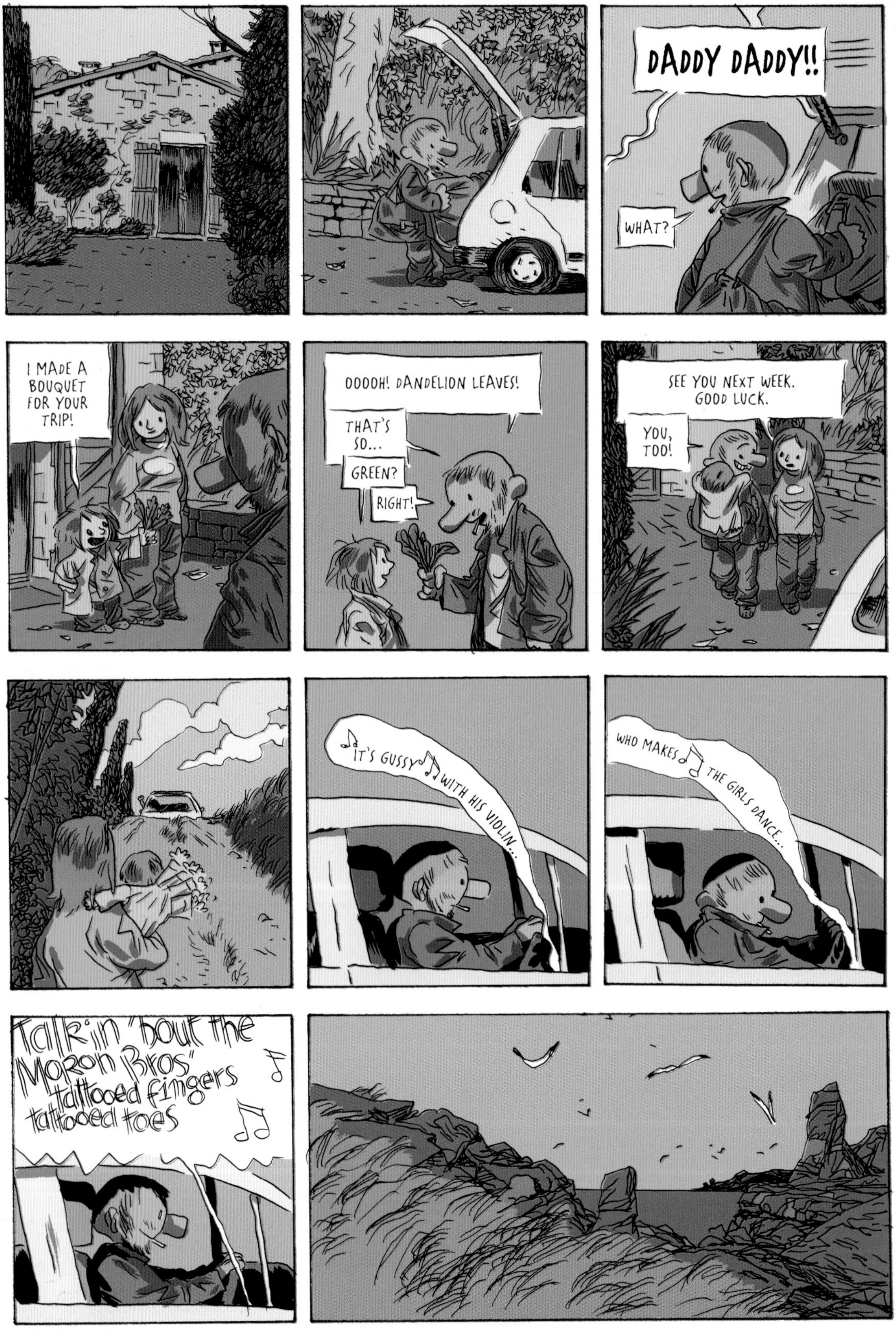
DADDY DADDY!!
WHAT?
I MADE A BOUQUET FOR YOUR TRIP!
OOOOH! DANDELION LEAVES!
THAT'S SO...
GREEN?
RIGHT!
SEE YOU NEXT WEEK. GOOD LUCK.
YOU, TOO!
IT'S GUSSY WITH HIS VIOLIN...
WHO MAKES THE GIRLS DANCE...
Talkin' 'bout the Moron Bros' tattooed fingers tattooed toes

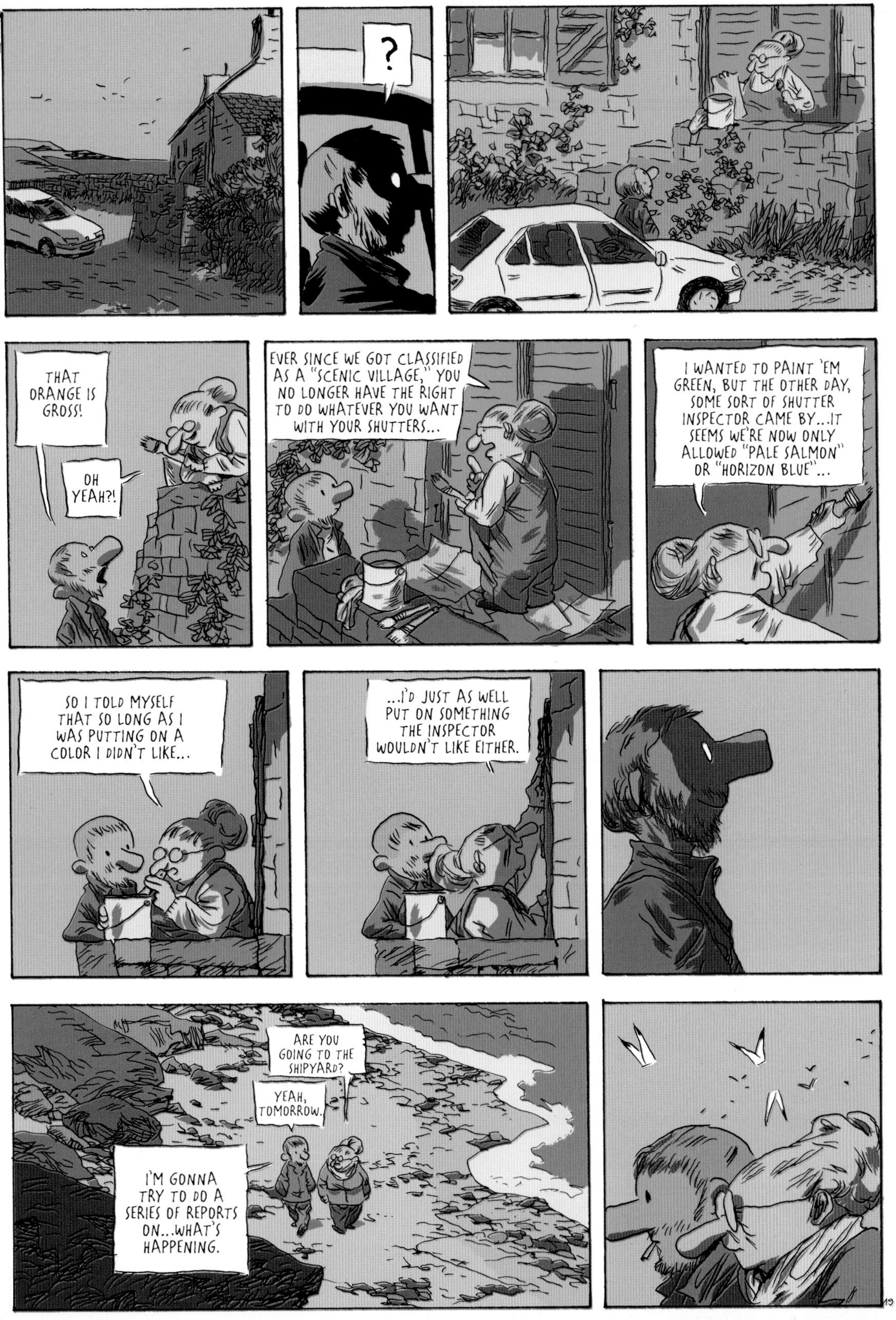
?
THAT ORANGE IS GROSS!
OH YEAH?!
EVER SINCE WE GOT CLASSIFIED AS A "SCENIC VILLAGE," YOU NO LONGER HAVE THE RIGHT TO DO WHATEVER YOU WANT WITH YOUR SHUTTERS...
I WANTED TO PAINT 'EM GREEN, BUT THE OTHER DAY, SOME SORT OF SHUTTER INSPECTOR CAME BY...IT SEEMS WE'RE NOW ONLY ALLOWED "PALE SALMON" OR "HORIZON BLUE"...
SO I TOLD MYSELF THAT SO LONG AS I WAS PUTTING ON A COLOR I DIDN'T LIKE...
...I'D JUST AS WELL PUT ON SOMETHING THE INSPECTOR WOULDN'T LIKE EITHER.
ARE YOU GOING TO THE SHIPYARD?
YEAH, TOMORROW.
I'M GONNA TRY TO DO A SERIES OF REPORTS ON...WHAT'S HAPPENING.

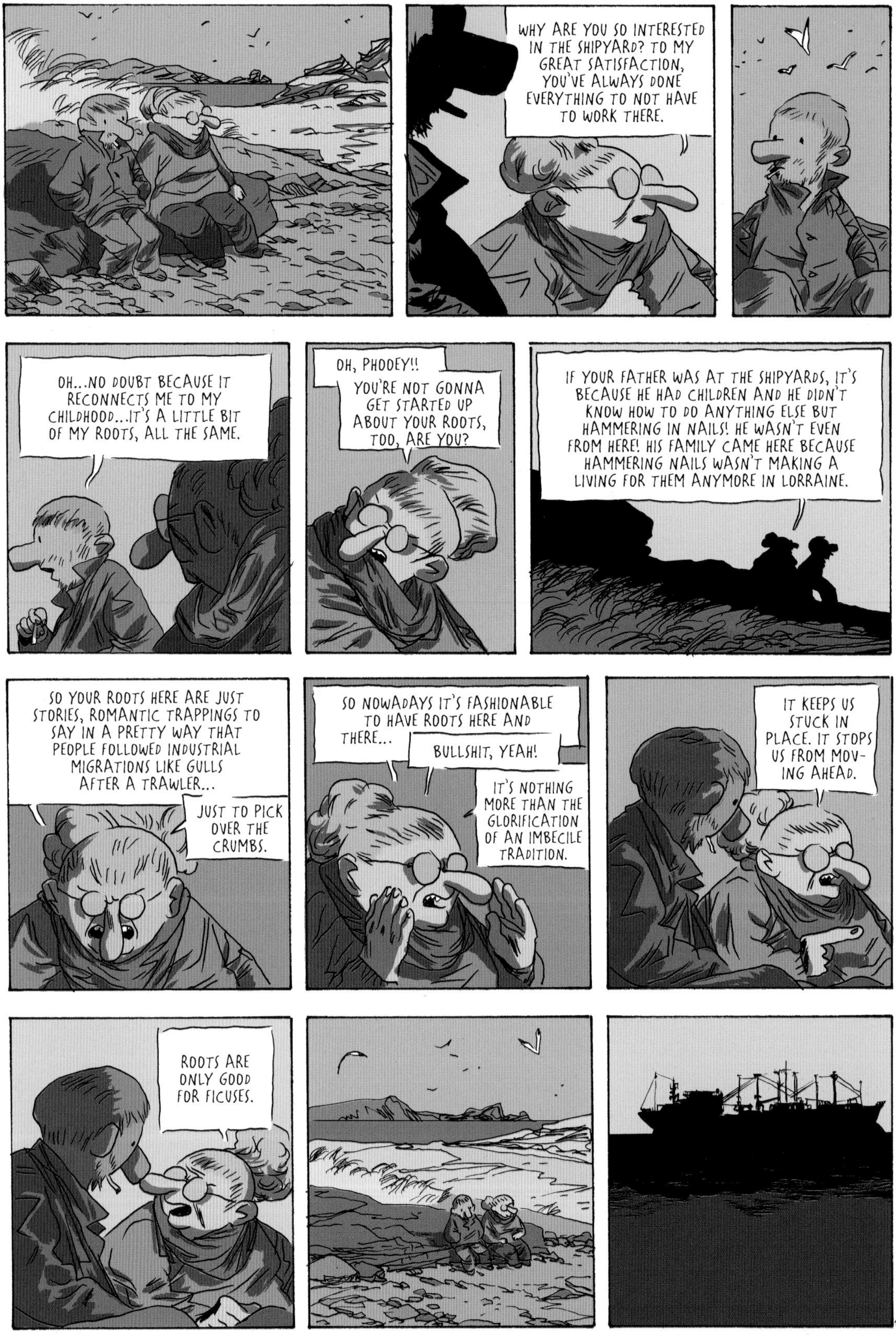
WHY ARE YOU SO INTERESTED IN THE SHIPYARD? TO MY GREAT SATISFACTION, YOU'VE ALWAYS DONE EVERYTHING TO NOT HAVE TO WORK THERE.
OH...NO DOUBT BECAUSE IT RECONNECTS ME TO MY CHILDHOOD...IT'S A LITTLE BIT OF MY ROOTS, ALL THE SAME.
OH, PHOOEY!!
YOU'RE NOT GONNA GET STARTED UP ABOUT YOUR ROOTS, TOO, ARE YOU?
IF YOUR FATHER WAS AT THE SHIPYARDS, IT'S BECAUSE HE HAD CHILDREN AND HE DIDN'T KNOW HOW TO DO ANYTHING ELSE BUT HAMMERING IN NAILS! HE WASN'T EVEN FROM HERE! HIS FAMILY CAME HERE BECAUSE HAMMERING NAILS WASN'T MAKING A LIVING FOR THEM ANYMORE IN LORRAINE.
SO YOUR ROOTS HERE ARE JUST STORIES, ROMANTIC TRAPPINGS TO SAY IN A PRETTY WAY THAT PEOPLE FOLLOWED INDUSTRIAL MIGRATIONS LIKE GULLS AFTER A TRAWLER...
JUST TO PICK OVER THE CRUMBS.
SO NOWADAYS IT'S FASHIONABLE TO HAVE ROOTS HERE AND THERE...
BULLSHIT, YEAH!
IT'S NOTHING MORE THAN THE GLORIFICATION OF AN IMBECILE TRADITION.
IT KEEPS US STUCK IN PLACE. IT STOPS US FROM MOVING AHEAD.
ROOTS ARE ONLY GOOD FOR FICUSES.

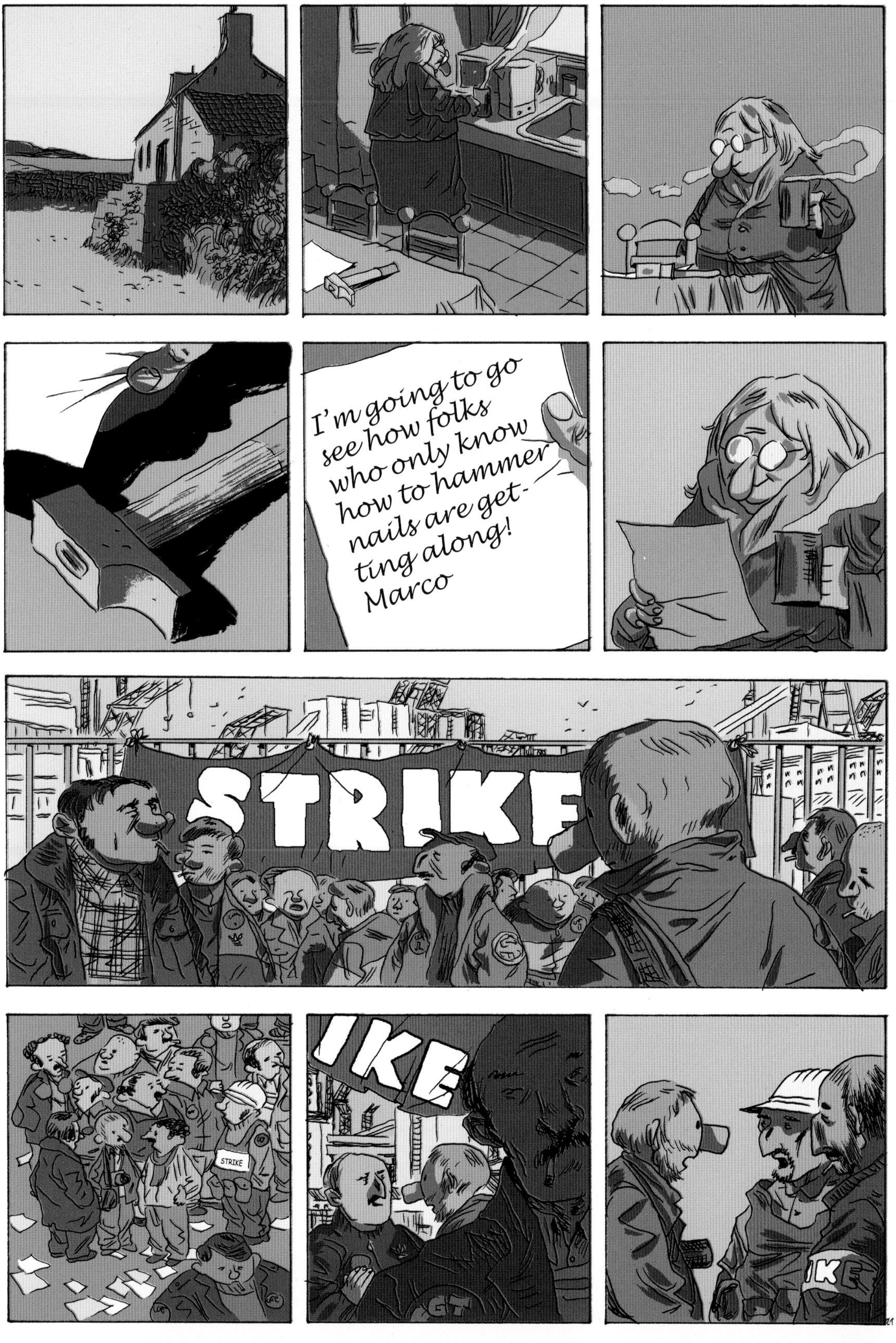
I'm going to go see how folks who only know how to hammer nails are getting along!
Marco
STRIKE
IKE
STRIKE
IKE

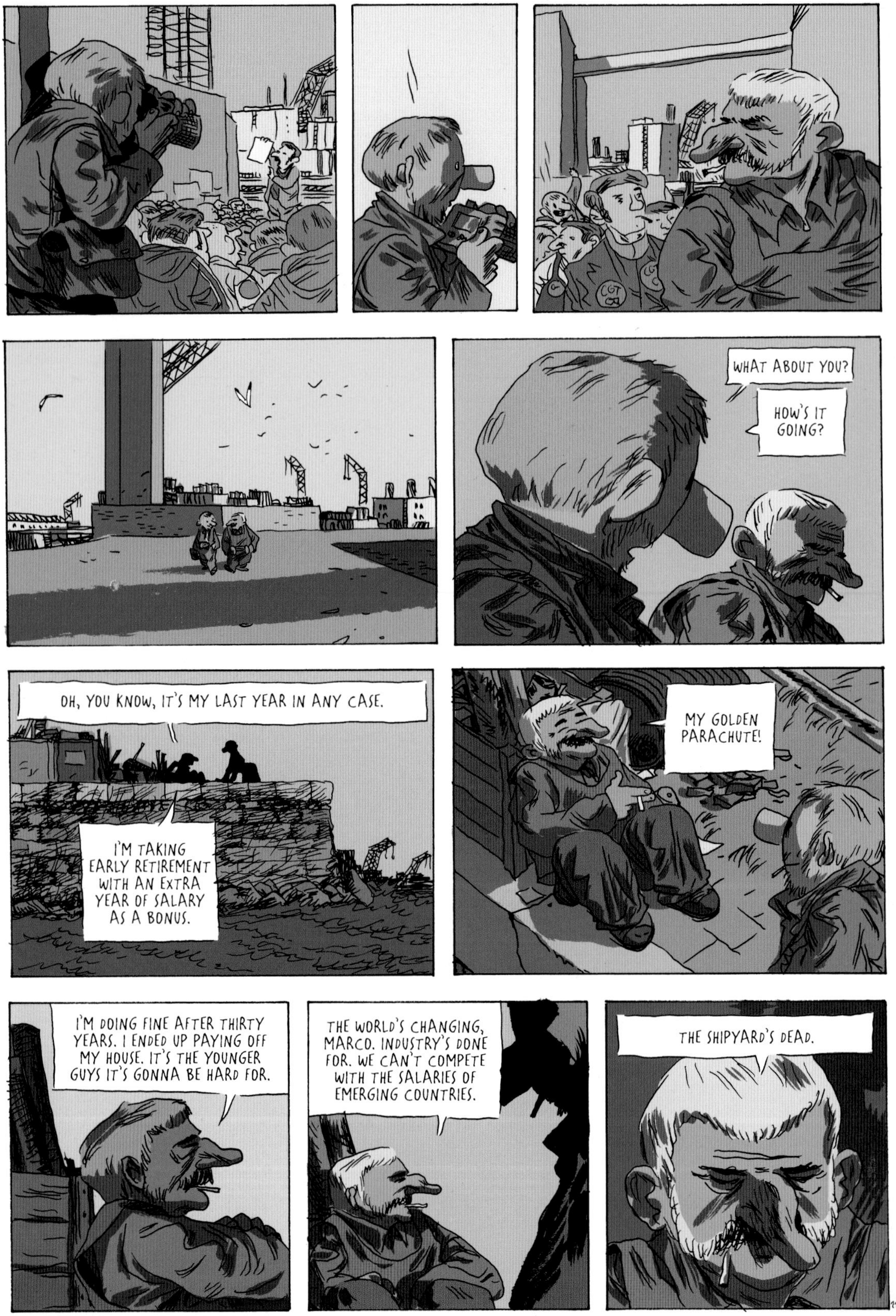

WHAT ABOUT YOU?
HOW'S IT GOING?
OH, YOU KNOW, IT'S MY LAST YEAR IN ANY CASE.
I'M TAKING EARLY RETIREMENT WITH AN EXTRA YEAR OF SALARY AS A BONUS.
MY GOLDEN PARACHUTE!
I'M DOING FINE AFTER THIRTY YEARS. I ENDED UP PAYING OFF MY HOUSE. IT'S THE YOUNGER GUYS IT'S GONNA BE HARD FOR.
THE WORLD'S CHANGING, MARCO. INDUSTRY'S DONE FOR. WE CAN'T COMPETE WITH THE SALARIES OF EMERGING COUNTRIES.
THE SHIPYARD'S DEAD.

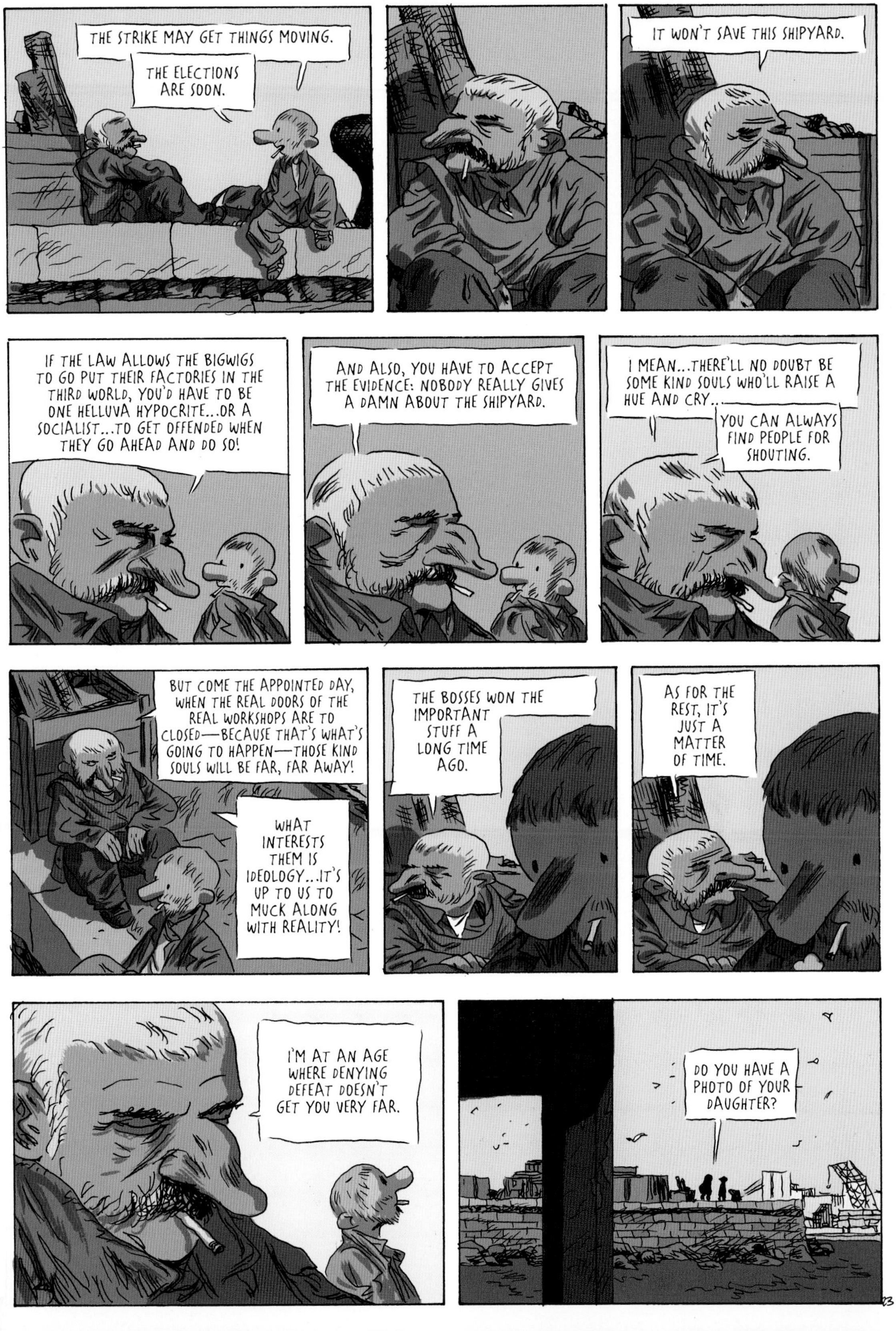

THE STRIKE MAY GET THINGS MOVING.
THE ELECTIONS ARE SOON.
IT WON'T SAVE THIS SHIPYARD.
IF THE LAW ALLOWS THE BIGWIGS TO GO PUT THEIR FACTORIES IN THE THIRD WORLD, YOU'D HAVE TO BE ONE HELLUVA HYPOCRITE...OR A SOCIALIST...TO GET OFFENDED WHEN THEY GO AHEAD AND DO SO!
AND ALSO, YOU HAVE TO ACCEPT THE EVIDENCE: NOBODY REALLY GIVES A DAMN ABOUT THE SHIPYARD.
I MEAN...THERE'LL NO DOUBT BE SOME KIND SOULS WHO'LL RAISE A HUE AND CRY...
YOU CAN ALWAYS FIND PEOPLE FOR SHOUTING.
BUT COME THE APPOINTED DAY, WHEN THE REAL DOORS OF THE REAL WORKSHOPS ARE TO CLOSED—BECAUSE THAT'S WHAT'S GOING TO HAPPEN—THOSE KIND SOULS WILL BE FAR, FAR AWAY!
WHAT INTERESTS THEM IS IDEOLOGY...IT'S UP TO US TO MUCK ALONG WITH REALITY!
THE BOSSES WON THE IMPORTANT STUFF A LONG TIME AGO.
AS FOR THE REST, IT'S JUST A MATTER OF TIME.
I'M AT AN AGE WHERE DENYING DEFEAT DOESN'T GET YOU VERY FAR.
DO YOU HAVE A PHOTO OF YOUR DAUGHTER?

PURE DESPAIR POSES SUCH FUNDAMENTAL QUESTIONS, IT CANNOT BE ACCOMMODATED BY IDEOLOGY.

THE IDEOLOGICAL SWINDLE IS TO CONVINCE PEOPLE THAT A TRUTH EXISTS. WHAT'S REAL IS THEN ONLY OF IMPORTANCE INSOFAR AS IT CAN BEND ITSELF TO CONFORM TO THE IDEOLOGY.

HOWEVER, THE STREETS OR METASTASES, FOR EXAMPLE, ARE UTTERLY INDIFFERENT TO THE STOCK MARKET INDEX OR TO THE PARTY LINE.

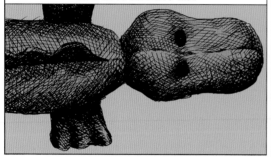

ONE MIGHT OBJECT THAT THEY'RE EVERY BIT AS MUCH SO AS POETRY IS, BUT ONE WOULD BE WRONG.

FREED FROM ALL LOGIC, POETRY IS THE ONLY WAY TO NOTICE WHAT IS PRECIOUS.

DEPARDON, BRASSENS, MIYAZAKI, BONNARD, JARMUSH, SEMPÉ, TOM WAITS, CÉZANNE, MONTY PYTHON, MONET...

...BREL, DESPROGES, KLEE, CARTIER-BRESSON, SPRINGSTEEN, CÉLINE, HARVEY KEITEL, BAUDELAIRE, VAN GOGH...

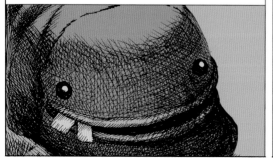

...POETRY REDEEMS EVERYTHING.

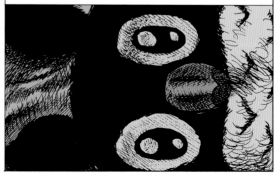

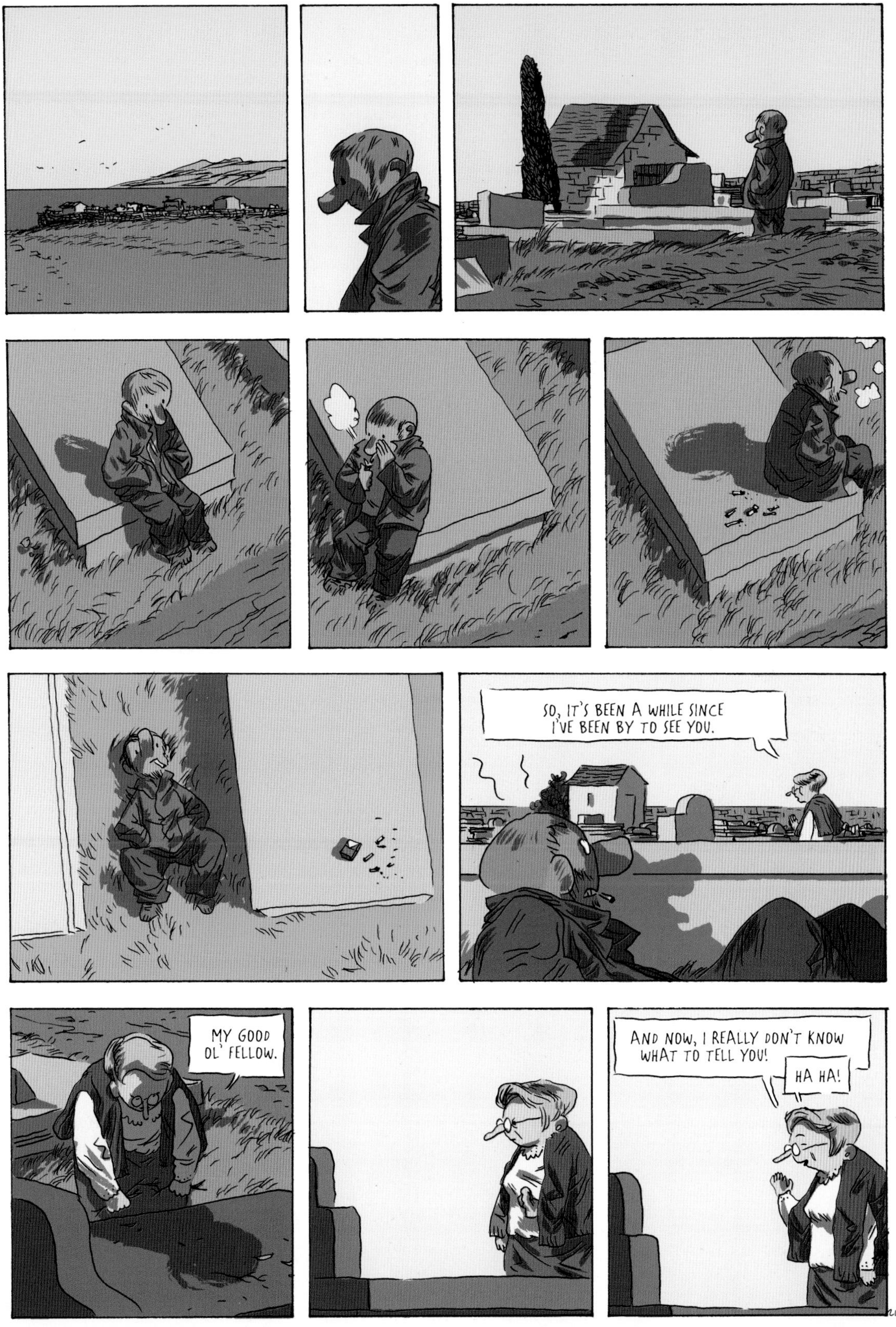
SO, IT'S BEEN A WHILE SINCE I'VE BEEN BY TO SEE YOU.
MY GOOD OL' FELLOW.
AND NOW, I REALLY DON'T KNOW WHAT TO TELL YOU!
HA HA!

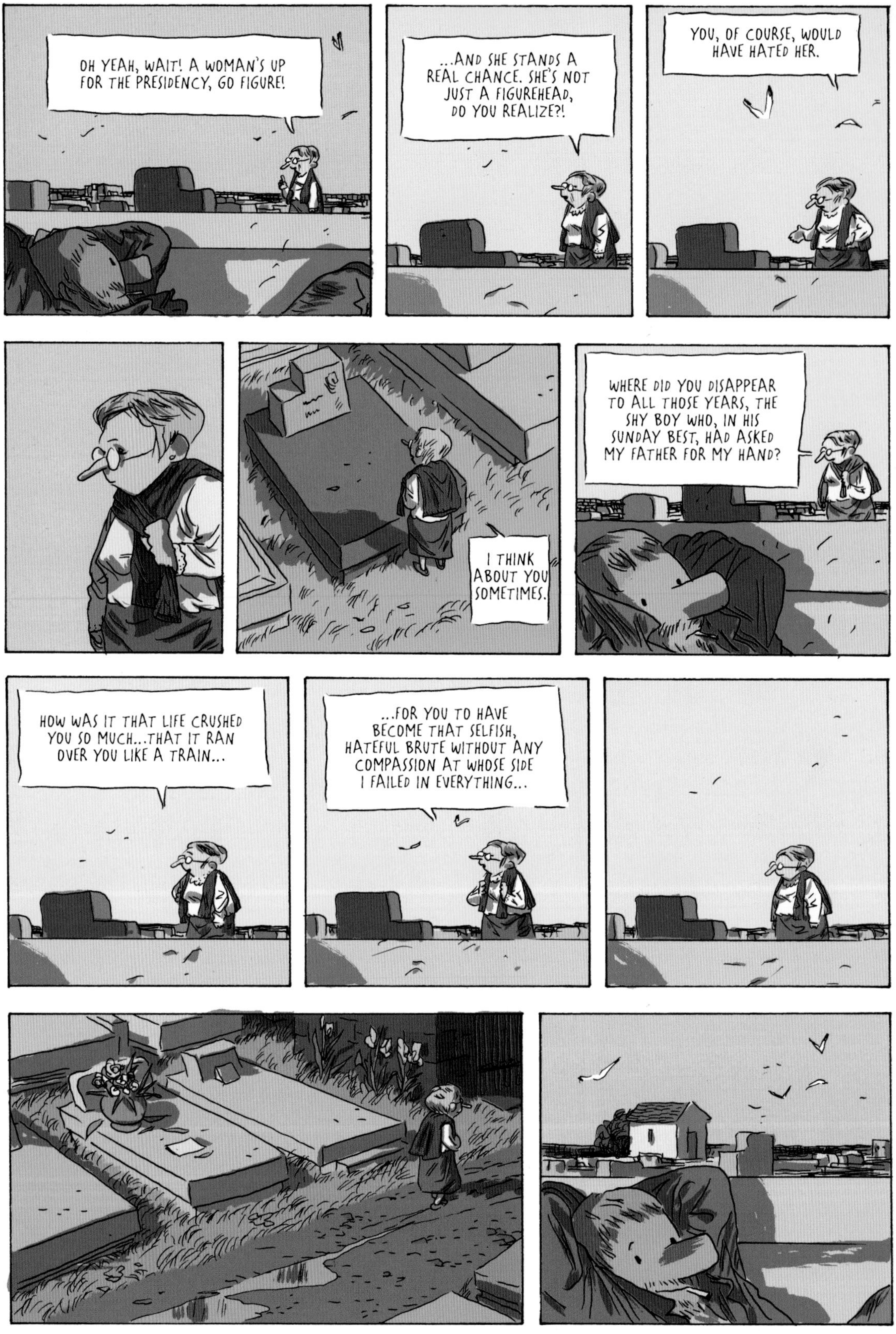
OH YEAH, WAIT! A WOMAN'S UP FOR THE PRESIDENCY, GO FIGURE!
...AND SHE STANDS A REAL CHANCE. SHE'S NOT JUST A FIGUREHEAD, DO YOU REALIZE?!
YOU, OF COURSE, WOULD HAVE HATED HER.
I THINK ABOUT YOU SOMETIMES.
WHERE DID YOU DISAPPEAR TO ALL THOSE YEARS, THE SHY BOY WHO, IN HIS SUNDAY BEST, HAD ASKED MY FATHER FOR MY HAND?
HOW WAS IT THAT LIFE CRUSHED YOU SO MUCH...THAT IT RAN OVER YOU LIKE A TRAIN...
...FOR YOU TO HAVE BECOME THAT SELFISH, HATEFUL BRUTE WITHOUT ANY COMPASSION AT WHOSE SIDE I FAILED IN EVERYTHING...

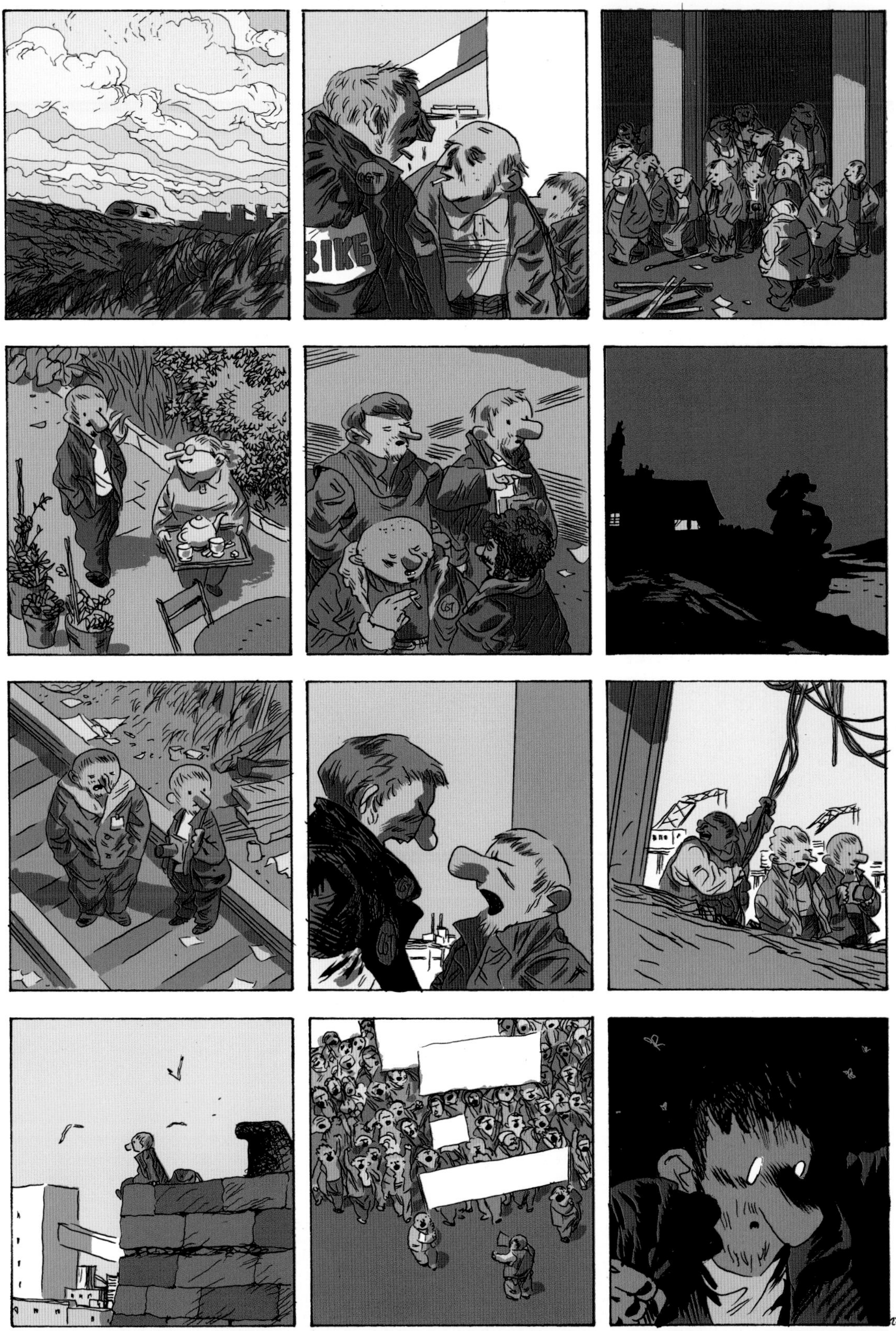
RIKE
CGT

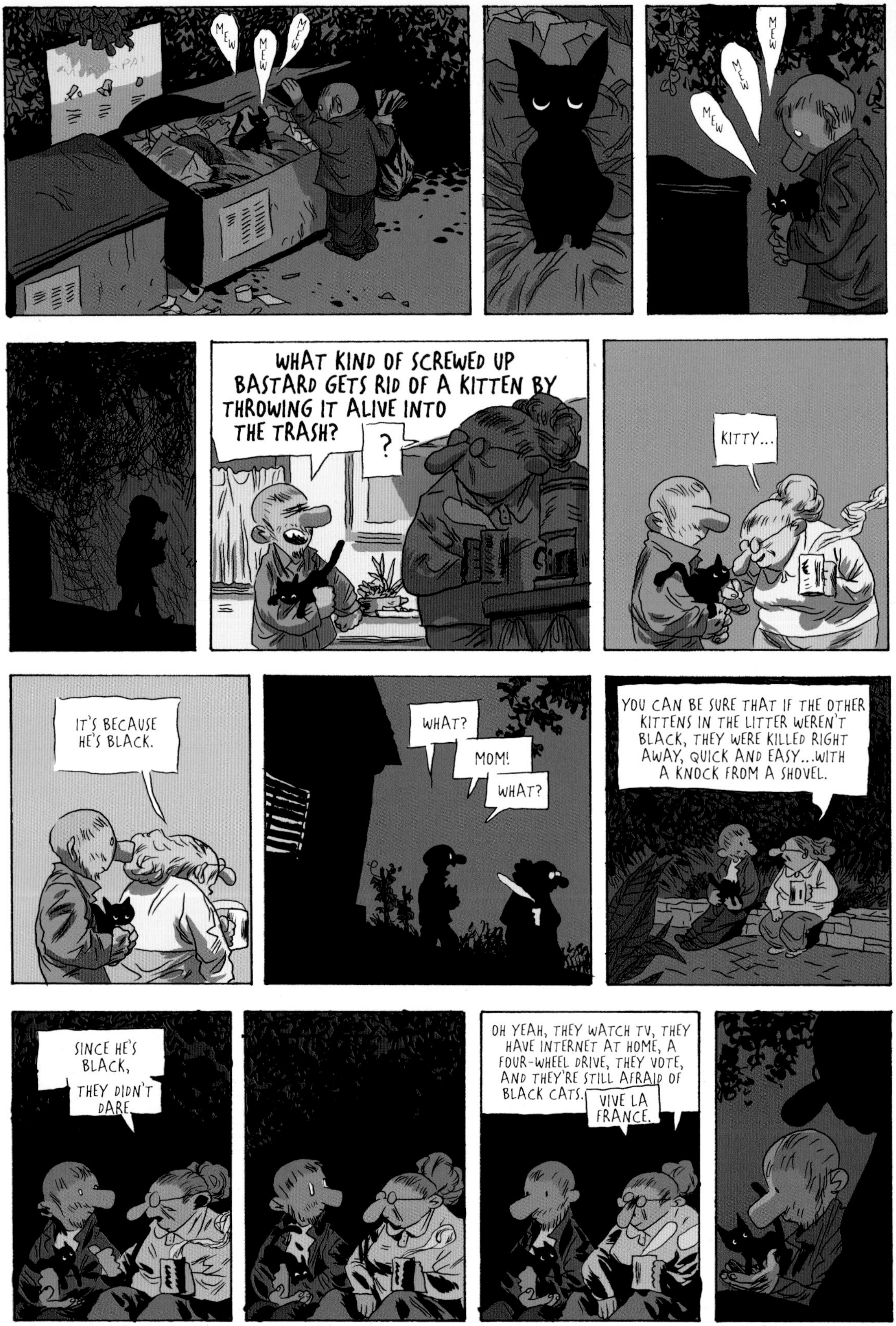
MEW
MEW
MEW
MEW
MEW
MEW
WHAT KIND OF SCREWED UP BASTARD GETS RID OF A KITTEN BY THROWING IT ALIVE INTO THE TRASH?
?
KITTY...
IT'S BECAUSE HE'S BLACK.
WHAT?
MOM!
WHAT?
YOU CAN BE SURE THAT IF THE OTHER KITTENS IN THE LITTER WEREN'T BLACK, THEY WERE KILLED RIGHT AWAY, QUICK AND EASY...WITH A KNOCK FROM A SHOVEL.
SINCE HE'S BLACK,
THEY DIDN'T DARE.
OH YEAH, THEY WATCH TV, THEY HAVE INTERNET AT HOME, A FOUR-WHEEL DRIVE, THEY VOTE, AND THEY'RE STILL AFRAID OF BLACK CATS.
VIVE LA FRANCE.

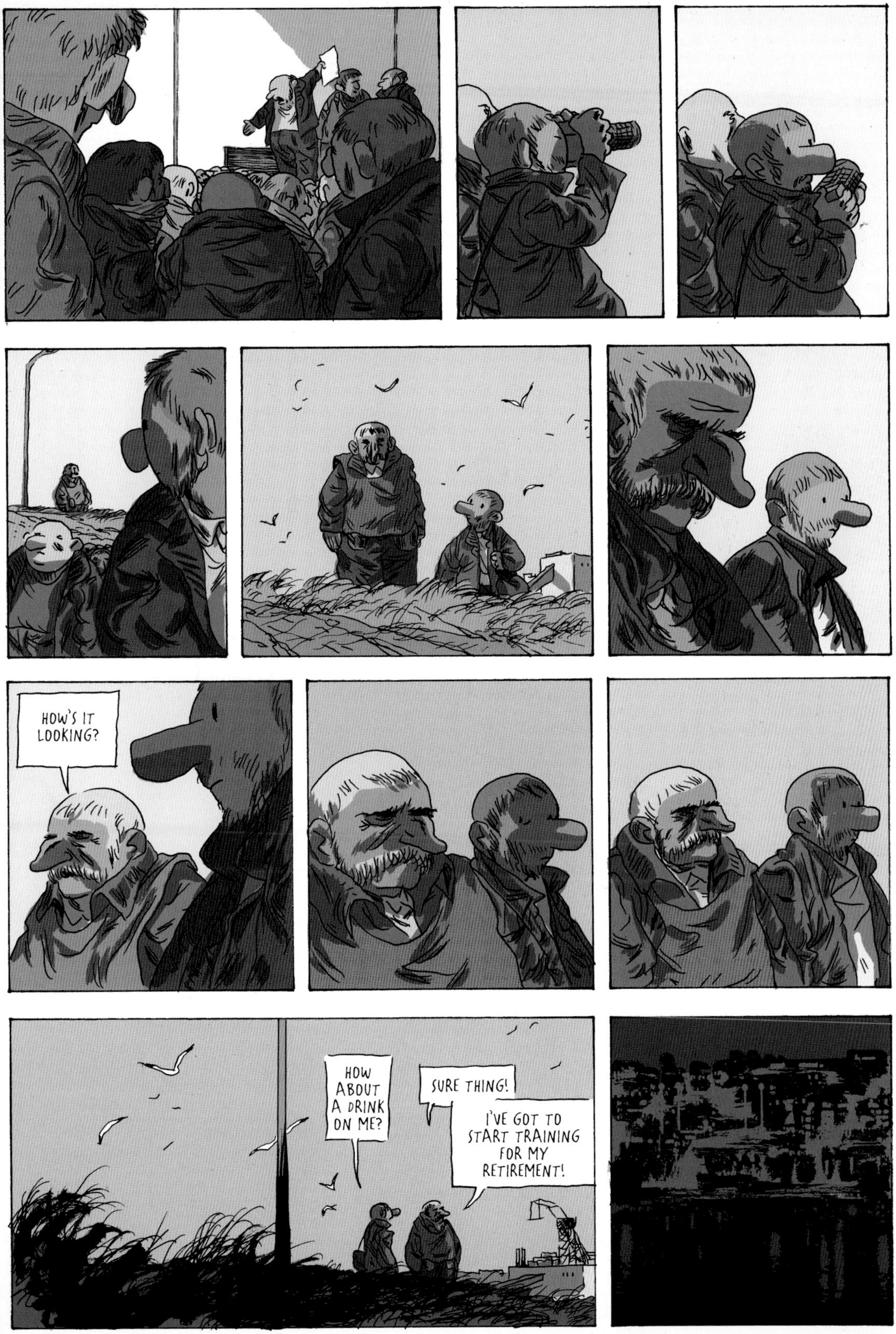
HOW'S IT LOOKING?
HOW ABOUT A DRINK ON ME?
SURE THING!
I'VE GOT TO START TRAINING FOR MY RETIREMENT!

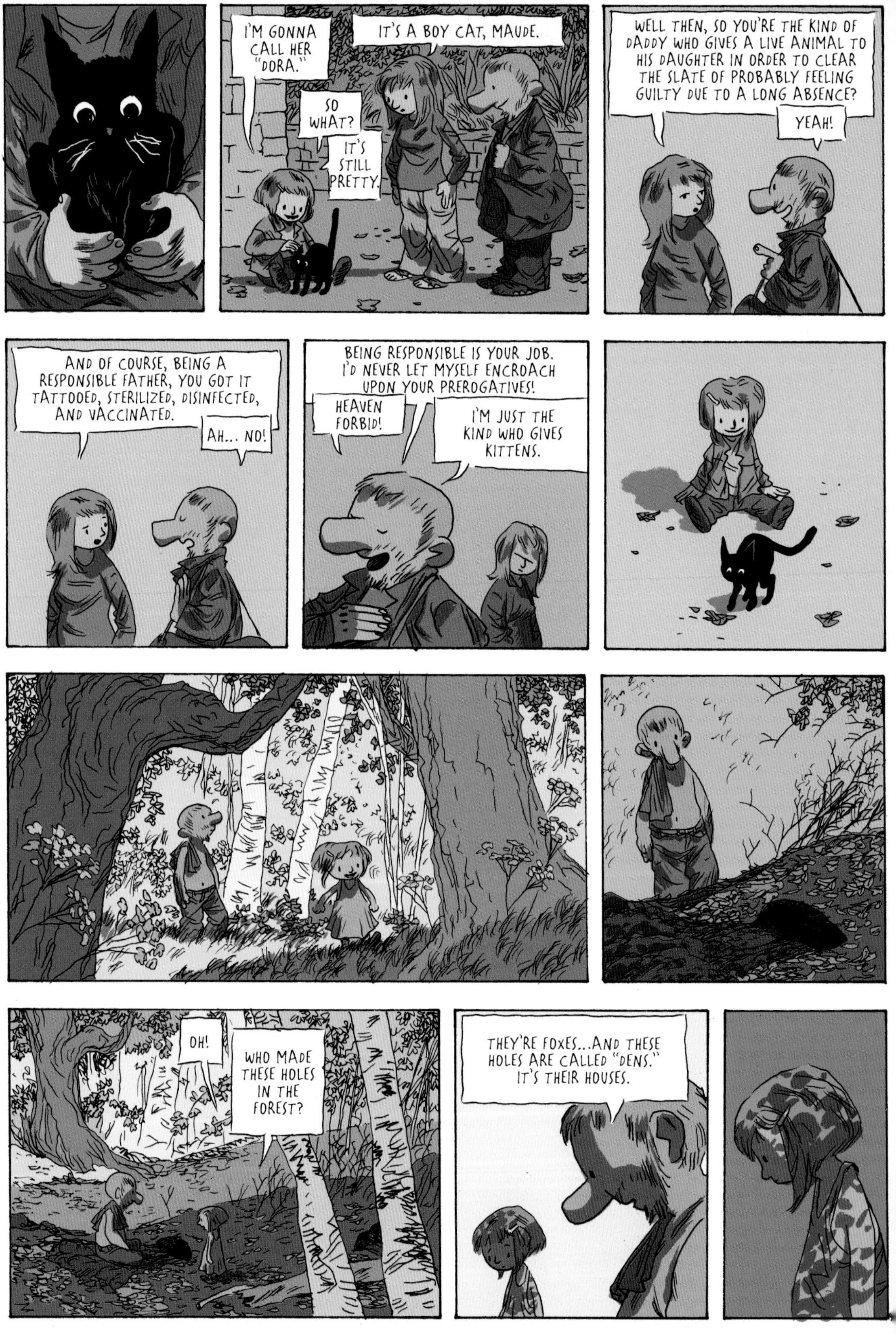
I'M GONNA CALL HER "DORA."
IT'S A BOY CAT, MAUDE.
SO WHAT?
IT'S STILL PRETTY.
WELL THEN, SO YOU'RE THE KIND OF DADDY WHO GIVES A LIVE ANIMAL TO HIS DAUGHTER IN ORDER TO CLEAR THE SLATE OF PROBABLY FEELING GUILTY DUE TO A LONG ABSENCE?
YEAH!
AND OF COURSE, BEING A RESPONSIBLE FATHER, YOU GOT IT TATTOOED, STERILIZED, DISINFECTED, AND VACCINATED.
AH... NO!
BEING RESPONSIBLE IS YOUR JOB. I'D NEVER LET MYSELF ENCROACH UPON YOUR PREROGATIVES!
HEAVEN FORBID!
I'M JUST THE KIND WHO GIVES KITTENS.
OH!
WHO MADE THESE HOLES IN THE FOREST?
THEY'RE FOXES...AND THESE HOLES ARE CALLED "DENS." IT'S THEIR HOUSES.

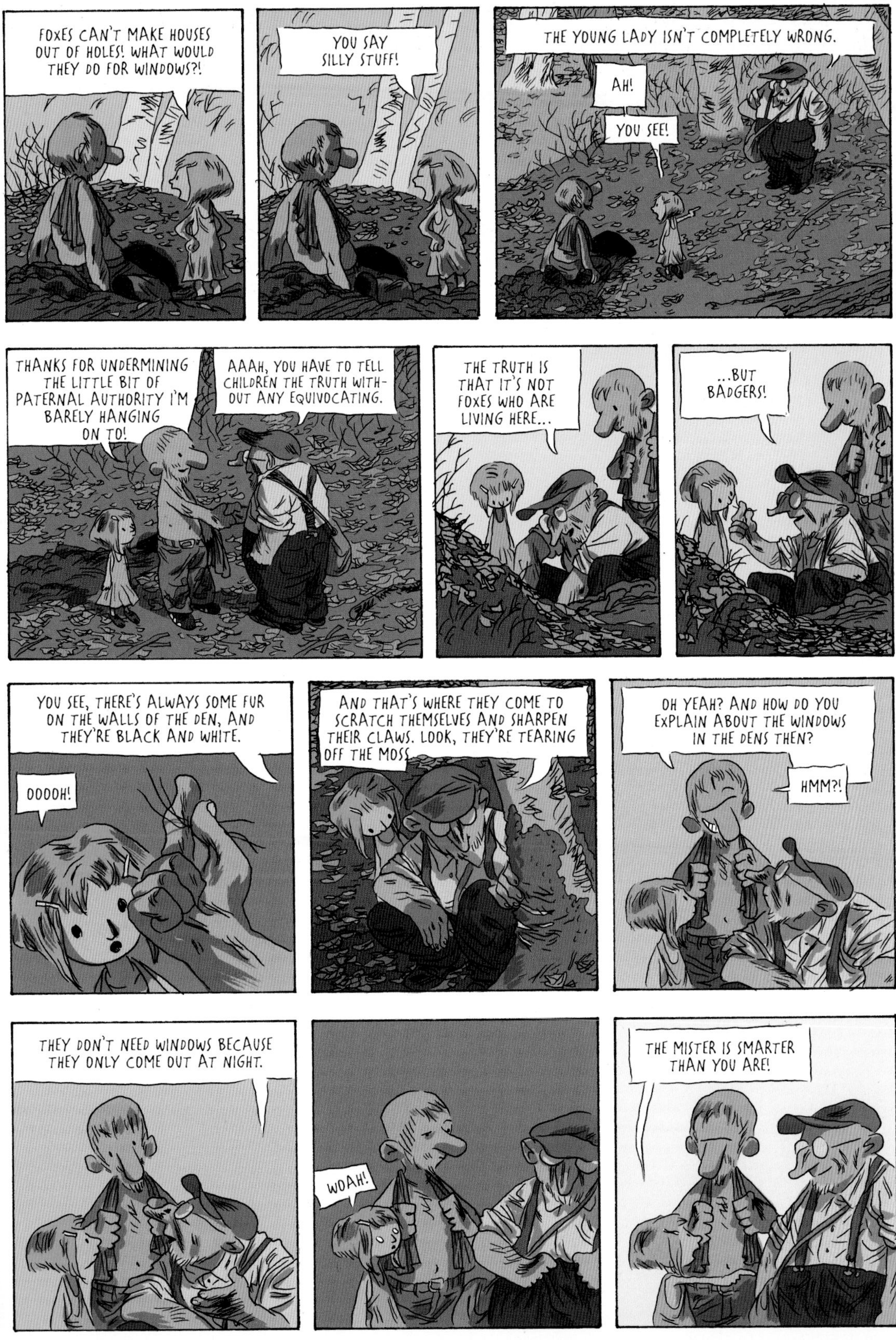
FOXES CAN'T MAKE HOUSES OUT OF HOLES! WHAT WOULD THEY DO FOR WINDOWS?!
YOU SAY SILLY STUFF!
THE YOUNG LADY ISN'T COMPLETELY WRONG.
AH!
YOU SEE!
THANKS FOR UNDERMINING THE LITTLE BIT OF PATERNAL AUTHORITY I'M BARELY HANGING ON TO!
AAAH, YOU HAVE TO TELL CHILDREN THE TRUTH WITHOUT ANY EQUIVOCATING.
THE TRUTH IS THAT IT'S NOT FOXES WHO ARE LIVING HERE...
...BUT BADGERS!
YOU SEE, THERE'S ALWAYS SOME FUR ON THE WALLS OF THE DEN, AND THEY'RE BLACK AND WHITE.
OOOOH!
AND THAT'S WHERE THEY COME TO SCRATCH THEMSELVES AND SHARPEN THEIR CLAWS. LOOK, THEY'RE TEARING OFF THE MOSS.
OH YEAH? AND HOW DO YOU EXPLAIN ABOUT THE WINDOWS IN THE DENS THEN?
HMM?!
THEY DON'T NEED WINDOWS BECAUSE THEY ONLY COME OUT AT NIGHT.
WOAH!
THE MISTER IS SMARTER THAN YOU ARE!

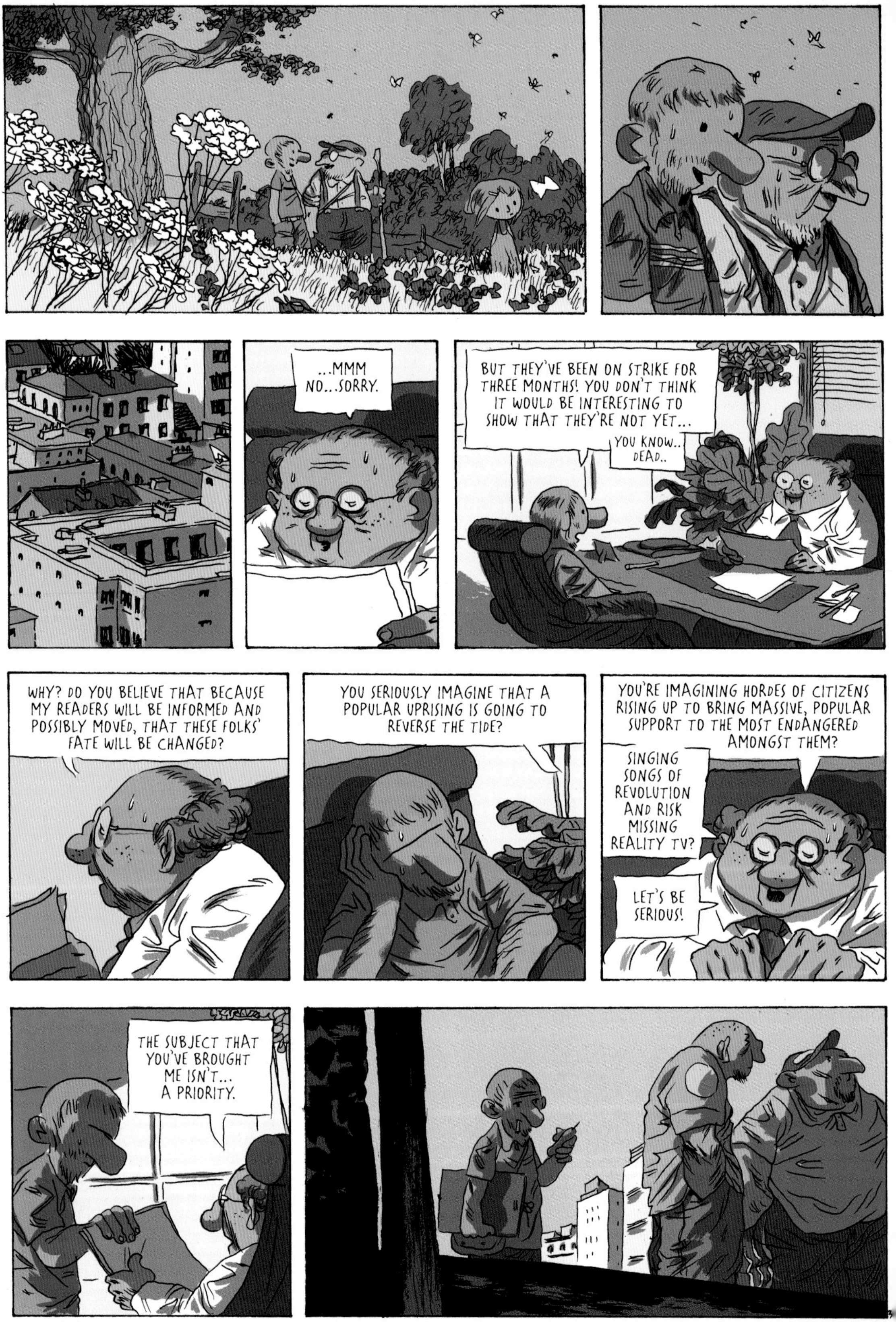
...MMM NO...SORRY.
BUT THEY'VE BEEN ON STRIKE FOR THREE MONTHS! YOU DON'T THINK IT WOULD BE INTERESTING TO SHOW THAT THEY'RE NOT YET...
YOU KNOW.. DEAD..
WHY? DO YOU BELIEVE THAT BECAUSE MY READERS WILL BE INFORMED AND POSSIBLY MOVED, THAT THESE FOLKS' FATE WILL BE CHANGED?
YOU SERIOUSLY IMAGINE THAT A POPULAR UPRISING IS GOING TO REVERSE THE TIDE?
YOU'RE IMAGINING HORDES OF CITIZENS RISING UP TO BRING MASSIVE, POPULAR SUPPORT TO THE MOST ENDANGERED AMONGST THEM?
SINGING SONGS OF REVOLUTION AND RISK MISSING REALITY TV?
LET'S BE SERIOUS!
THE SUBJECT THAT YOU'VE BROUGHT ME ISN'T... A PRIORITY.

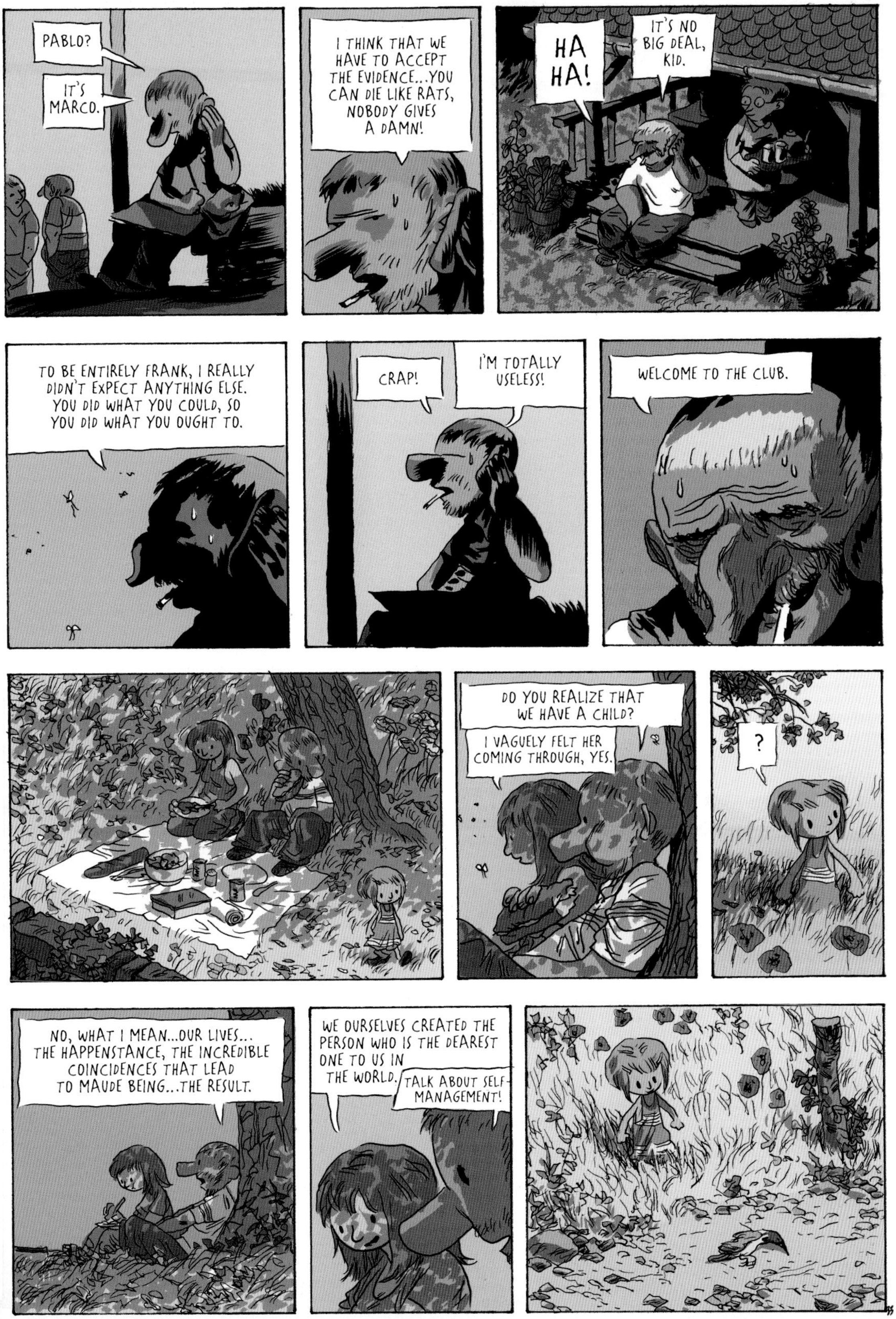
PABLO?
IT'S MARCO.
I THINK THAT WE HAVE TO ACCEPT THE EVIDENCE...YOU CAN DIE LIKE RATS, NOBODY GIVES A DAMN!
HA HA!
IT'S NO BIG DEAL, KID.
TO BE ENTIRELY FRANK, I REALLY DIDN'T EXPECT ANYTHING ELSE. YOU DID WHAT YOU COULD, SO YOU DID WHAT YOU OUGHT TO.
CRAP!
I'M TOTALLY USELESS!
WELCOME TO THE CLUB.
DO YOU REALIZE THAT WE HAVE A CHILD?
I VAGUELY FELT HER COMING THROUGH, YES.
?
NO, WHAT I MEAN...OUR LIVES... THE HAPPENSTANCE, THE INCREDIBLE COINCIDENCES THAT LEAD TO MAUDE BEING...THE RESULT.
WE OURSELVES CREATED THE PERSON WHO IS THE DEAREST ONE TO US IN THE WORLD.
TALK ABOUT SELF-MANAGEMENT!

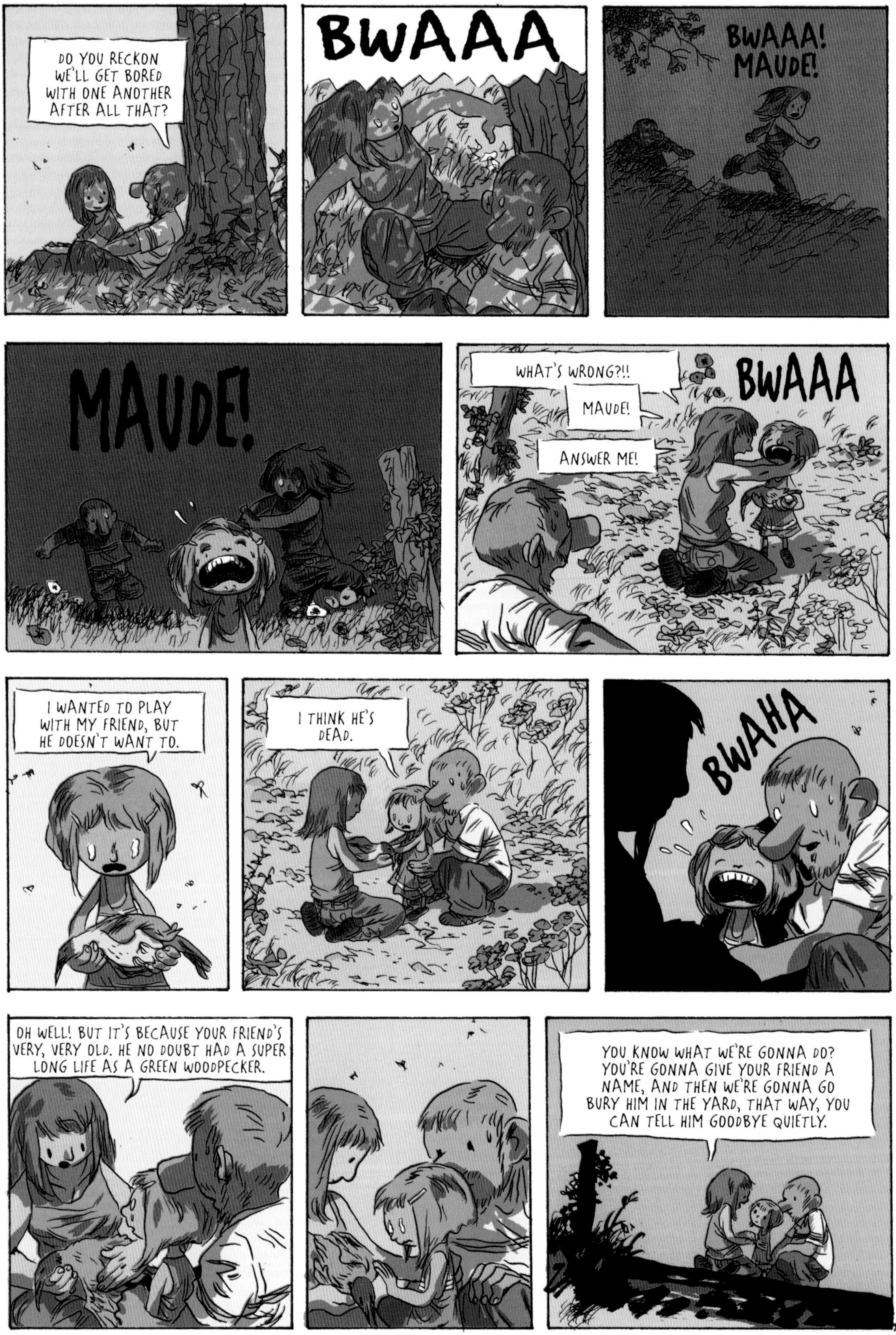

DO YOU RECKON WE'LL GET BORED WITH ONE ANOTHER AFTER ALL THAT?
BWAAA
BWAAA! MAUDE!
MAUDE!
WHAT'S WRONG?!!
MAUDE!
ANSWER ME!
BWAAA
I WANTED TO PLAY WITH MY FRIEND, BUT HE DOESN'T WANT TO.
I THINK HE'S DEAD.
BWAHA
OH WELL! BUT IT'S BECAUSE YOUR FRIEND'S VERY, VERY OLD. HE NO DOUBT HAD A SUPER LONG LIFE AS A GREEN WOODPECKER.
YOU KNOW WHAT WE'RE GONNA DO? YOU'RE GONNA GIVE YOUR FRIEND A NAME, AND THEN WE'RE GONNA GO BURY HIM IN THE YARD, THAT WAY, YOU CAN TELL HIM GOODBYE QUIETLY.

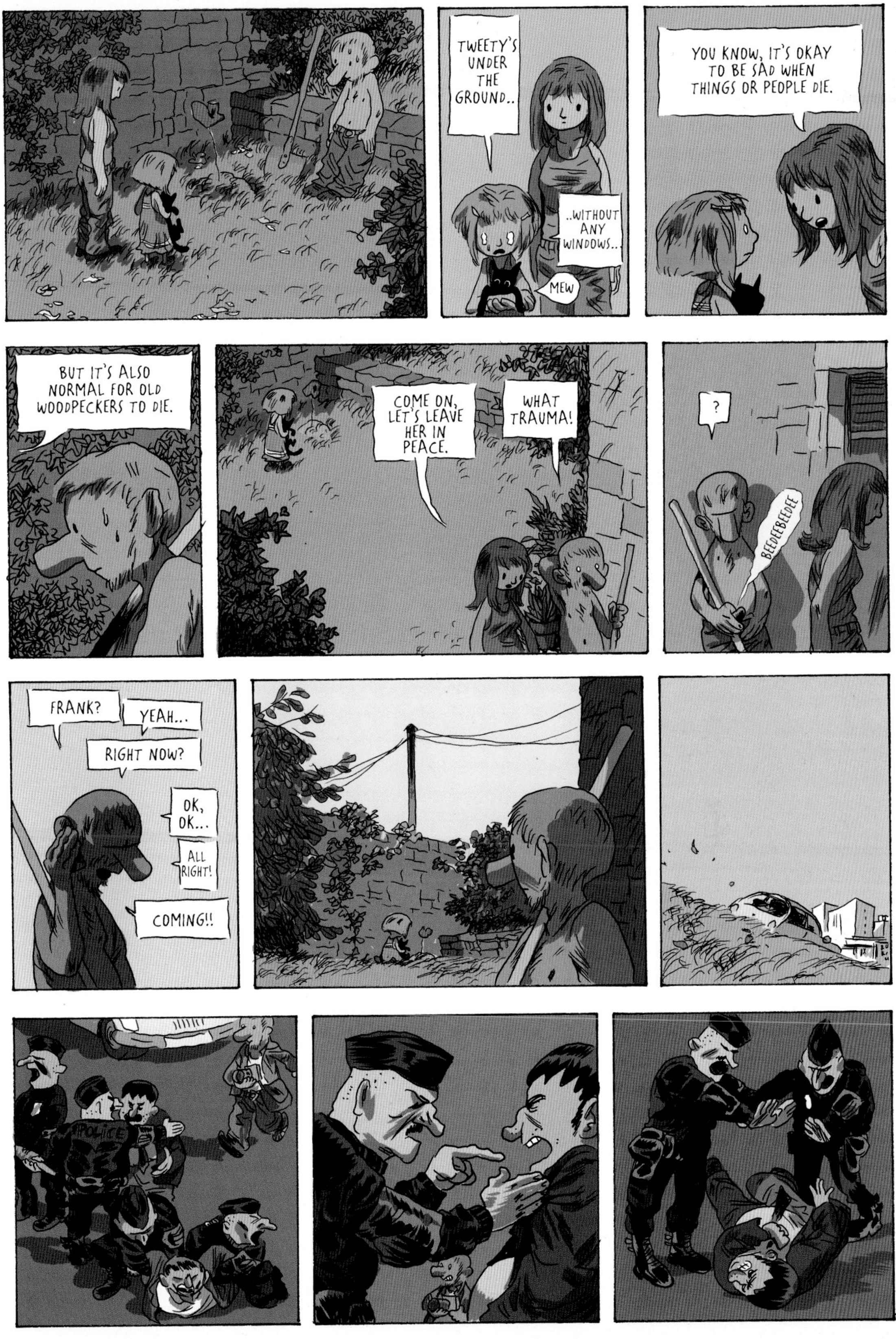
TWEETY'S UNDER THE GROUND..
..WITHOUT ANY WINDOWS..
MEW
YOU KNOW, IT'S OKAY TO BE SAD WHEN THINGS OR PEOPLE DIE.
BUT IT'S ALSO NORMAL FOR OLD WOODPECKERS TO DIE.
COME ON, LET'S LEAVE HER IN PEACE.
WHAT TRAUMA!
?
BEEDEEBEEDEE
FRANK?
YEAH...
RIGHT NOW?
OK, OK...
ALL RIGHT!
COMING!!
POLICE

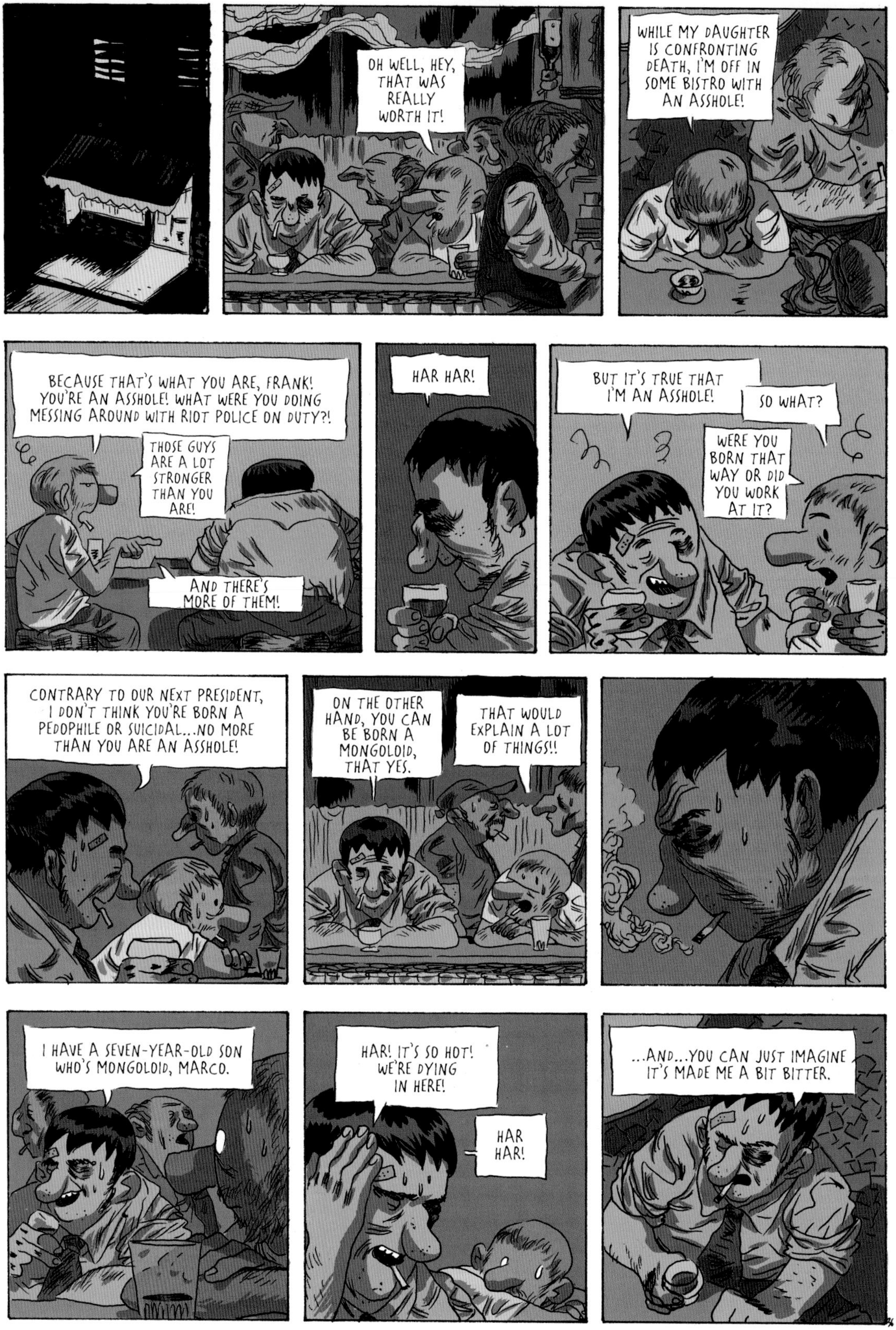
OH WELL, HEY, THAT WAS REALLY WORTH IT!
WHILE MY DAUGHTER IS CONFRONTING DEATH, I'M OFF IN SOME BISTRO WITH AN ASSHOLE!
BECAUSE THAT'S WHAT YOU ARE, FRANK! YOU'RE AN ASSHOLE! WHAT WERE YOU DOING MESSING AROUND WITH RIOT POLICE ON DUTY?!
THOSE GUYS ARE A LOT STRONGER THAN YOU ARE!
AND THERE'S MORE OF THEM!
HAR HAR!
BUT IT'S TRUE THAT I'M AN ASSHOLE!
SO WHAT?
WERE YOU BORN THAT WAY OR DID YOU WORK AT IT?
CONTRARY TO OUR NEXT PRESIDENT, I DON'T THINK YOU'RE BORN A PEDOPHILE OR SUICIDAL...NO MORE THAN YOU ARE AN ASSHOLE!
ON THE OTHER HAND, YOU CAN BE BORN A MONGOLOID, THAT YES.
THAT WOULD EXPLAIN A LOT OF THINGS!!
I HAVE A SEVEN-YEAR-OLD SON WHO'S MONGOLOID, MARCO.
HAR! IT'S SO HOT! WE'RE DYING IN HERE!
HAR HAR!
...AND...YOU CAN JUST IMAGINE IT'S MADE ME A BIT BITTER.

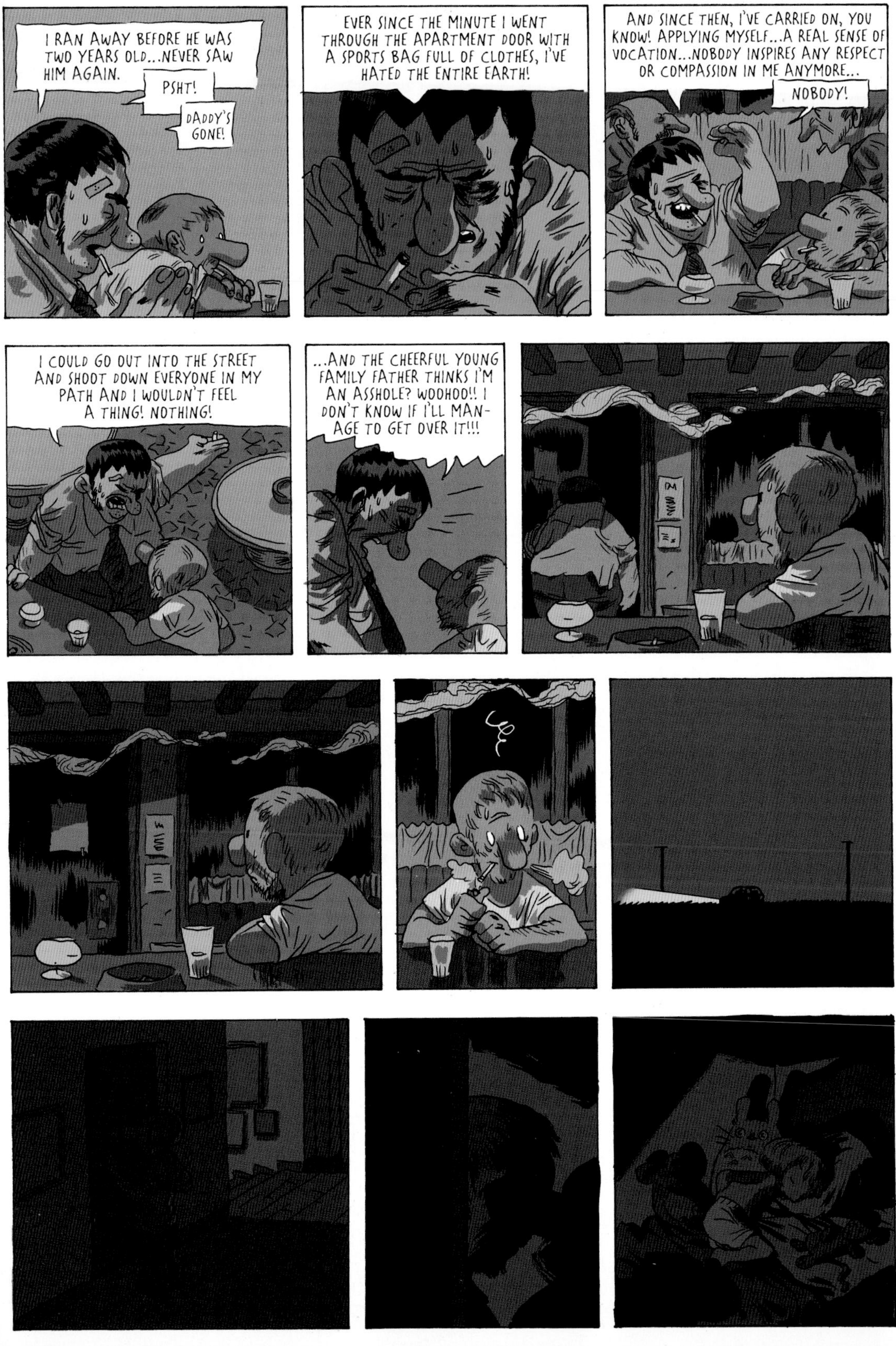
I RAN AWAY BEFORE HE WAS TWO YEARS OLD...NEVER SAW HIM AGAIN.
PSHT!
DADDY'S GONE!
EVER SINCE THE MINUTE I WENT THROUGH THE APARTMENT DOOR WITH A SPORTS BAG FULL OF CLOTHES, I'VE HATED THE ENTIRE EARTH!
AND SINCE THEN, I'VE CARRIED ON, YOU KNOW! APPLYING MYSELF...A REAL SENSE OF VOCATION...NOBODY INSPIRES ANY RESPECT OR COMPASSION IN ME ANYMORE...
NOBODY!
I COULD GO OUT INTO THE STREET AND SHOOT DOWN EVERYONE IN MY PATH AND I WOULDN'T FEEL A THING! NOTHING!
...AND THE CHEERFUL YOUNG FAMILY FATHER THINKS I'M AN ASSHOLE? WOOHOO!! I DON'T KNOW IF I'LL MAN-AGE TO GET OVER IT!!!

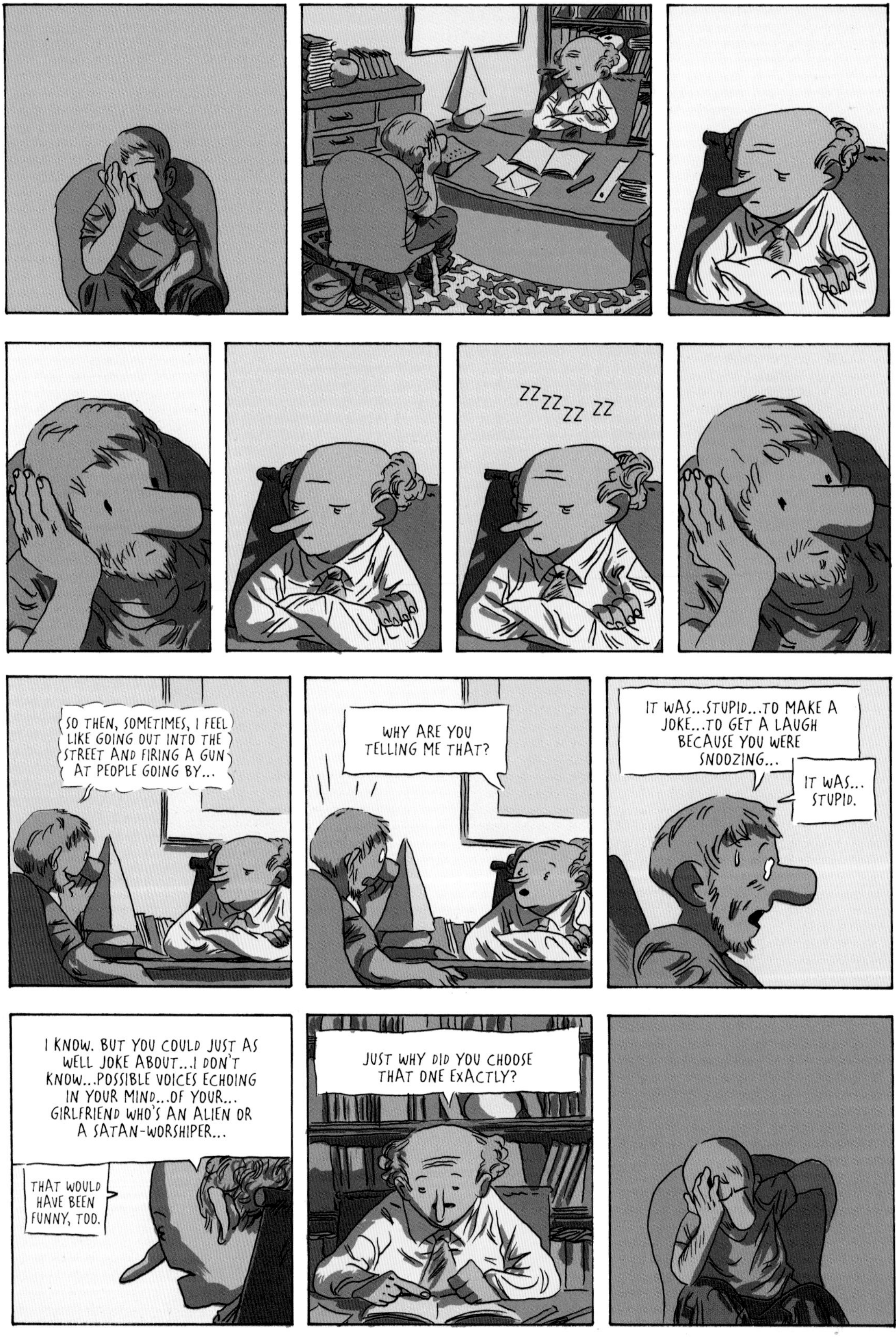
ZZZZZ ZZ
SO THEN, SOMETIMES, I FEEL LIKE GOING OUT INTO THE STREET AND FIRING A GUN AT PEOPLE GOING BY...
WHY ARE YOU TELLING ME THAT?
IT WAS...STUPID...TO MAKE A JOKE...TO GET A LAUGH BECAUSE YOU WERE SNOOZING...
IT WAS... STUPID.
I KNOW. BUT YOU COULD JUST AS WELL JOKE ABOUT...I DON'T KNOW...POSSIBLE VOICES ECHOING IN YOUR MIND...OF YOUR... GIRLFRIEND WHO'S AN ALIEN OR A SATAN-WORSHIPER...
THAT WOULD HAVE BEEN FUNNY, TOO.
JUST WHY DID YOU CHOOSE THAT ONE EXACTLY?

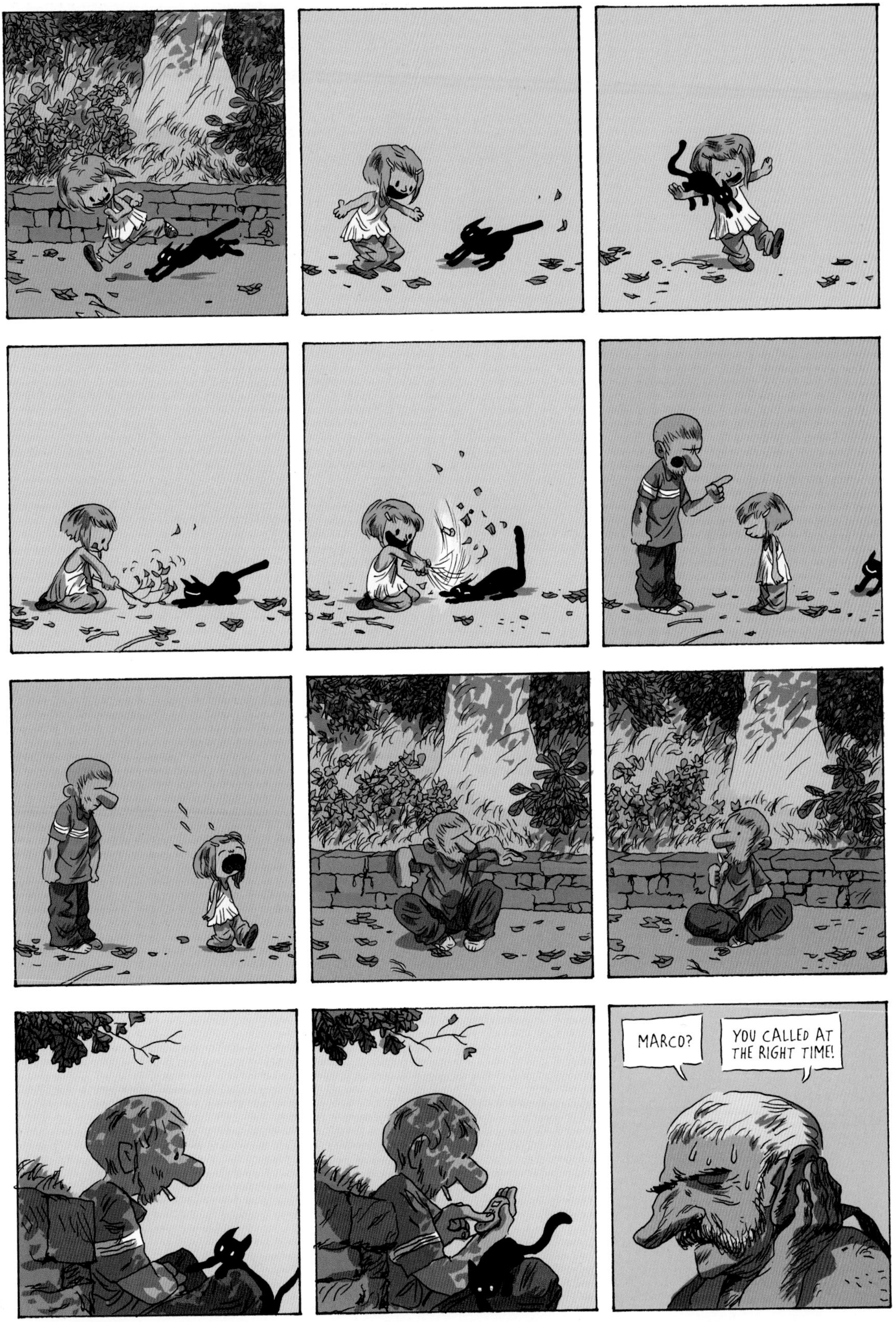
MARCO?
YOU CALLED AT THE RIGHT TIME!

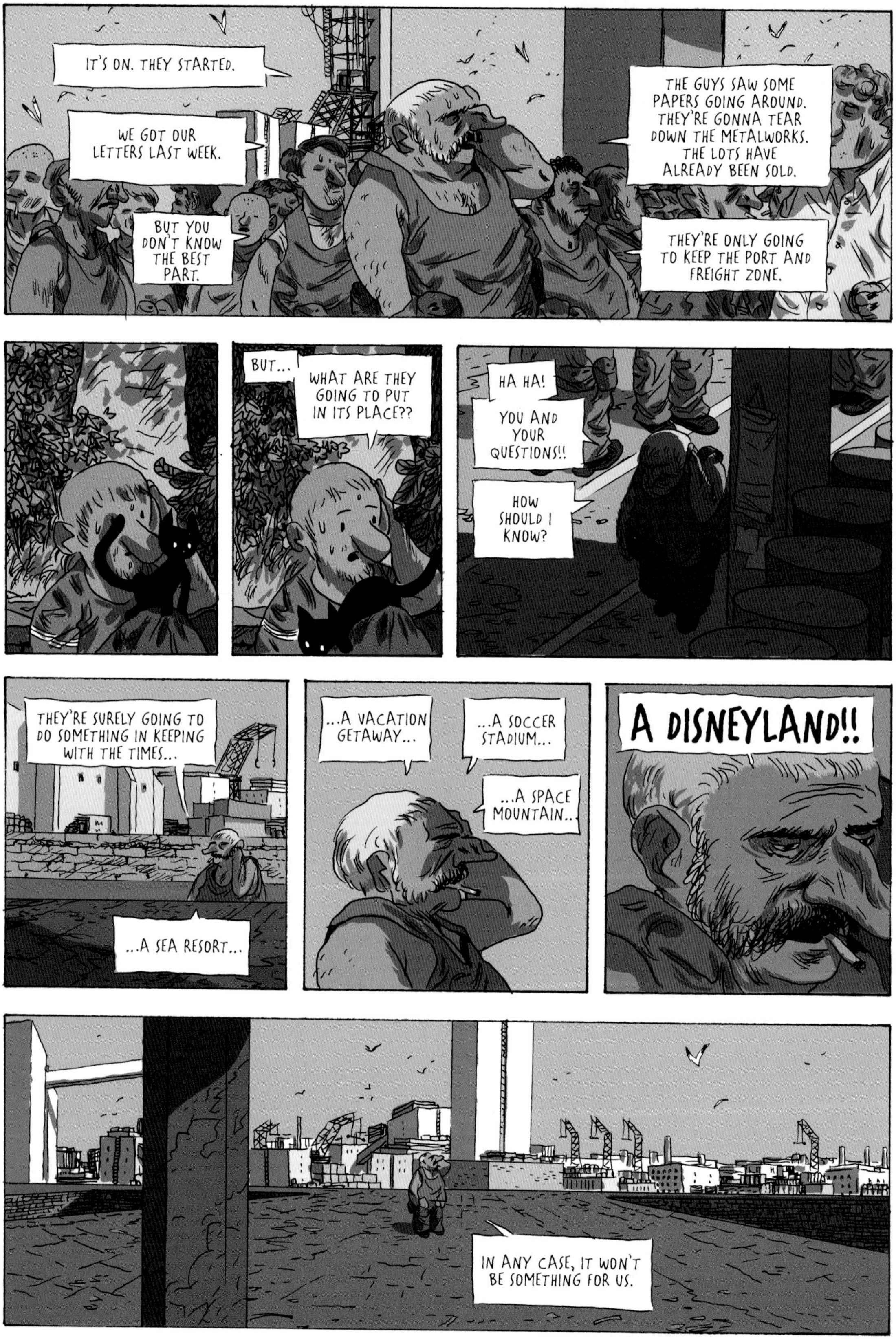
IT'S ON. THEY STARTED.
WE GOT OUR LETTERS LAST WEEK.
BUT YOU DON'T KNOW THE BEST PART.
THE GUYS SAW SOME PAPERS GOING AROUND. THEY'RE GONNA TEAR DOWN THE METALWORKS. THE LOTS HAVE ALREADY BEEN SOLD.
THEY'RE ONLY GOING TO KEEP THE PORT AND FREIGHT ZONE.
BUT...
WHAT ARE THEY GOING TO PUT IN ITS PLACE??
HA HA!
YOU AND YOUR QUESTIONS!!
HOW SHOULD I KNOW?
THEY'RE SURELY GOING TO DO SOMETHING IN KEEPING WITH THE TIMES...
...A SEA RESORT...
...A VACATION GETAWAY...
...A SOCCER STADIUM...
...A SPACE MOUNTAIN...
A DISNEYLAND!!
IN ANY CASE, IT WON'T BE SOMETHING FOR US.

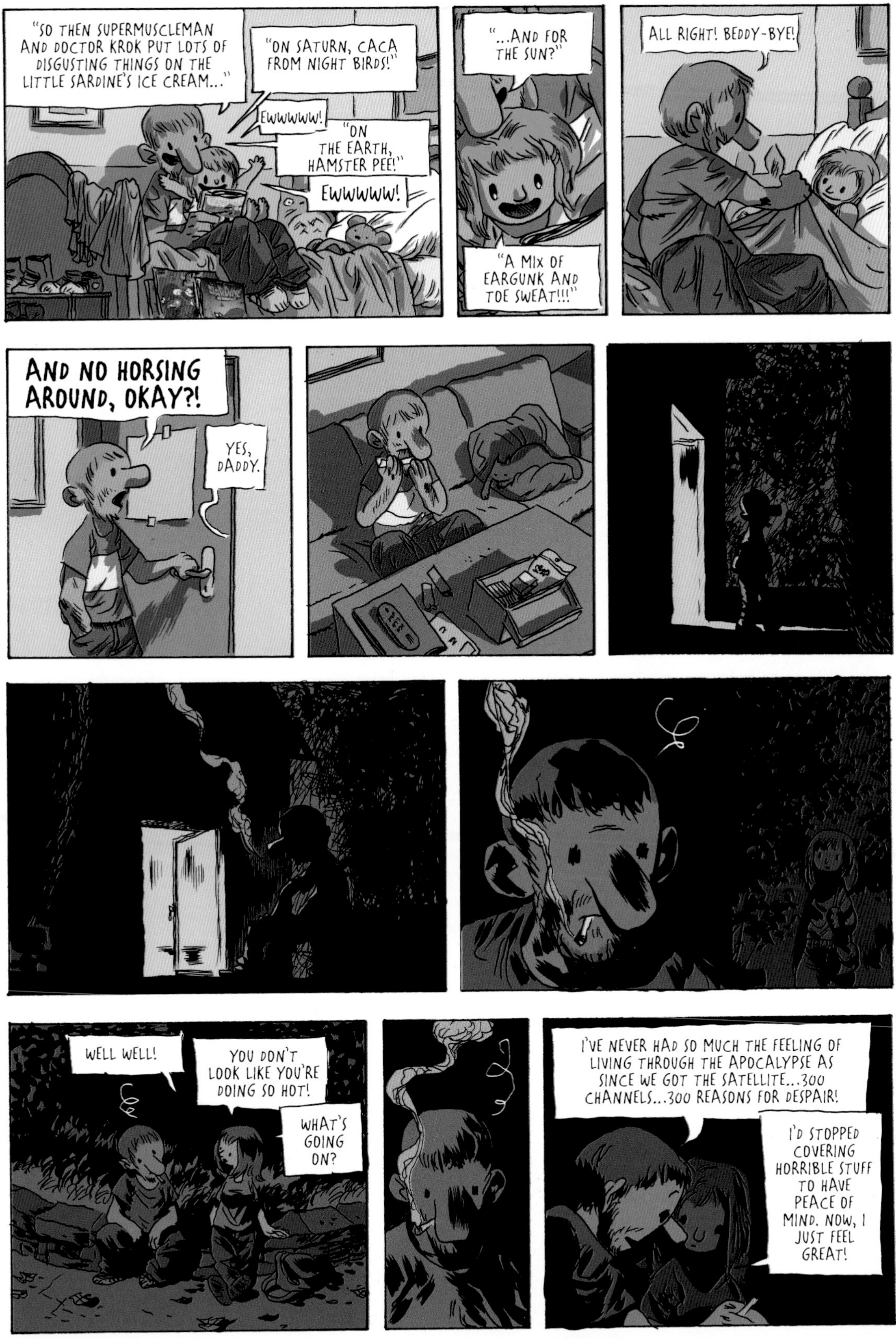
"SO THEN SUPERMUSCLEMAN AND DOCTOR KROK PUT LOTS OF DISGUSTING THINGS ON THE LITTLE SARDINE'S ICE CREAM..."
"ON SATURN, CACA FROM NIGHT BIRDS!"
EWWWWW!
"ON THE EARTH, HAMSTER PEE!"
EWWWWW!
"...AND FOR THE SUN?"
"A MIX OF EARGUNK AND TOE SWEAT!!!"
ALL RIGHT! BEDDY-BYE!
AND NO HORSING AROUND, OKAY?!
YES, DADDY.
WELL WELL!
YOU DON'T LOOK LIKE YOU'RE DOING SO HOT!
WHAT'S GOING ON?
I'VE NEVER HAD SO MUCH THE FEELING OF LIVING THROUGH THE APOCALYPSE AS SINCE WE GOT THE SATELLITE...300 CHANNELS...300 REASONS FOR DESPAIR!
I'D STOPPED COVERING HORRIBLE STUFF TO HAVE PEACE OF MIND. NOW, I JUST FEEL GREAT!

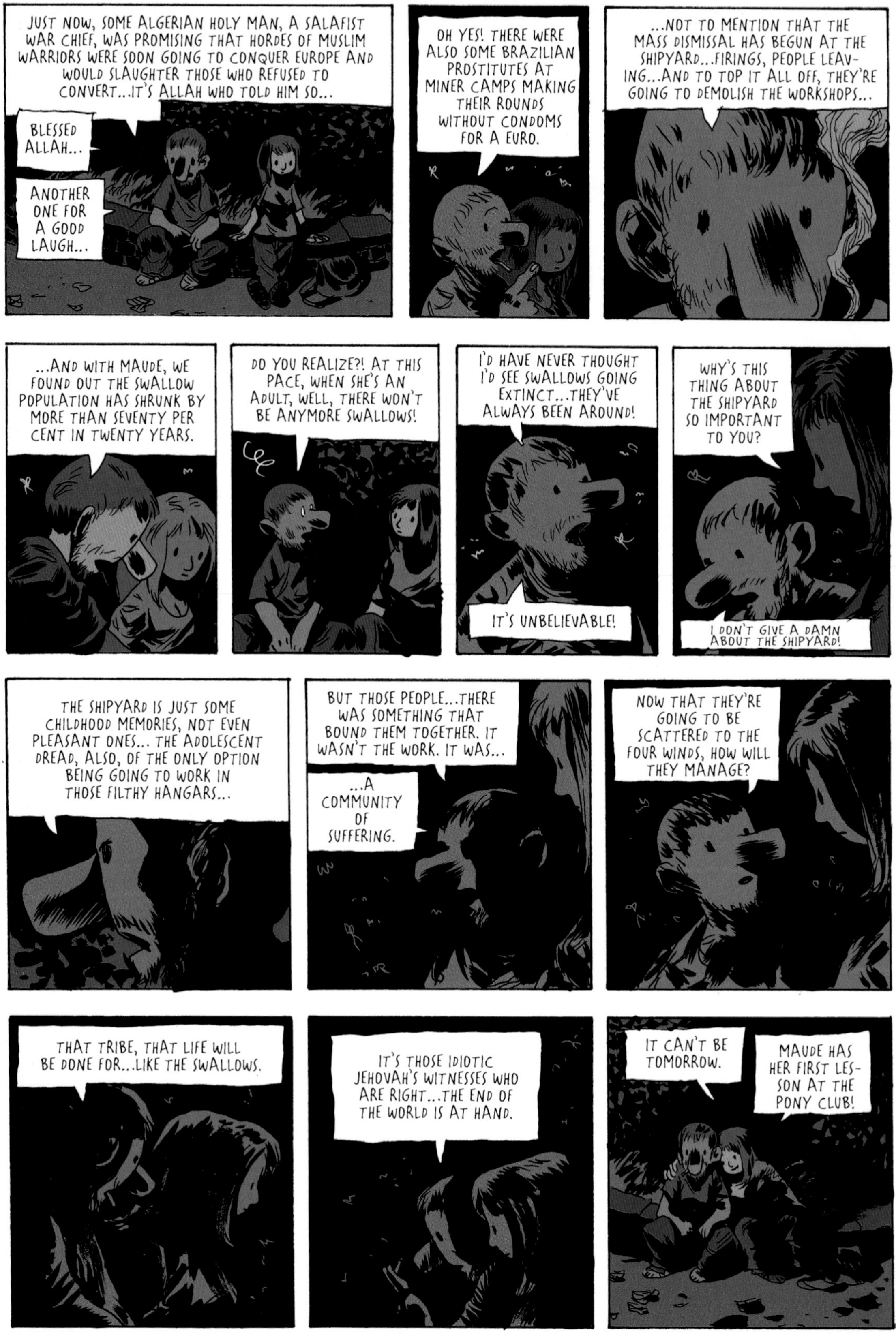
JUST NOW, SOME ALGERIAN HOLY MAN, A SALAFIST WAR CHIEF, WAS PROMISING THAT HORDES OF MUSLIM WARRIORS WERE SOON GOING TO CONQUER EUROPE AND WOULD SLAUGHTER THOSE WHO REFUSED TO CONVERT...IT'S ALLAH WHO TOLD HIM SO...
BLESSED ALLAH...
ANOTHER ONE FOR A GOOD LAUGH...
OH YES! THERE WERE ALSO SOME BRAZILIAN PROSTITUTES AT MINER CAMPS MAKING THEIR ROUNDS WITHOUT CONDOMS FOR A EURO.
...NOT TO MENTION THAT THE MASS DISMISSAL HAS BEGUN AT THE SHIPYARD...FIRINGS, PEOPLE LEAVING...AND TO TOP IT ALL OFF, THEY'RE GOING TO DEMOLISH THE WORKSHOPS...
...AND WITH MAUDE, WE FOUND OUT THE SWALLOW POPULATION HAS SHRUNK BY MORE THAN SEVENTY PER CENT IN TWENTY YEARS.
DO YOU REALIZE?! AT THIS PACE, WHEN SHE'S AN ADULT, WELL, THERE WON'T BE ANYMORE SWALLOWS!
I'D HAVE NEVER THOUGHT I'D SEE SWALLOWS GOING EXTINCT...THEY'VE ALWAYS BEEN AROUND!
IT'S UNBELIEVABLE!
WHY'S THIS THING ABOUT THE SHIPYARD SO IMPORTANT TO YOU?
I DON'T GIVE A DAMN ABOUT THE SHIPYARD!
THE SHIPYARD IS JUST SOME CHILDHOOD MEMORIES, NOT EVEN PLEASANT ONES... THE ADOLESCENT DREAD, ALSO, OF THE ONLY OPTION BEING GOING TO WORK IN THOSE FILTHY HANGARS...
BUT THOSE PEOPLE...THERE WAS SOMETHING THAT BOUND THEM TOGETHER. IT WASN'T THE WORK. IT WAS...
...A COMMUNITY OF SUFFERING.
NOW THAT THEY'RE GOING TO BE SCATTERED TO THE FOUR WINDS, HOW WILL THEY MANAGE?
THAT TRIBE, THAT LIFE WILL BE DONE FOR...LIKE THE SWALLOWS.
IT'S THOSE IDIOTIC JEHOVAH'S WITNESSES WHO ARE RIGHT...THE END OF THE WORLD IS AT HAND.
IT CAN'T BE TOMORROW.
MAUDE HAS HER FIRST LESSON AT THE PONY CLUB!

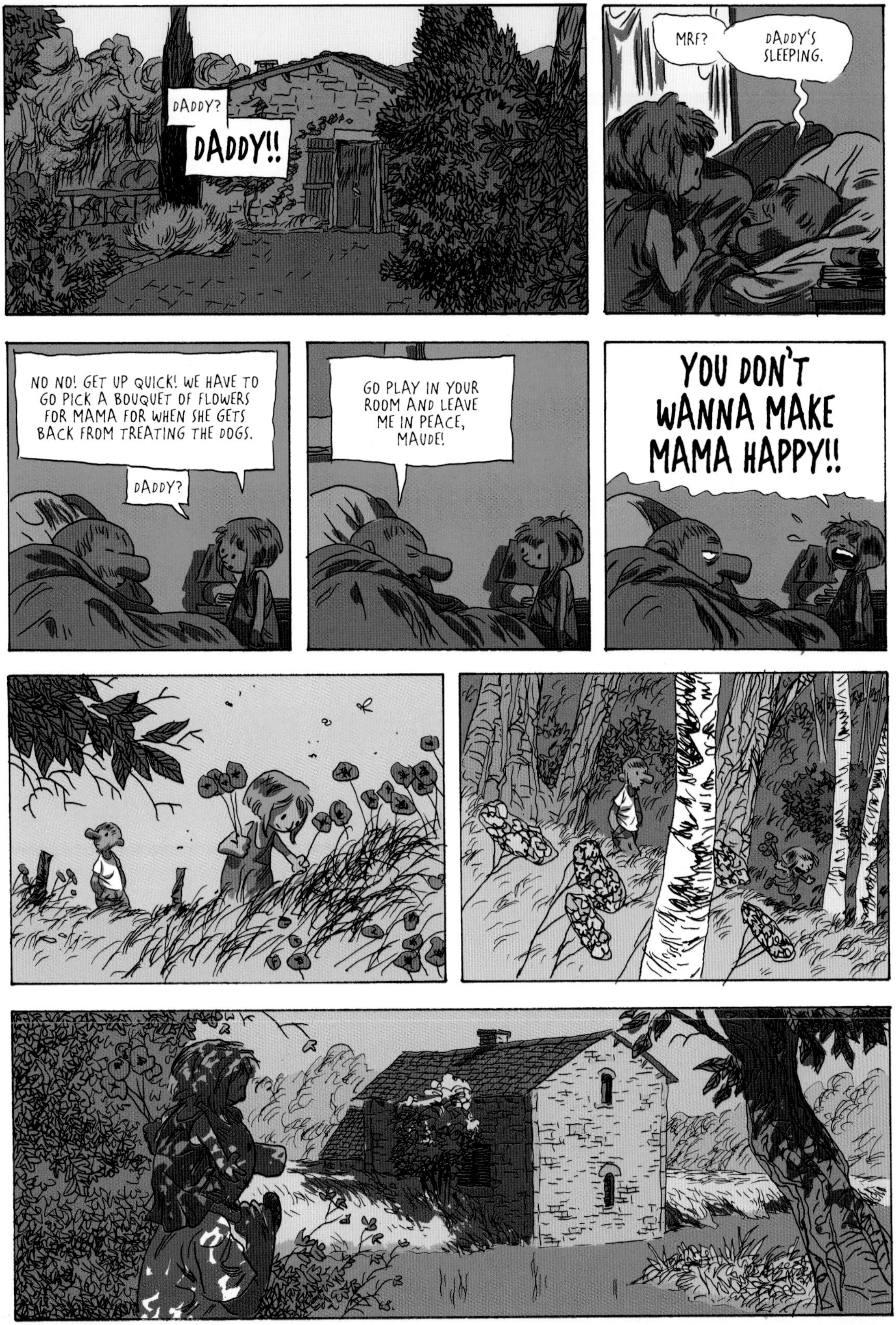
DADDY?
DADDY!!
MRF?
DADDY'S SLEEPING.
NO NO! GET UP QUICK! WE HAVE TO GO PICK A BOUQUET OF FLOWERS FOR MAMA FOR WHEN SHE GETS BACK FROM TREATING THE DOGS.
DADDY?
GO PLAY IN YOUR ROOM AND LEAVE ME IN PEACE, MAUDE!
YOU DON'T WANNA MAKE MAMA HAPPY!!

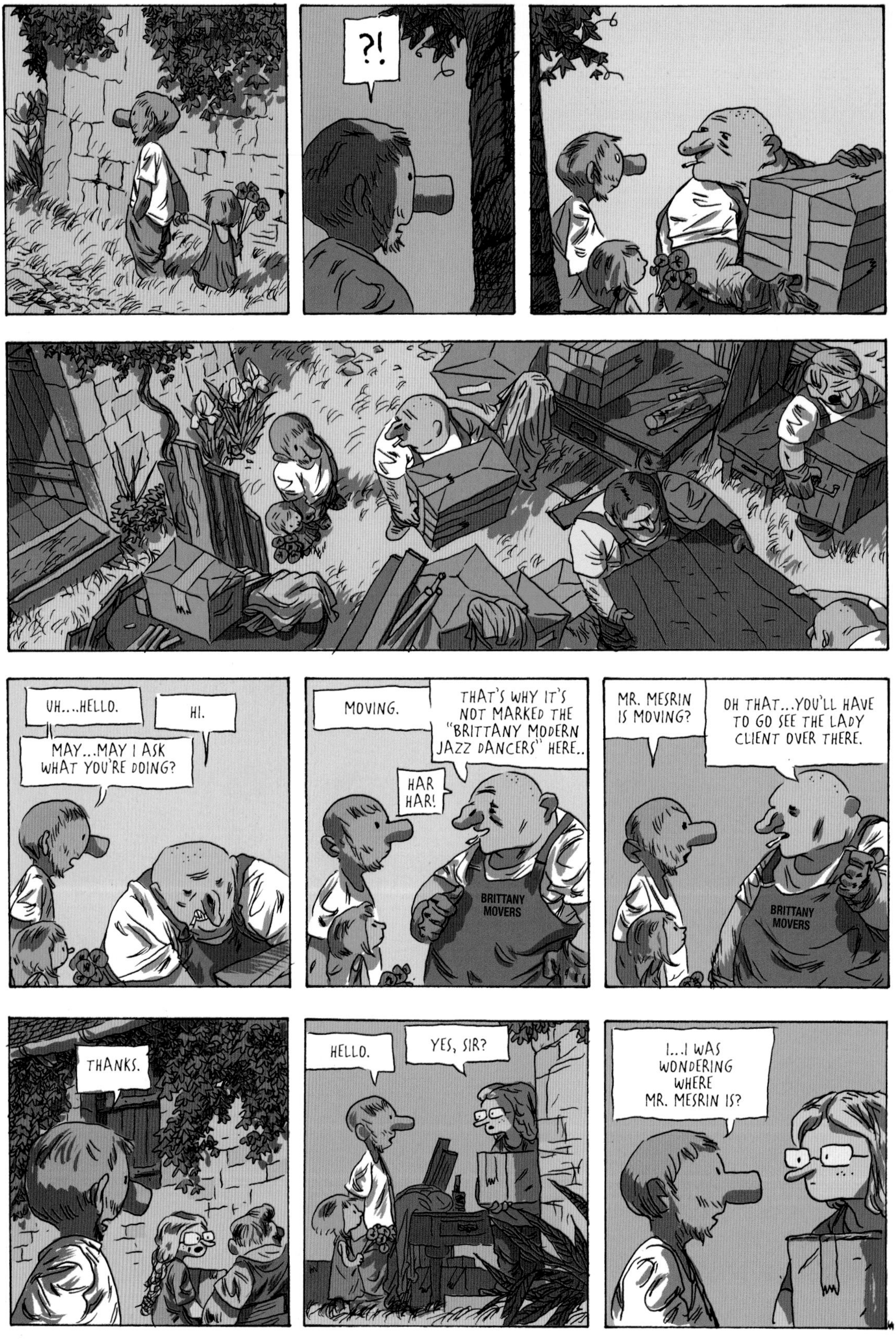

?!
UH...HELLO.
HI.
MAY...MAY I ASK WHAT YOU'RE DOING?
MOVING.
THAT'S WHY IT'S NOT MARKED THE "BRITTANY MODERN JAZZ DANCERS" HERE..
HAR HAR!
BRITTANY MOVERS
MR. MESRIN IS MOVING?
OH THAT...YOU'LL HAVE TO GO SEE THE LADY CLIENT OVER THERE.
BRITTANY MOVERS
THANKS.
HELLO.
YES, SIR?
I...I WAS WONDERING WHERE MR. MESRIN IS?

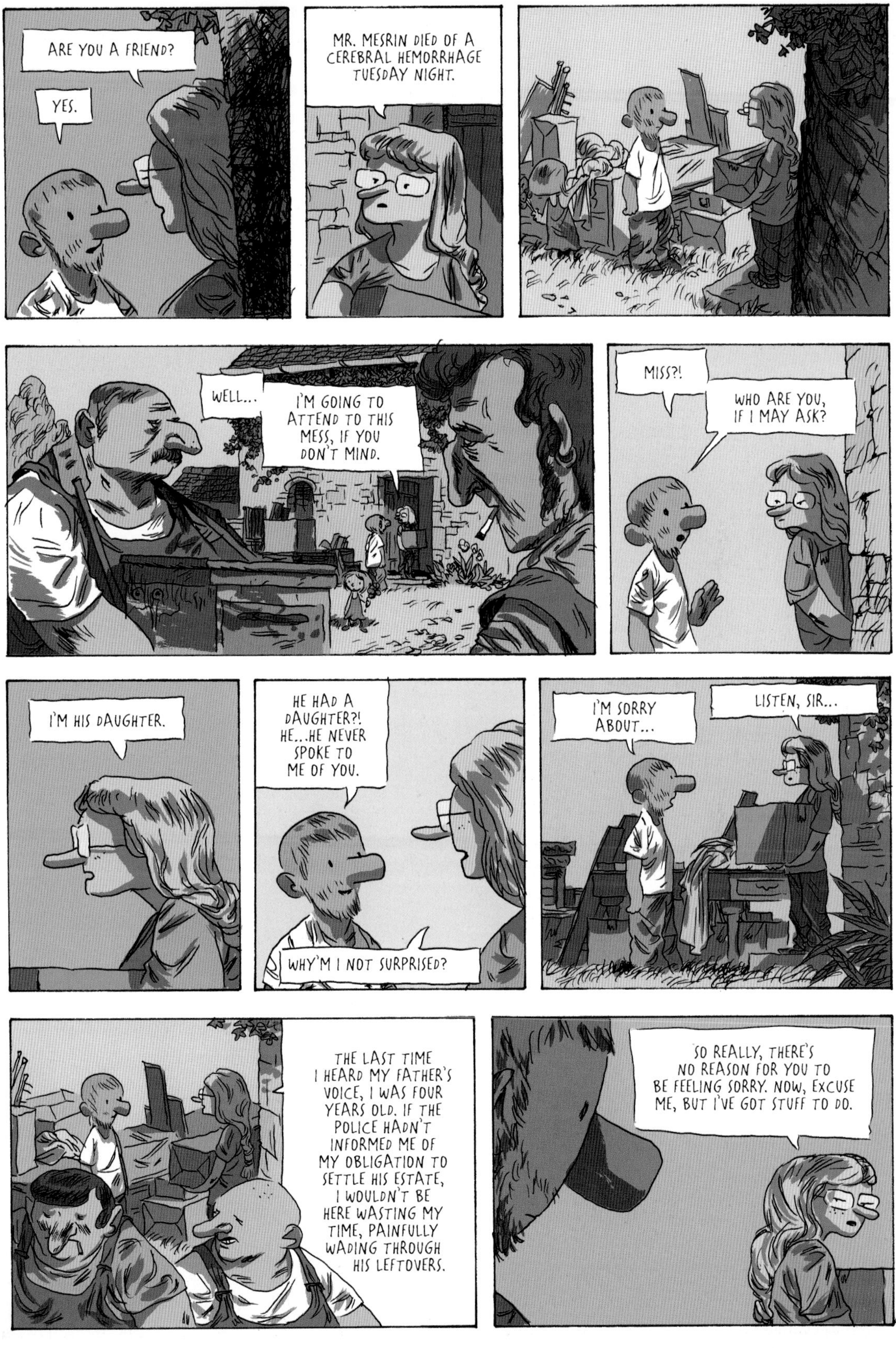
ARE YOU A FRIEND?
YES.
MR. MESRIN DIED OF A CEREBRAL HEMORRHAGE TUESDAY NIGHT.
WELL...
I'M GOING TO ATTEND TO THIS MESS, IF YOU DON'T MIND.
MISS?!
WHO ARE YOU, IF I MAY ASK?
I'M HIS DAUGHTER.
HE HAD A DAUGHTER?! HE...HE NEVER SPOKE TO ME OF YOU.
WHY'M I NOT SURPRISED?
I'M SORRY ABOUT...
LISTEN, SIR...
THE LAST TIME I HEARD MY FATHER'S VOICE, I WAS FOUR YEARS OLD. IF THE POLICE HADN'T INFORMED ME OF MY OBLIGATION TO SETTLE HIS ESTATE, I WOULDN'T BE HERE WASTING MY TIME, PAINFULLY WADING THROUGH HIS LEFTOVERS.
SO REALLY, THERE'S NO REASON FOR YOU TO BE FEELING SORRY. NOW, EXCUSE ME, BUT I'VE GOT STUFF TO DO.

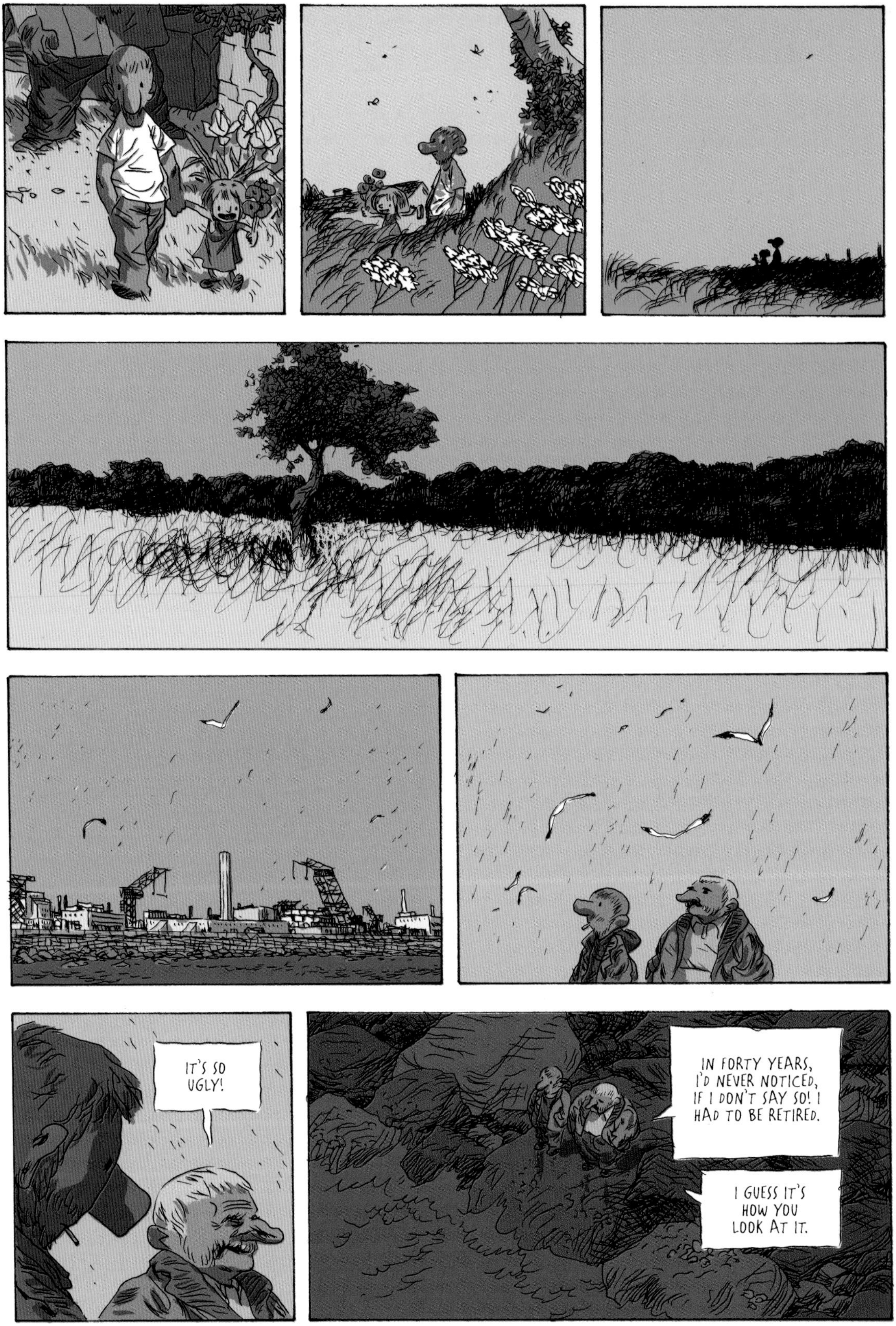
IT'S SO UGLY!
IN FORTY YEARS, I'D NEVER NOTICED, IF I DON'T SAY SO! I HAD TO BE RETIRED.
I GUESS IT'S HOW YOU LOOK AT IT.

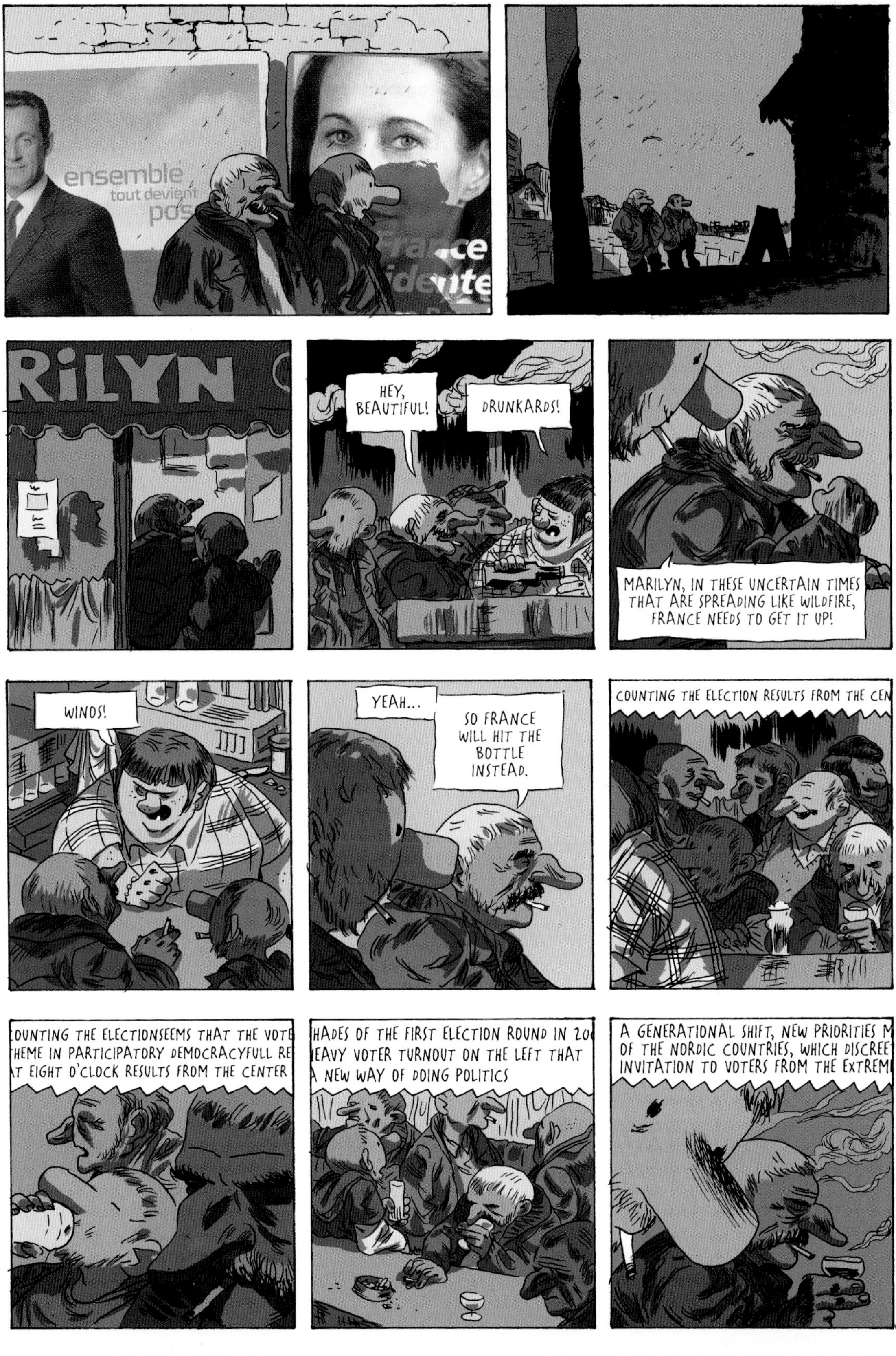
ensemble
tout devient
RiLYN
HEY, BEAUTIFUL!
DRUNKARDS!
MARILYN, IN THESE UNCERTAIN TIMES THAT ARE SPREADING LIKE WILDFIRE, FRANCE NEEDS TO GET IT UP!
WINOS!
YEAH...
SO FRANCE WILL HIT THE BOTTLE INSTEAD.
COUNTING THE ELECTION RESULTS FROM THE CEN
COUNTING THE ELECTIONSEEMS THAT THE VOTE
THEME IN PARTICIPATORY DEMOCRACYFULL RE
T EIGHT O'CLOCK RESULTS FROM THE CENTER
HADES OF THE FIRST ELECTION ROUND IN 20
EAVY VOTER TURNOUT ON THE LEFT THAT
A NEW WAY OF DOING POLITICS
A GENERATIONAL SHIFT, NEW PRIORITIES M
OF THE NORDIC COUNTRIES, WHICH DISCREET
INVITATION TO VOTERS FROM THE EXTREM

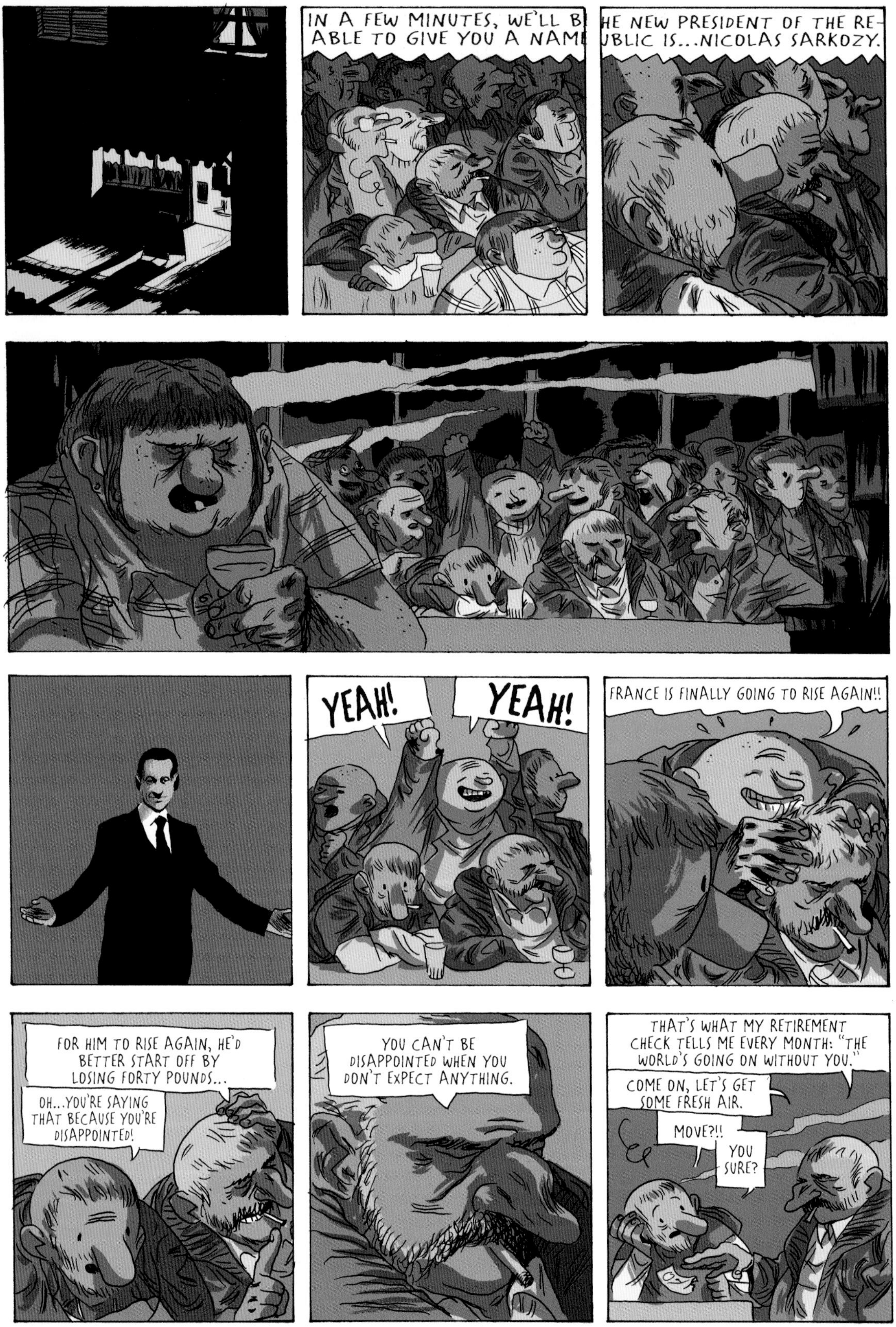

IN A FEW MINUTES, WE'LL BE ABLE TO GIVE YOU A NAME
THE NEW PRESIDENT OF THE REPUBLIC IS...NICOLAS SARKOZY.
YEAH!
YEAH!
FRANCE IS FINALLY GOING TO RISE AGAIN!!
FOR HIM TO RISE AGAIN, HE'D BETTER START OFF BY LOSING FORTY POUNDS...
OH...YOU'RE SAYING THAT BECAUSE YOU'RE DISAPPOINTED!
YOU CAN'T BE DISAPPOINTED WHEN YOU DON'T EXPECT ANYTHING.
THAT'S WHAT MY RETIREMENT CHECK TELLS ME EVERY MONTH: "THE WORLD'S GOING ON WITHOUT YOU."
COME ON, LET'S GET SOME FRESH AIR.
MOVE?!!
YOU SURE?

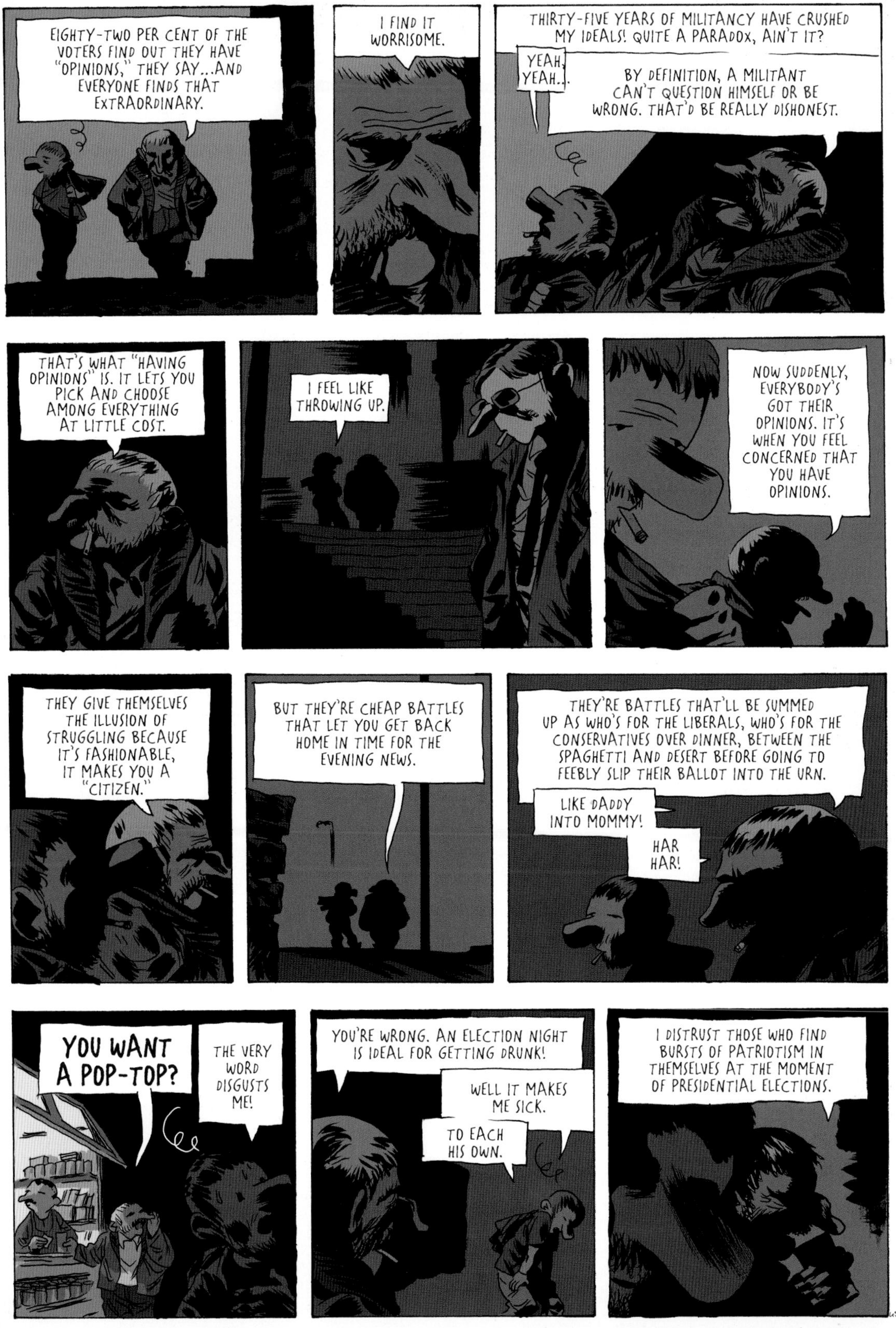
EIGHTY-TWO PER CENT OF THE VOTERS FIND OUT THEY HAVE "OPINIONS," THEY SAY...AND EVERYONE FINDS THAT EXTRAORDINARY.
I FIND IT WORRISOME.
THIRTY-FIVE YEARS OF MILITANCY HAVE CRUSHED MY IDEALS! QUITE A PARADOX, AIN'T IT?
YEAH. YEAH...
BY DEFINITION, A MILITANT CAN'T QUESTION HIMSELF OR BE WRONG. THAT'D BE REALLY DISHONEST.
THAT'S WHAT "HAVING OPINIONS" IS. IT LETS YOU PICK AND CHOOSE AMONG EVERYTHING AT LITTLE COST.
I FEEL LIKE THROWING UP.
NOW SUDDENLY, EVERYBODY'S GOT THEIR OPINIONS. IT'S WHEN YOU FEEL CONCERNED THAT YOU HAVE OPINIONS.
THEY GIVE THEMSELVES THE ILLUSION OF STRUGGLING BECAUSE IT'S FASHIONABLE, IT MAKES YOU A "CITIZEN."
BUT THEY'RE CHEAP BATTLES THAT LET YOU GET BACK HOME IN TIME FOR THE EVENING NEWS.
THEY'RE BATTLES THAT'LL BE SUMMED UP AS WHO'S FOR THE LIBERALS, WHO'S FOR THE CONSERVATIVES OVER DINNER, BETWEEN THE SPAGHETTI AND DESERT BEFORE GOING TO FEEBLY SLIP THEIR BALLOT INTO THE URN.
LIKE DADDY INTO MOMMY!
HAR HAR!
YOU WANT A POP-TOP?
THE VERY WORD DISGUSTS ME!
YOU'RE WRONG. AN ELECTION NIGHT IS IDEAL FOR GETTING DRUNK!
WELL IT MAKES ME SICK.
TO EACH HIS OWN.
I DISTRUST THOSE WHO FIND BURSTS OF PATRIOTISM IN THEMSELVES AT THE MOMENT OF PRESIDENTIAL ELECTIONS.

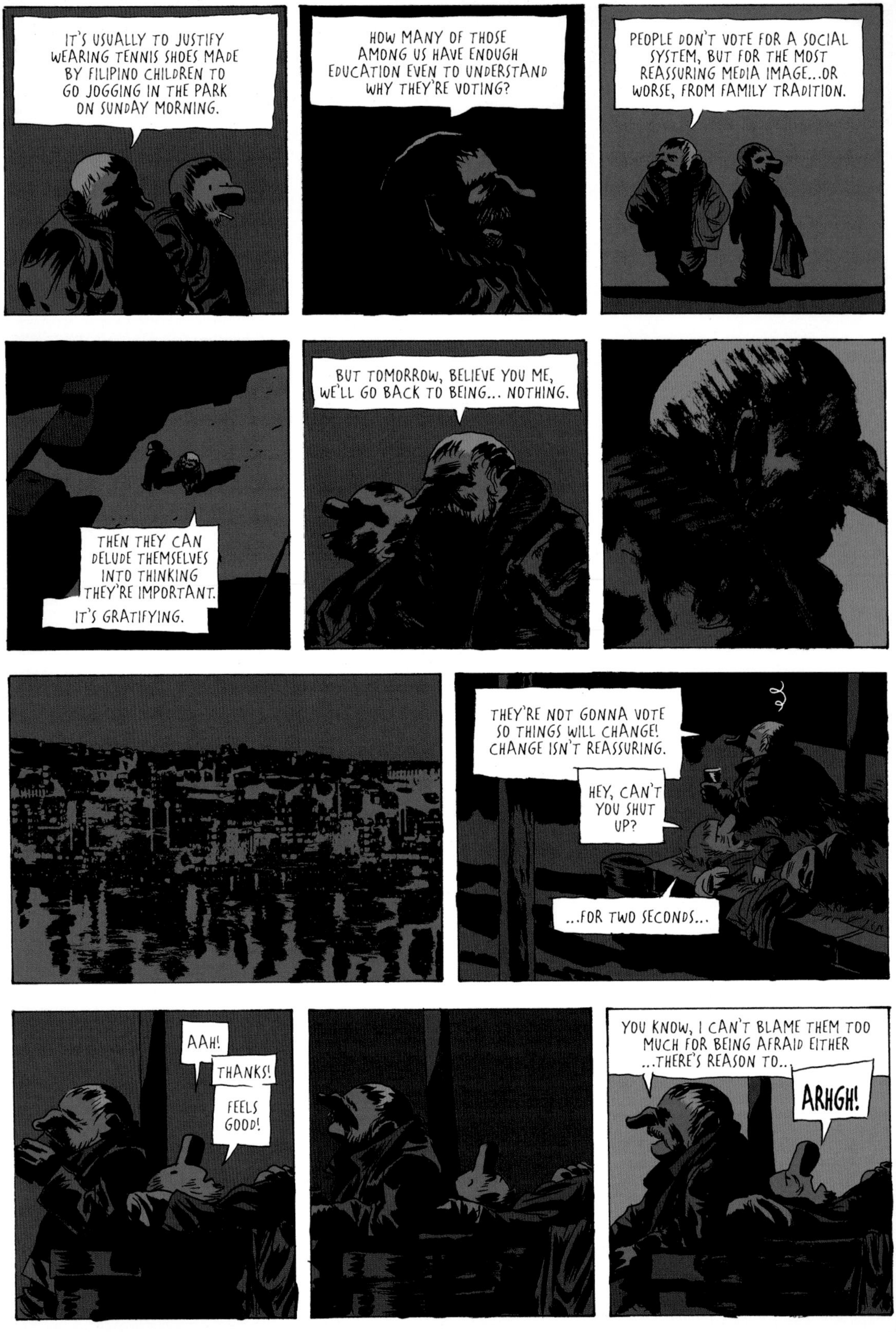
IT'S USUALLY TO JUSTIFY WEARING TENNIS SHOES MADE BY FILIPINO CHILDREN TO GO JOGGING IN THE PARK ON SUNDAY MORNING.
HOW MANY OF THOSE AMONG US HAVE ENOUGH EDUCATION EVEN TO UNDERSTAND WHY THEY'RE VOTING?
PEOPLE DON'T VOTE FOR A SOCIAL SYSTEM, BUT FOR THE MOST REASSURING MEDIA IMAGE...OR WORSE, FROM FAMILY TRADITION.
THEN THEY CAN DELUDE THEMSELVES INTO THINKING THEY'RE IMPORTANT.
IT'S GRATIFYING.
BUT TOMORROW, BELIEVE YOU ME, WE'LL GO BACK TO BEING... NOTHING.
THEY'RE NOT GONNA VOTE SO THINGS WILL CHANGE! CHANGE ISN'T REASSURING.
HEY, CAN'T YOU SHUT UP?
...FOR TWO SECONDS...
AAH!
THANKS!
FEELS GOOD!
YOU KNOW, I CAN'T BLAME THEM TOO MUCH FOR BEING AFRAID EITHER ...THERE'S REASON TO...
ARHGH!

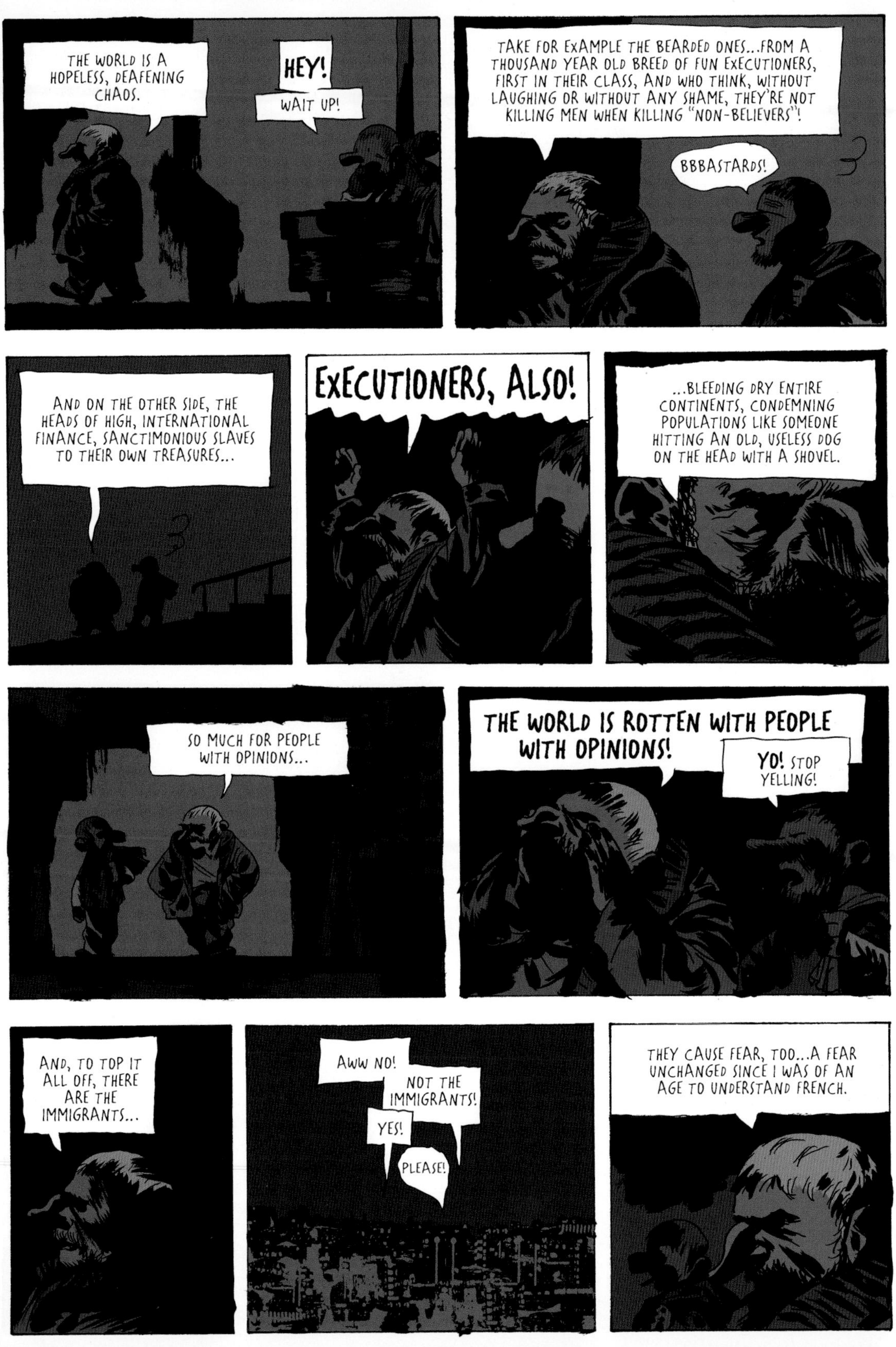
THE WORLD IS A HOPELESS, DEAFENING CHAOS.
HEY!
WAIT UP!
TAKE FOR EXAMPLE THE BEARDED ONES...FROM A THOUSAND YEAR OLD BREED OF FUN EXECUTIONERS, FIRST IN THEIR CLASS, AND WHO THINK, WITHOUT LAUGHING OR WITHOUT ANY SHAME, THEY'RE NOT KILLING MEN WHEN KILLING "NON-BELIEVERS"!
BBBASTARDS!
AND ON THE OTHER SIDE, THE HEADS OF HIGH, INTERNATIONAL FINANCE, SANCTIMONIOUS SLAVES TO THEIR OWN TREASURES...
EXECUTIONERS, ALSO!
...BLEEDING DRY ENTIRE CONTINENTS, CONDEMNING POPULATIONS LIKE SOMEONE HITTING AN OLD, USELESS DOG ON THE HEAD WITH A SHOVEL.
SO MUCH FOR PEOPLE WITH OPINIONS...
THE WORLD IS ROTTEN WITH PEOPLE WITH OPINIONS!
YO! STOP YELLING!
AND, TO TOP IT ALL OFF, THERE ARE THE IMMIGRANTS...
AWW NO!
NOT THE IMMIGRANTS!
YES!
PLEASE!
THEY CAUSE FEAR, TOO...A FEAR UNCHANGED SINCE I WAS OF AN AGE TO UNDERSTAND FRENCH.

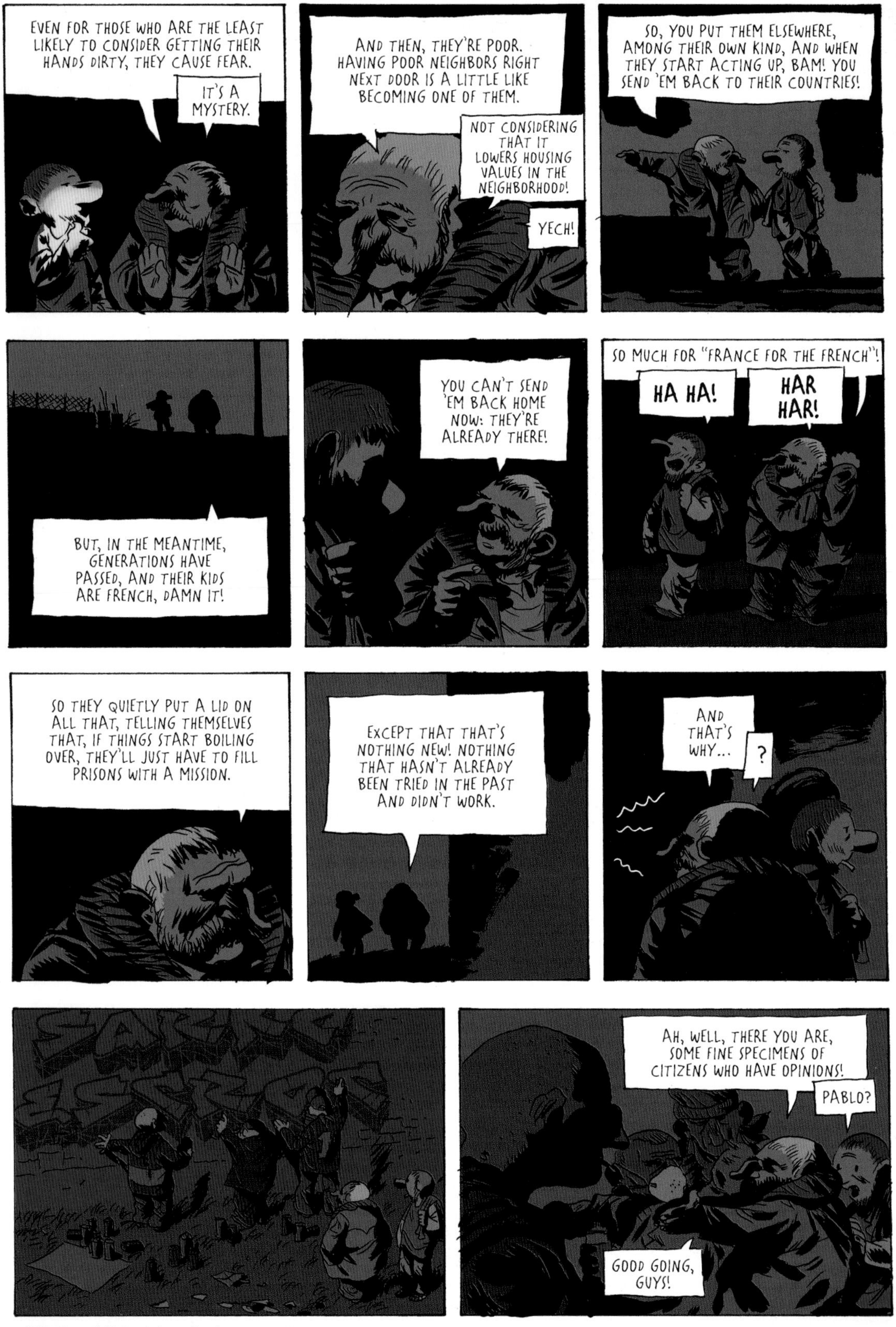
EVEN FOR THOSE WHO ARE THE LEAST LIKELY TO CONSIDER GETTING THEIR HANDS DIRTY, THEY CAUSE FEAR.
IT'S A MYSTERY.
AND THEN, THEY'RE POOR. HAVING POOR NEIGHBORS RIGHT NEXT DOOR IS A LITTLE LIKE BECOMING ONE OF THEM.
NOT CONSIDERING THAT IT LOWERS HOUSING VALUES IN THE NEIGHBORHOOD!
YECH!
SO, YOU PUT THEM ELSEWHERE, AMONG THEIR OWN KIND, AND WHEN THEY START ACTING UP, BAM! YOU SEND 'EM BACK TO THEIR COUNTRIES!
BUT, IN THE MEANTIME, GENERATIONS HAVE PASSED, AND THEIR KIDS ARE FRENCH, DAMN IT!
YOU CAN'T SEND 'EM BACK HOME NOW: THEY'RE ALREADY THERE!
SO MUCH FOR "FRANCE FOR THE FRENCH"!
HA HA!
HAR HAR!
SO THEY QUIETLY PUT A LID ON ALL THAT, TELLING THEMSELVES THAT, IF THINGS START BOILING OVER, THEY'LL JUST HAVE TO FILL PRISONS WITH A MISSION.
EXCEPT THAT THAT'S NOTHING NEW! NOTHING THAT HASN'T ALREADY BEEN TRIED IN THE PAST AND DIDN'T WORK.
AND THAT'S WHY...
?
AH, WELL, THERE YOU ARE, SOME FINE SPECIMENS OF CITIZENS WHO HAVE OPINIONS!
PABLO?
GOOD GOING, GUYS!

GRAFFITI: SARKOZY YOU CROOK

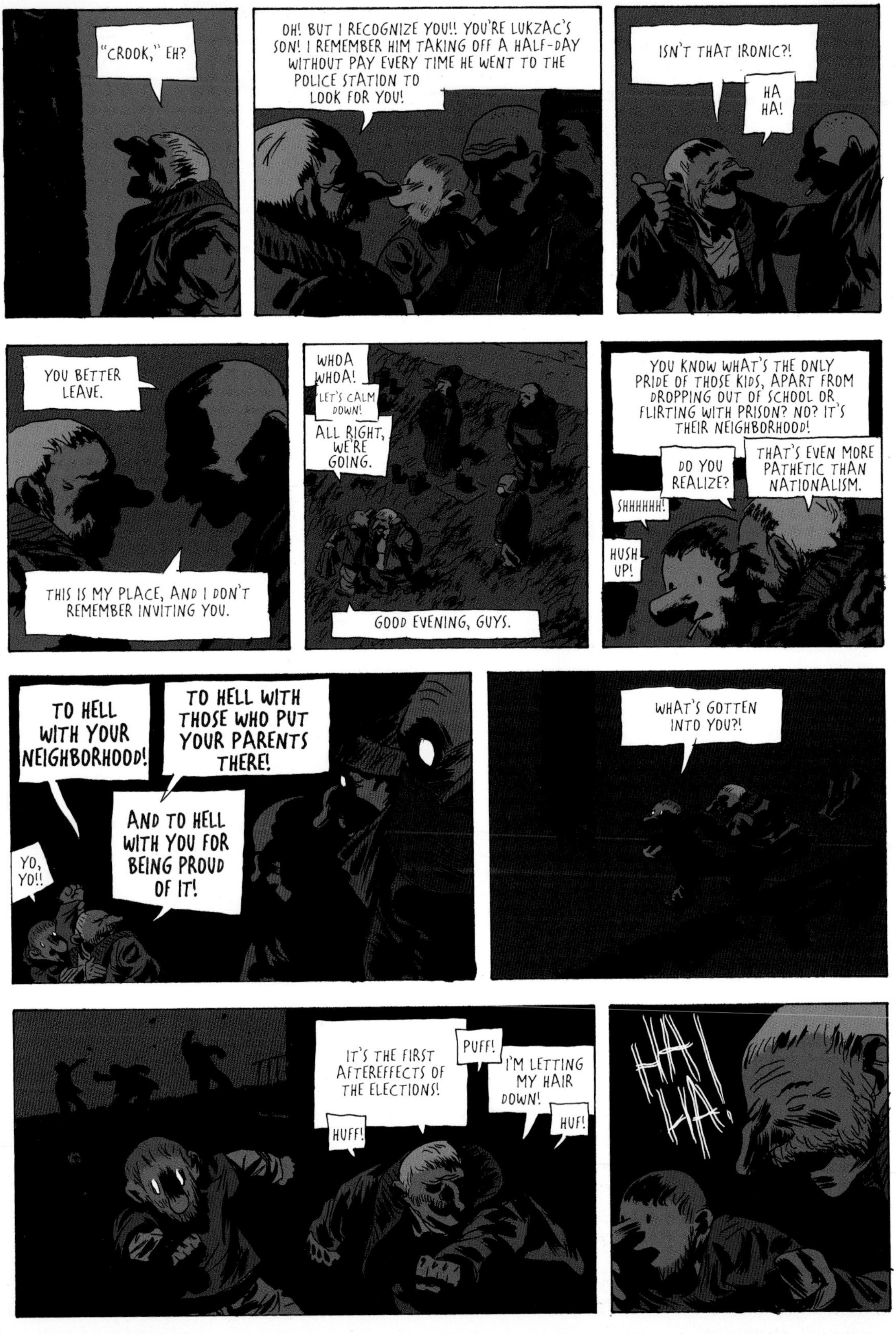
"CROOK," EH?
OH! BUT I RECOGNIZE YOU!! YOU'RE LUKZAC'S SON! I REMEMBER HIM TAKING OFF A HALF-DAY WITHOUT PAY EVERY TIME HE WENT TO THE POLICE STATION TO LOOK FOR YOU!
ISN'T THAT IRONIC?!
HA HA!
YOU BETTER LEAVE.
THIS IS MY PLACE, AND I DON'T REMEMBER INVITING YOU.
WHOA WHOA!
LET'S CALM DOWN!
ALL RIGHT, WE'RE GOING.
GOOD EVENING, GUYS.
YOU KNOW WHAT'S THE ONLY PRIDE OF THOSE KIDS, APART FROM DROPPING OUT OF SCHOOL OR FLIRTING WITH PRISON? NO? IT'S THEIR NEIGHBORHOOD!
DO YOU REALIZE?
THAT'S EVEN MORE PATHETIC THAN NATIONALISM.
SHHHHHH!
HUSH UP!
TO HELL WITH YOUR NEIGHBORHOOD!
TO HELL WITH THOSE WHO PUT YOUR PARENTS THERE!
AND TO HELL WITH YOU FOR BEING PROUD OF IT!
YO, YO!!
WHAT'S GOTTEN INTO YOU?!
IT'S THE FIRST AFTEREFFECTS OF THE ELECTIONS!
PUFF!
I'M LETTING MY HAIR DOWN!
HUFF!
HUF!
HA! HA!

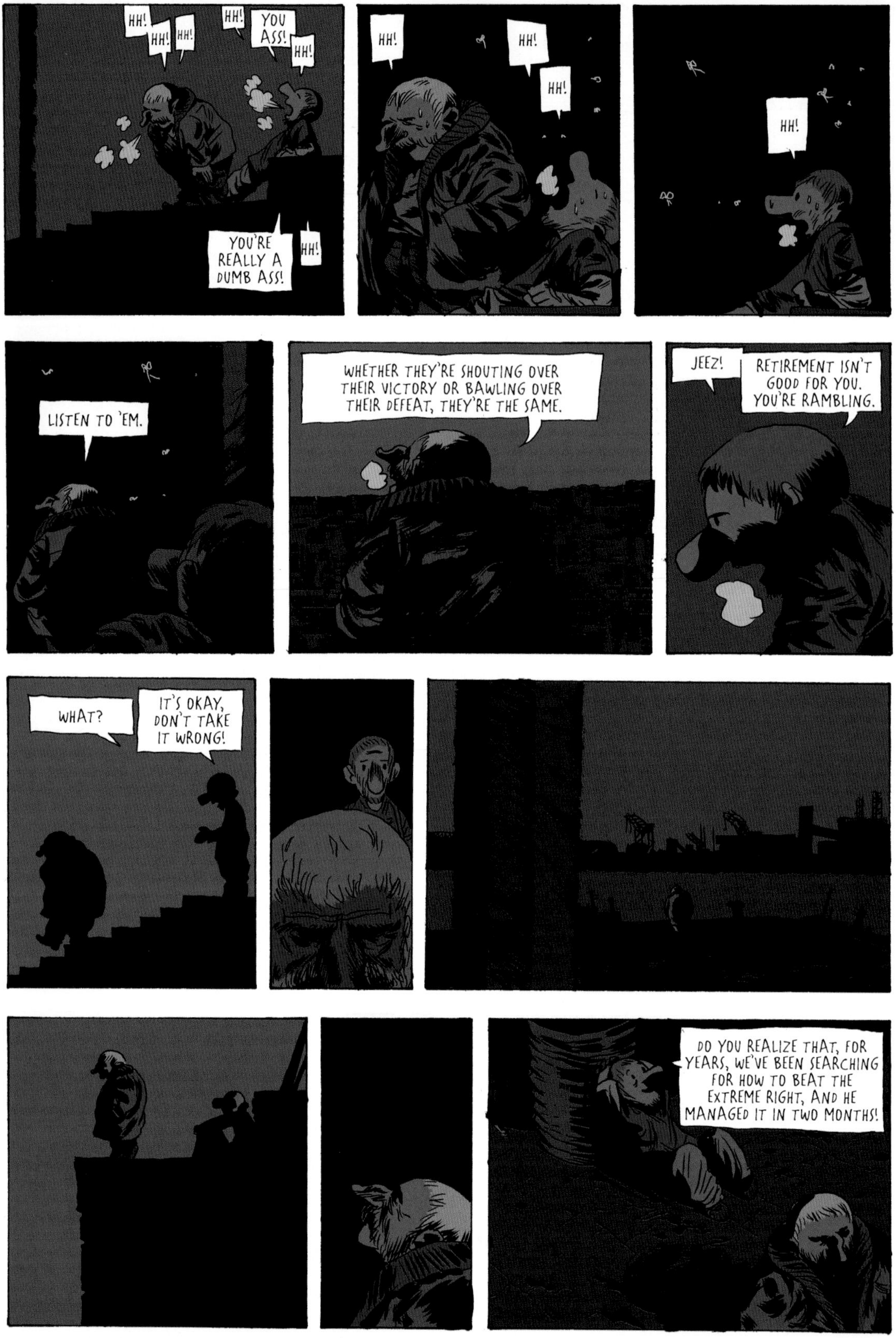

HH!
HH!
HH!
HH!
YOU ASS!
HH!
YOU'RE REALLY A DUMB ASS!
HH!
HH!
HH!
HH!
HH!
LISTEN TO 'EM.
WHETHER THEY'RE SHOUTING OVER THEIR VICTORY OR BAWLING OVER THEIR DEFEAT, THEY'RE THE SAME.
JEEZ!
RETIREMENT ISN'T GOOD FOR YOU. YOU'RE RAMBLING.
WHAT?
IT'S OKAY, DON'T TAKE IT WRONG!
DO YOU REALIZE THAT, FOR YEARS, WE'VE BEEN SEARCHING FOR HOW TO BEAT THE EXTREME RIGHT, AND HE MANAGED IT IN TWO MONTHS!

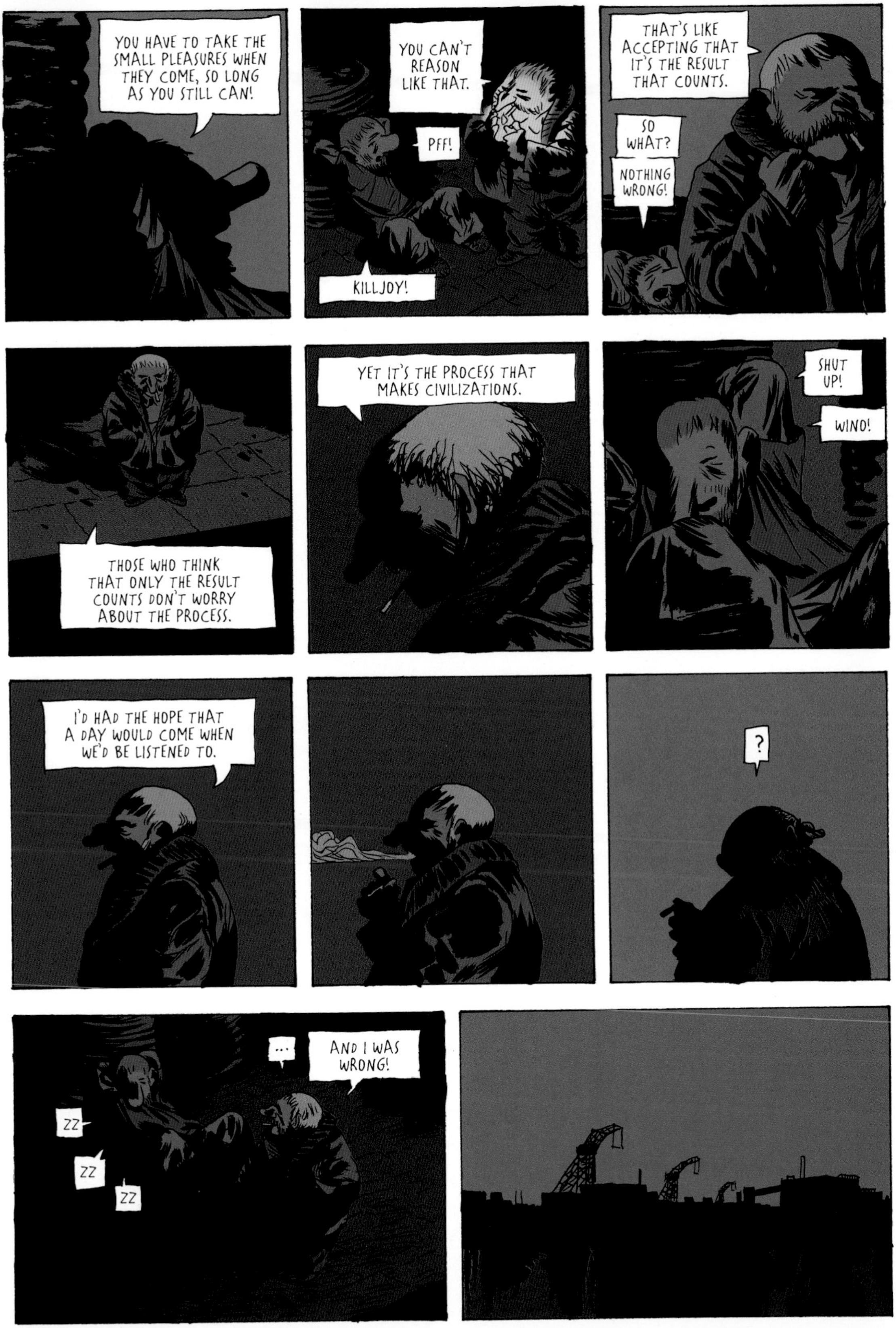
YOU HAVE TO TAKE THE SMALL PLEASURES WHEN THEY COME, SO LONG AS YOU STILL CAN!
YOU CAN'T REASON LIKE THAT.
PFF!
KILLJOY!
THAT'S LIKE ACCEPTING THAT IT'S THE RESULT THAT COUNTS.
SO WHAT?
NOTHING WRONG!
THOSE WHO THINK THAT ONLY THE RESULT COUNTS DON'T WORRY ABOUT THE PROCESS.
YET IT'S THE PROCESS THAT MAKES CIVILIZATIONS.
SHUT UP!
WINO!
I'D HAD THE HOPE THAT A DAY WOULD COME WHEN WE'D BE LISTENED TO.
?
ZZ
ZZ
ZZ
...
AND I WAS WRONG!

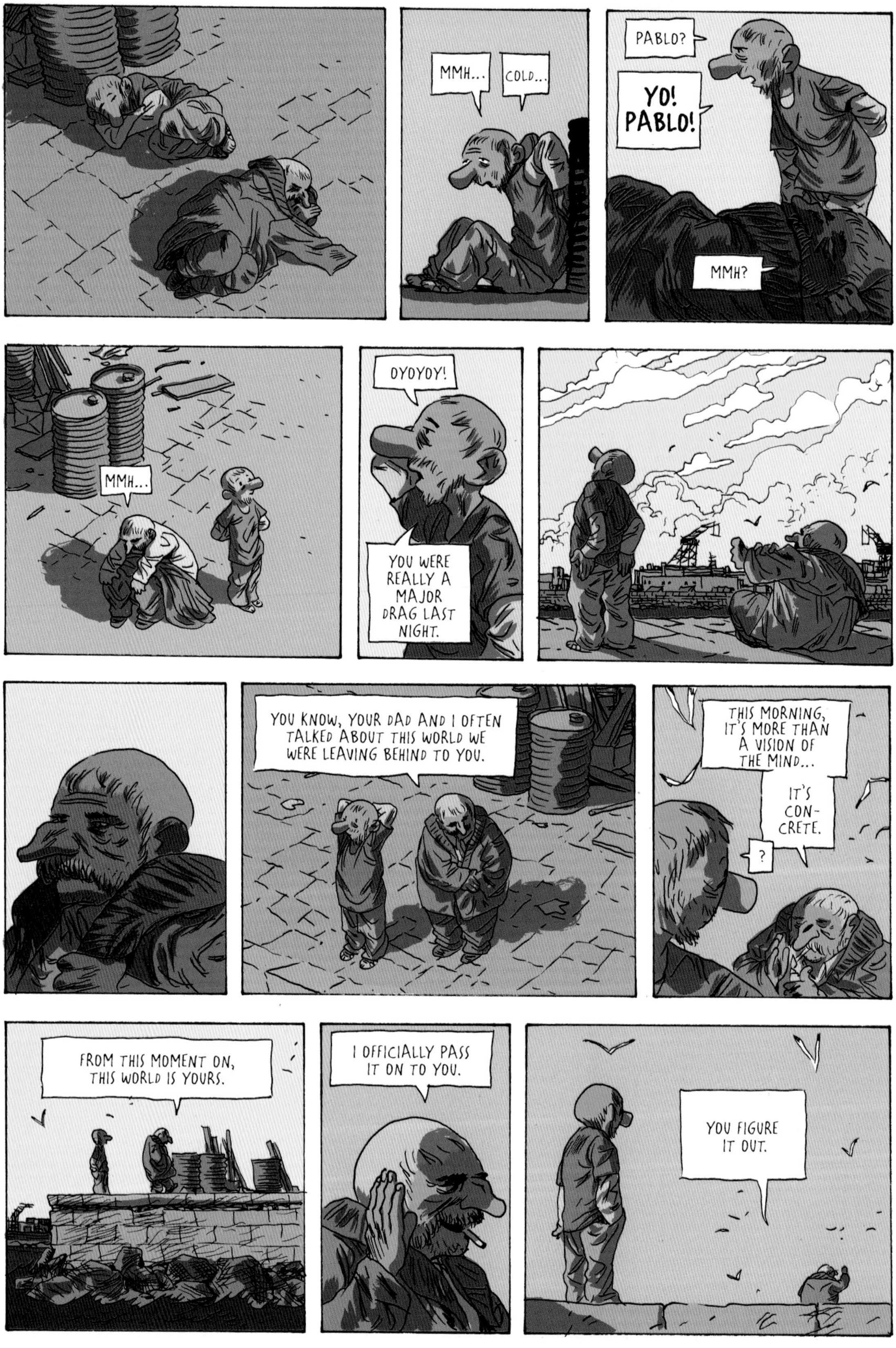
MMH...
COLD...
PABLO?
YO! PABLO!
MMH?
MMH...
OYOYOY!
YOU WERE REALLY A MAJOR DRAG LAST NIGHT.
YOU KNOW, YOUR DAD AND I OFTEN TALKED ABOUT THIS WORLD WE WERE LEAVING BEHIND TO YOU.
THIS MORNING, IT'S MORE THAN A VISION OF THE MIND...
IT'S CON-CRETE.
?
FROM THIS MOMENT ON, THIS WORLD IS YOURS.
I OFFICIALLY PASS IT ON TO YOU.
YOU FIGURE IT OUT.

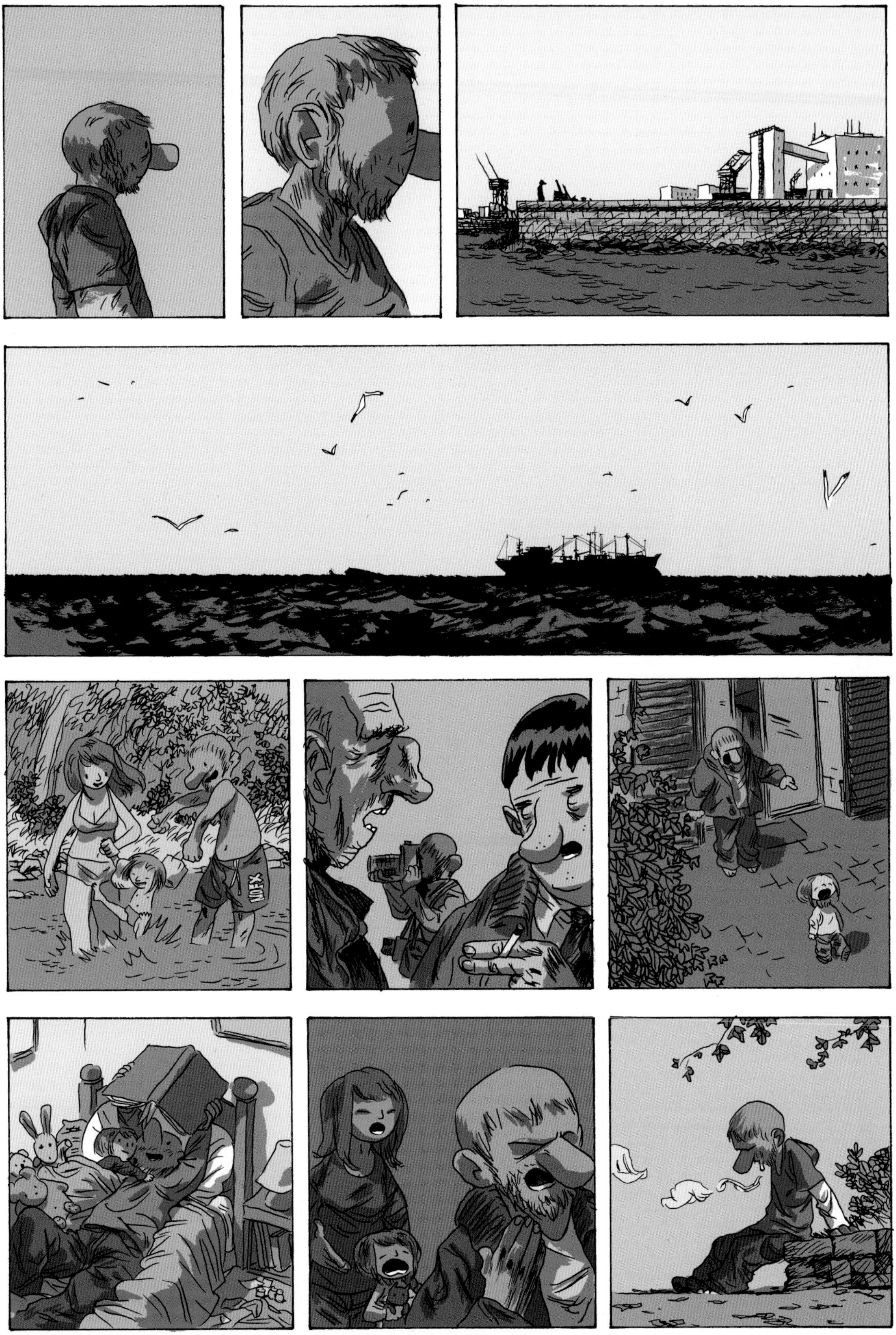

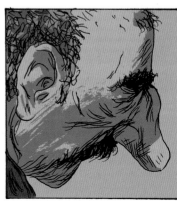

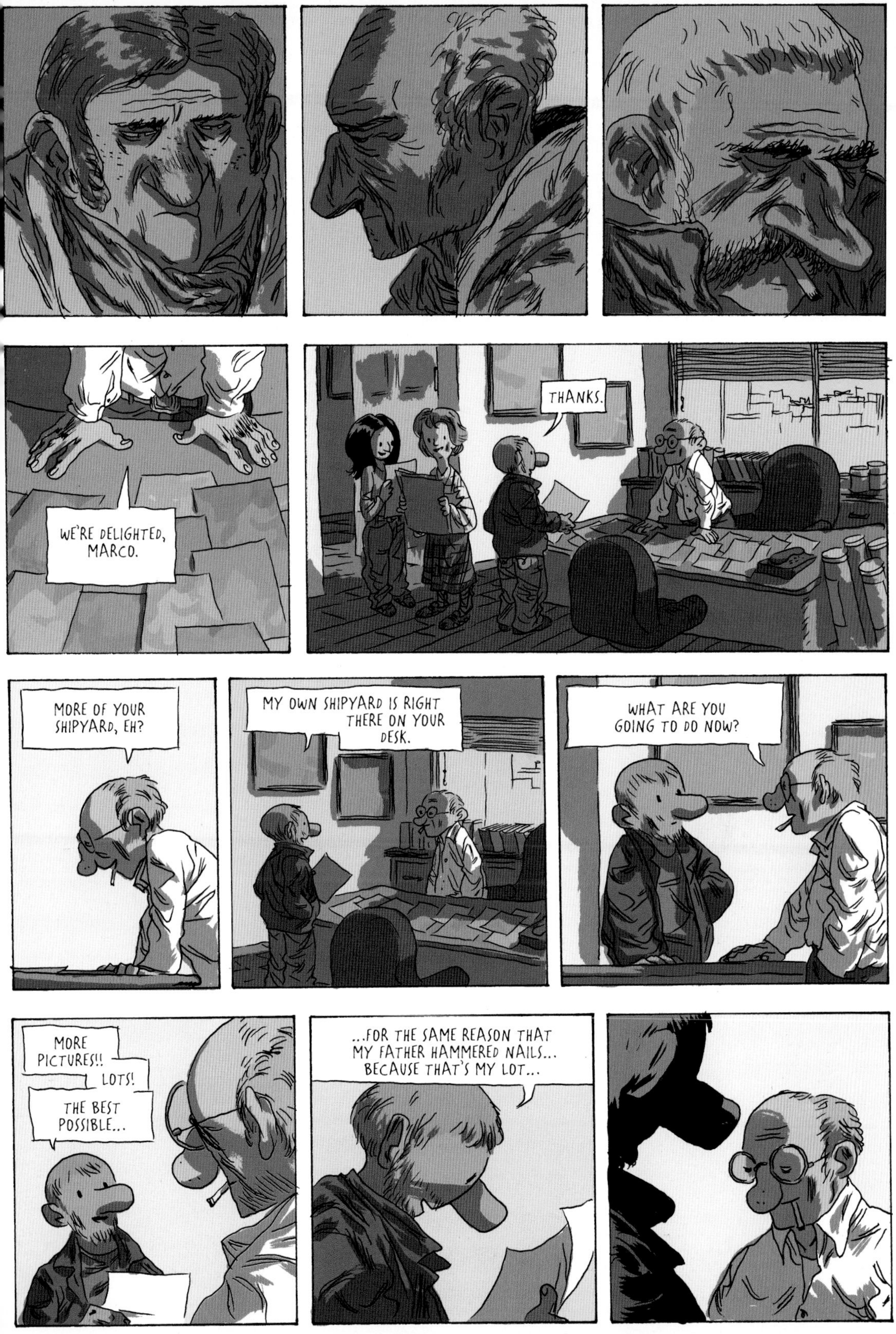

THANKS.
WE'RE DELIGHTED, MARCO.
MORE OF YOUR SHIPYARD, EH?
MY OWN SHIPYARD IS RIGHT THERE ON YOUR DESK.
WHAT ARE YOU GOING TO DO NOW?
MORE PICTURES!!
LOTS!
THE BEST POSSIBLE...
...FOR THE SAME REASON THAT MY FATHER HAMMERED NAILS... BECAUSE THAT'S MY LOT...

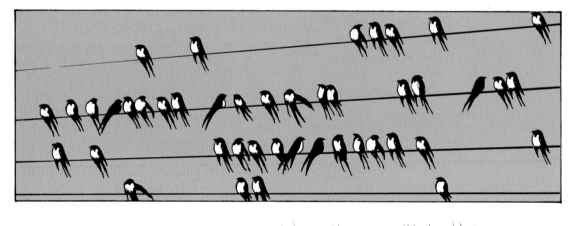

pour Lilie et Lenni   le 5 sept 2007   Manu Larcenet